CRUSADING AS AN ACT OF VENGEANCE, 1095–1216

For Matt

Crusading as an Act of Vengeance, 1095–1216

SUSANNA A. THROOP
Ursinus College, Collegeville, PA, USA

ASHGATE

Published by
Ashgate Publishing Limited
Wey Court East
Union Road
Farnham
Surrey, GU9 7PT
England

Ashgate Publishing Company
Suite 420
101 Cherry Street
Burlington
VT 05401-4405
USA

www.ashgate.com

British Library Cataloguing in Publication Data
Throop, Susanna A.
 Crusading as an act of vengeance, 1095–1216.
 1. Revenge – Religious aspects – History – To 1500. 2. Crusades.
 I. Title
 940.1'8–dc22

Library of Congress Cataloging-in-Publication Data
Throop, Susanna A.
 Crusading as an act of vengeance, 1095-1216 / Susanna A. Throop.
  p. cm.
 Includes bibliographical references and index.
 ISBN 978-0-7546-6582-3 (hardcover : alk. paper)—ISBN 978-1-4094-2400-0
 (ebook) 1. Crusades—13th-15th centuries. 2. Revenge—Europe—History—To 1500.
 3. Revenge—Social aspects—Europe—History—To 1500. 4. Revenge—Political aspects—
 Europe—History—To 1500. 5. Revenge—Religious aspects—Christianity. 6. Europe—
 History—476-1492. I. Title.
 D160.T49 2010
 909.07—dc22

2010038449

ISBN 9780754665823 (hbk)
ISBN 9781409424000 (ebk)

MIX
Paper from
responsible sources
FSC® C018575
www.fsc.org

Printed and bound in Great Britain by the
MPG Books Group, UK

Contents

Acknowledgments   vii

List of Abbreviations   ix

Introduction   1

1   The Meanings of *Vindicta*, *Ultio* and *Venjance*   11

2   Early Years: Crusading as Vengeance, 1095–1137   43

3   A Growing Appeal: Crusading as Vengeance, 1138–1197   73

4   Popular—or Papal? Crusading as Vengeance, 1198–1216   117

5   *Zelus*: An Emotional Component of Crusading as Vengeance   145

Conclusion   173

Appendix 1: Historiographical Overview   189

Appendix 2: Resumé of the Sources   195

Bibliography   207

Index   223

Acknowledgments

This work began as my doctoral research at the University of Cambridge. It would never have gotten off the ground without generous assistance from 2001 through 2005 from the Gates Cambridge Trust and my college, Trinity Hall. I would especially like to thank Christopher Padfield, then Tutor for Graduate Students at Trinity Hall, for his support and encouragement.

To my Ph.D. supervisor, Jonathan Riley-Smith, I owe an immense professional and personal debt of gratitude. He vastly improved my skills as a historian with kind guidance, insightful criticism, and the highest expectations. He also believed enthusiastically in me and my research, and provided considerable support during a personally stressful time. I hope that someday I may be as wise, compassionate, and generous a teacher.

I am grateful to many institutions in the U.S. and the U.K. for their help and support while working on this project: the University of Cambridge, the University of Edinburgh, the National Library of Scotland, the University of Glasgow, the University of New Hampshire, and Ursinus College, as well as all the schools involved with the Boston Library Consortium (especially Boston College). Without their assistance and access to their collections, the project would not have been possible.

Scholars on both sides of the Atlantic have helped me refine my ideas and strengthen weak points. In particular, many thanks to Jonathan Riley-Smith, Norman Housley, Hugh Clark, Dallett Hemphill, Ross Doughty, Richard King, Walt Greason, and David McAllister for reading portions of the manuscript. I am also grateful to Paul Hyams, Miri Rubin, Carl Watkins, Nick Paul, Caroline Smith, Iben Schmidt, Jochen Schenck, Rebecca Rist, and William Purkis. In addition, medievalists at the University of Cambridge, the University of Edinburgh, the University of St. Andrews, the Institute for Historical Research in London, and the International Medieval Congress at Leeds listened to papers of mine and provided invaluable suggestions and insight. Thanks are also owed to my students in History 300B (*The Crusades*) at Ursinus. In a matter of months, they showed me new ways to think about the sources and my conclusions.

Numerous friends and family members have been rooting for this book for years now. In particular, I would like to thank past colleagues at the University of New Hampshire-Manchester and Brookstone. There are many individuals who deserve mention, but I am especially grateful to Tamsin Palmer, George and Deborah Brown, Pamala Abbott, John and Sally Bowkett, Paul Love, Hollie Bowen, Benjamin Throop, Paul and Elaine Hyams, Elizabeth Macaulay Lewis, Carol Lambert, Paul Donovan, Shelagh Walsh, and Pam Rodenhizer.

Last here only because he is so obviously first, I want to thank my husband, Matthew Abbott. He started believing in me back when we were lowly undergraduates, and he hasn't stopped since (knock on wood). Without him urging me to apply for a Gates Cambridge Scholarship, and to be bold enough to contact the eminent Professor Riley-Smith, this research would never have gotten started. Without his tireless love, encouragement, and support, this book would never have been finished. Thank you, Matt, for everything.

NB: Many of the above-mentioned individuals have saved me from embarrassing errors. Any that remain are, of course, completely my own fault.

List of Abbreviations

AQDGM	Ausgewählte Quellen zur Deutschen Geschichte des Mittelalters
CCCM	Corpus Christianorum, Continuatio Mediaevalis
CFM	Les Classiques Français du Moyen Âge
CHF	Les Classiques de l'Histoire de France au Moyen Âge
DHC	Documents relatifs à l'Histoire des Croisades
MGHHT	Monumenta Germaniae Historica, Hebräische Texte aus dem Mittelalterlichen Deutschland
MGHSS	Monumenta Germaniae Historica, Series Scriptores
OFCC	The Old French Crusade Cycle
PL	Patrologia Latina
RHCOc.	Recueil des Historiens des Croisades, Historiens Occidentaux
RHGF	Recueil des Historiens des Gaules et de la France
RS	Rerum Brittanicarum Medii Aevi Scriptores
SBO	S. Bernardi Opera Omnia
TLF	Textes Littéraires Français

NB: With the exception of the Hebrew sources, all translations are my own unless otherwise noted.

Introduction

Sometime in the late twelfth century, roughly around the year 1180, a French scribe wrote down a version of a popular *chanson* that presumably had been making the rounds. This epic song engaged its audiences with what was arguably one of the most entertaining stories of the times, a narrative of religion, war, and honor that featured an impossible journey, menacing foreign enemies, strange and distant lands, do-or-die battles, treachery and betrayal, miracles and visions, and agonizing crises of faith.

This narrative was, of course, the story of the First Crusade until the crusaders' victory at Antioch. The primary concern of this particular version of the story was entertainment, not argument, yet all the same it provided audiences with a clearly stated justification for the events of the First Crusade: vengeance. Even within the first forty laisses of the poem, attention is drawn to the First Crusade as vengeance:

> but the noble barons who loved God and held him dear,
> went to *outremer* in order to avenge his body.[1]

As the *chanson* continues, it becomes clear why vengeance is required: the seizure of "Christian" lands, the desecration of the holy places, the abuse of pilgrims and eastern Christians, and even the crucifixion of Christ—all demand revenge. Not only does the narrative of the *chanson* draw the audience's attention to the motif of vengeance, but also characters within the poem, from Pope Urban II to the knight Rainald Porcet, are described envisioning the First Crusade as vengeance.[2] Vengeance drives the ideology of the *Chanson d'Antioche*, and also provides its internal narrative momentum, as crusaders in the text seek engagement after engagement with Muslims to avenge their fallen comrades.

Even a cursory examination of other twelfth-century texts reveals that the construction of crusading as vengeance was hardly an anomaly. Numerous chronicles, in many ways the meat-and-potatoes documents for historical research, also included the idea. To give but one example, the accepted and widely used account of Baldric of Bourgueil, written in the early twelfth century,

---

[1] *La Chanson d'Antioche*, ed. J. Nelson, OFCC 4 (Tuscaloosa, 2003), p. 49.
[2] Ibid., pp. 50 and 182.

depicted the crusaders driven by the obligation to avenge Christ as a fallen kinsman.[3] And notably, another twelfth-century *chanson de geste, La Venjance de Nostre Seigneur,* portrayed the Roman destruction of Jerusalem in 70 C.E. as revenge for the crucifixion.

It would be possible to dismiss an emphasis on vengeance in one lone text, like the *Chanson d'Antioche,* as exceptional and largely irrelevant. Carl Erdmann, the father of the modern study of crusading ideology, certainly did so when he described the emphasis on crusading as vengeance as "an obvious improvisation suggestive of how immature the idea of crusade still was."[4] But although even a quick survey of twelfth-century crusading texts reveals that the *Chanson d'Antioche* was not a singular, anomalous text, only recently have historians of the crusades begun to seriously investigate the presence of the idea of crusading as an act of vengeance.[5]

Understandably, to date the study of this idea has primarily concentrated on non-ecclesiastical phenomena such as feuding, purportedly a component of "secular" culture and the interpersonal obligations inherent in medieval society.[6] Some scholars have begun to elaborate the ways in which Christian theology contributed to the idea,[7] and many historians have noted the apparent relationship between ideas of vengeance on the Jews for the crucifixion and the crusading movement.[8] But until now, no one has tackled these topics directly in a comprehensive study.

The idea of crusading as vengeance merits a fuller discussion for two reasons. First, admittedly at the most basic level, because it is an area of crusading studies that is incomplete and, as it turns out, currently inaccurate. Although there can be no doubt that military obligation and notions of family honor contributed to the concept of crusading vengeance, we have not yet taken into full account the frequent references to the Biblical God of vengeance that reside alongside more "secular" themes in crusade narratives. Moreover, the general assumption remains that the idea of crusading as vengeance only flourished among the

---

[3]   *Baldric of Bourgueil, Historia Jerosolimitana,* in RHCOc. 4 (Paris, 1879), p. 101.

[4]   Carl Erdmann, *The Origin of the Idea of Crusading,* trans. M. W. Baldwin and W. Goffart (Princeton, 1977), p. 116.

[5]   That said, in the last seventy years many scholars have noted its existence. For a brief overview of the historiography of crusading as vengeance, please see Appendix 1 below.

[6]   Notably Jonathan Riley-Smith, Peter Partner, Jean Flori, and Tomaz Mastnak. For more information and references, see pages 190–92.

[7]   Notably John Gilchrist, John Cowdrey, and Phillipe Buc. For more information and references, see pages 190 and 92.

[8]   Notably Jonathan Riley-Smith, Susan Jacoby, Jean Flori, and Tomaz Mastnak. For more information and references, see pages 189–92.

laity, and only at the very beginning of the First Crusade, a vivid example of their limited comprehension of theological subtlety and the general emotional excitement that accompanied the expeditions of 1096.[9] But there has been no extensive study of the origin and evolution of the ideology to prove these points.

Second, and much more importantly, the topic of crusading as vengeance matters because of its potential impact on our understanding of contemporary perceptions of crusading. Our current understanding of crusade ideology is centered on the concepts of pilgrimage, penitential warfare, just war, holy war, the defense of the Church, liberation, Christian love, and the imitation of Christ.[10] Studying these ideological themes has challenged us to reconcile values that seem recognizably Christian to our modern minds (like charity and pilgrimage) with the bloody reality of crusading. They have pushed us to consider notions of justice and religion that only incompletely resemble our own—yet that nevertheless do bear some resemblance.

The idea of crusading as vengeance, on the other hand, compels us a step further, asking us to acknowledge the importance of an ideological theme that runs counter to our post-Enlightenment sensibilities in virtually every way. Moreover, we cannot retreat to the position that those vengeful crusaders, were, after all, simply "primitive" or amoral human beings, because it is so clear that the idea of crusading as vengeance was seen at the time as perfectly compatible

---

[9] This assumption is largely based on two of Riley-Smith's seminal works: *The First Crusade and the Idea of Crusading* (London, 1986) and *The First Crusaders, 1095–1131* (Cambridge, 1997). See also page 4 and 189–90.

[10] I hope to undertake a synthesis of recent work on ideas of crusading in the twelfth century in the future. For those new to the subject, good places to start are Jonathan Riley-Smith, *The Crusades: A History* (2nd edn, New Haven, 2005), pp. 1–25; and Christopher Tyerman, *God's War: A New History of the Crusades* (Cambridge MA, 2006), pp. 27–57. Other useful scholarship on ideas of crusading not previously cited in this chapter includes: Jonathan Riley-Smith, "Crusading as an Act of Love," *History*, 65 (1980): 177–92; Benjamin Z. Kedar, *Crusade and Mission: European Approaches Toward the Muslims* (Princeton, 1984); Norman Daniel, "Crusade Propaganda," in H. W. Hazard and N. P. Zacour (eds), *A History of the Crusades 6: The Impact of the Crusades on Europe* (Madison WI, 1989), pp. 39–97; Michael Markowski, "Peter of Blois and the Conception of the Third Crusade," in B. Z. Kedar (ed.), *The Horns of Hattin* (Jerusalem, 1992), pp. 261–9; H. E. J. Cowdrey, "Martyrdom and the First Crusade," *The Crusades and Latin Monasticism, 11th–12th Centuries* (Aldershot, 1999), pp. 46–56; Jonathan Phillips, "Ideas of Crusade and Holy War in De Expugnatione Lyxbonensi (The Conquest of Lisbon)," in Robert Swanson (ed.), *Holy Land, Holy Lands, and Christian History*, Studies in Church History 36 (2000), pp. 123–41; William Purkis, "Elite and Popular Perceptions of Imitatio Christi in Twelfth-Century Crusade Spirituality," in K. Cooper and J. Gregory (eds), *Elite and Popular Religion*, Studies in Church History 42 (Woodbridge, 2006), pp. 54–64.

with the other components of crusading ideology that we may find easier to stomach: love, penance, defense, liberation, and even the desire to emulate Christ. In addition, the frequency and enthusiasm with which the idea was used by writers in the Church—and not only when writing to the laity—prevents us from clinging to the idea that crusading as vengeance was purely secular and socio-political, an unsophisticated carry-over from the violent and chaotic society inhabited by the men with swords (and arrows and lances) who actually prosecuted the crusades. By confronting the ways in which it seemed perfectly reasonable (indeed, desirable) to view crusading as vengeance in the twelfth century, and what contemporary sources in fact meant when they talked about "vengeance," we are faced with the fact that many of our own assumptions about justice, religious violence, and the morality of revenge are cultural constructs, too.

Moreover, the current consensus about crusading as vengeance—that the idea was secular in origin, most dominant during the First Crusade, and filtered out of crusading ideology by monastic revisionists working in the early twelfth century[11]—all too easily corresponds to a progressive view of medieval history. From this perspective, practices like feud and ideas like vengeance were more dominant in the early Middle Ages, and were gradually replaced with state-sponsored justice. The intellectual premise underlying this perspective is that concepts of justice replaced concepts of vengeance, because justice is a more sophisticated idea than vengeance. In addition, this perspective contains an inherent moral judgment—that feud and vengeance are "primitive," "barbaric," and, in some obscure way, less desirable. At its most extreme, the implication is that as human societies clawed their way out of the "dark ages" towards the light of the Renaissance, they gradually abandoned such practices as vengeance and took up more enlightened customs, customs which just so happen to more and more closely resemble our own form of civilization.[12] Ironically, then, there is a risk in acknowledging that the idea of crusading as vengeance was more prominent, in a later period, than we might have expected. The risk is that we will simply conclude that the "primitiveness" of the Middle Ages lasted longer, and the "barbaric" nature of the crusades was more dominant, than we have thought. Fortunately, as this book demonstrates, the evidence continually pushes us away from such a reactionary judgment, towards an appreciation of the wide range

---

[11]   Riley-Smith, *The First Crusade and the Idea of Crusading*, pp. 49, 55 and 154. For more detail, see pages 189–90.

[12]   The "long history of vengeance may be a history of the civilizing process—how states and societies repressed the urge to do violence" (Daniel Lord Smail and Kelly Gibson (eds), *Vengeance in Medieval Europe: A Reader* (Toronto, 2009), p. xvii).

of themes (many of them quite sophisticated) that contributed to the twelfth-century understanding of crusading as vengeance.

To be sure, this work does not deny the relative importance of other ideological elements of crusading. The theme of crusading as vengeance is for the most part a theme written between the lines, a theme taken for granted, perhaps both by medieval contemporaries of the crusades and by present-day historians.[13] Indeed, the almost subconscious nature of the idea of crusade as vengeance is what makes it worth investigating. By doing so we are going beyond the glossy surface of the twelfth century to look at a pervasive aspect of culture that was assumed to make sense by those living at the time.

It is in truth very difficult to study the history of any idea, and especially when the idea in question is ambiguous, and heavily weighted both then and now with moral value. A brief explanation of the methodology with which I have attempted to read my sources, and the nature of the sources themselves, is therefore in order.[14] Of primary importance are questions of language, meaning, and translation. After all, if I simply were to investigate the events and discourse that seem to me to relate to vengeance, I would be looking at modern ideas of vengeance in medieval texts, not the medieval ideas themselves. In trying to analyze what those medieval ideas were, the medieval words become vitally significant, and serve almost as signposts in the texts, highlighting that "here is a matter that was considered to relate to vengeance." Given this, it was important to decide which medieval terms should be considered to signify "vengeance," and, if more than multiple terms were to be considered, would it be accurate to group them together and at the same time exclude other terms?

At the beginning I decided to limit the field of research as much as possible, and so chose to focus on the root-words *vindicta*, *ultio*, and *venjance*, and for the purpose of discussion and comparison I have translated these terms into the modern English *vengeance*. There is reason to believe that *vindicta*, *ultio*, and *venjance* were understood as roughly equivalent in the Middle Ages: Hebrew words such as *nâqam* were translated into both *vindicta* and *ultio* in the Latin Vulgate, and *vindicta* was translated into the Old French *venjance*, as in the case of the Latin poem *Vindicta Salvatoris* and its vernacular equivalent, *La Venjance de Nostre Seigneur*. It is also reasonable to translate the medieval

---

[13] As opposed to the "consciously present and largely unproblematic" categories usually investigated. For this phrase and further discussion, see Marcus Bull, "Views of Muslims and of Jerusalem in Miracle Stories, c. 1000–c. 1200: Reflections on the Study of First Crusaders' Motivations," in Marcus Bull and Norman Housley (eds), *The Experience of Crusading 1: Western Approaches* (Cambridge, 2003), pp. 13–38.

[14] A more comprehensive overview of the primary sources I used in this study can be found in Appendix 2 at the end of the book.

terms as the modern English *vengeance* for similar reasons. However, my choice of the specific term *vengeance* is based on linguistic similarity, and by no means implies perfect conceptual equivalence. *Vengeance* is a modern English word with its own accompanying baggage of meaning, emotional significance, and moral value, and there is no way to verify that without exception it corresponds exactly to concepts designated by words in historical languages.[15]

For the sake of clarity I have restricted my research to the words discussed above, despite the abundance of similar nouns like *retributio*. Medieval writers gave *retributio* both positive (in the sense of reward) and negative (in the sense of punishment) connotations, making it semantically distinct, though undoubtedly related to, *vindicta* and *ultio*.[16] The topic is difficult enough without complicating the question with a large number of terms that share a roughly similar meaning, or by using modern ideas of vengeance to frame medieval events. That said, future scholars will, I hope, both deepen our understanding of *vindicta* and *ultio*, and broaden our knowledge of related terms like *retributio*.

As a result of the methodology I have outlined above, if I use the word *vengeance* to discuss a certain passage or group of passages, it is because *vindicta*, *ultio*, or *venjance* were present in the medieval texts. It is worth repeating that I have not myself interpreted events as being "vengeful" or "acts of vengeance."[17]

My final chapter on vengeance and emotions requires an additional methodological explanation, since, of course, there is no way to reconstruct internal emotional feelings from the past, and a reliance on textual sources raises the question whether it is reasonable to analyze physical sensation through such a medium.[18] The last fifty years have seen an explosion of research on the emotions in the biological and social sciences, and this has provided a new basis for the analysis of emotion within specific historical contexts. One of the most significant insights to emerge is the recognition that emotion is more than just a

---

[15]   Though working independently of each other, François Bougard and I seem to have come to similar conclusions regarding the vocabulary. François Bougard, "Les Mots de la Vengeance," in Dominique Barthélemy, François Bougard, and Régine Le Jan (eds), *La Vengeance 400–1200* (Rome, 2006), pp. 1–6. See also page 12n below.

[16]   For example, *Gratian, Corpus Iuris Canonici*, ed. A. E. Richteri (2nd edn, 2 vols, Lipsiae, 1879), vol. 1, col. 896 (Causa 23 Q. 3 C. 1 *Quot sint differentiae retributionis*). Interestingly, modern theorists are asking the same sorts of questions about the relationship between revenge and retribution. See, for example, Peter French, *The Virtues of Vengeance* (Lawrence KS, 2001), pp. 67–8.

[17]   In this I was influenced by the discussion of the difficulties of researching words and concepts outlined by Susan Reynolds in *Fiefs and Vassals: The Medieval Evidence Reinterpreted* (Oxford, 1994), especially pp. 12–13.

[18]   I am just now beginning to look at representations of crusading as vengeance in medieval images and physical artifacts, and I hope others will do so as well.

universal physical sensation divorced from thought, reason and culture. William Reddy, in his guide to the study of emotions in the natural and social sciences, has noted that since 1989 research has emphasized the definition of emotion as an "overlearned cognitive habit."[19] Although emotion involves a quasi-autonomous physiological reaction, a racing heart or a flushed face, nevertheless the intellectual interpretation of that reaction is learned through culture. In essence, then, an "emotion" could be defined as the application of intellectual judgment to a sensation or series of events.[20]

If emotion is not just physical sensation, but also cultural interpretation, it may be possible to evaluate that cultural component through textual analysis. Language, the way in which a culture describes, discusses, and relates emotions to each other, is undoubtedly significant, since the interpretation of emotions is embedded in cultural discourse. Emotional experiences seem to be frequently shaped by the "emotional lexicon" of a given language and the behavior that stems from that lexicon.[21] This is given further weight by the fact that the words used to describe emotions impact the emotions themselves.[22] In other words, how people think about their feelings may be visible in the words they use to acknowledge or repress those feelings, and in the values they attribute to them.

In attempting to evaluate the emotions associated with the idea of crusading as vengeance in the Middle Ages, I have paid attention from the beginning to other words, phrases, and images frequently invoked alongside the vocabulary of vengeance. This attention revealed the significance of the word *zelus* in the sources. I have little doubt that *zelus* is just one of a number of clues to the emotions of vengeful crusading, and I hope my discussion of *zelus* will inspire other scholars to keep working on the topic of crusading emotions.

For this study I have utilized what I consider "crusading texts"— texts of virtually any genre written between 1095 and 1216 that were associated with western Europe's understanding of the crusading movement, including narratives, chronicles and entertainment literature as well as letters and other documents written by key figures in the twelfth-century crusades. This is a broad sweep of source material, and its breadth is not the result of carelessness, but is in fact vitally important. Because I am trying not only to determine whether the idea of vengeance played a role in "official" crusading documents, but

---

[19]   William M. Reddy, *The Navigation of Feeling: A Framework for the History of Emotions* (Cambridge, 2001), p. 17.

[20]   Paul Hyams, *Rancor and Reconciliation in Medieval England* (Ithaca NY, 2003), p. 36.

[21]   M. S. Rosaldo, *Knowledge and Passion: Ilongot Notions of Self and Social Life* (cited in Reddy, *The Navigation of Feeling*, p. 36).

[22]   Reddy, *The Navigation of Feeling*, p. 104.

additionally what the terms *vindicta* and *ultio* may have meant in general to medieval contemporaries who wrote about the crusades, there can be no hard and fast delimitations. Historical fields *may* have clear-cut boundaries—in the past, living ideas did not. To my mind, this approach rightly plants the history of the crusades back where it belongs, in the general history of twelfth-century European culture. I am aware, however, that some may disagree with this approach.

In addition, there will be those who raise the question of authorial intent and genre. Surely, one might protest, we cannot simply read a large group of contemporaneous sources without taking into account the specific, detailed context and genre in which each author was writing. There is some merit to this argument, especially if one inclines to the view that a text can never be viewed independently from its author, or to the opinion that we must, necessarily, separate the "elite" thinkers of the Middle Ages from the rough, unsophisticated mob. I would ask these critics to bear in mind that my deliberate goal has been to identify broad cultural themes, rather than individual proclivities. As a result, I have adopted a modified structuralist approach that separates "the author and authorial intentions from the text that results from the act of writing."[23] In a sense, then, I see this book as a skeleton, and I certainly do hope that future scholars will flesh out the story of the idea of crusading as vengeance, source by source, region by region, decade by decade. The best justification for my approach, however, is the evidence itself—the fact that, as this book demonstrates, dissimilar texts, written by dissimilar authors, in different languages, nevertheless contained ideas and passages that were remarkably alike.

With all that said, histories and chronicles, the core narrative sources that embody medieval attempts to give meaning to the crusades, have indeed formed the backbone of my research.[24] I have distinguished these and other sources by date of composition, rather than by the date of the events described within the texts. For the most part, sources written about a particular crusade will still be discussed within the same chapter, but there are exceptions. For example, Caffaro of Caschifelone wrote about the First Crusade in circa 1155, and thus I will discuss his account in Chapter Three, which deals with sources dating from approximately 1138 until 1197.[25] In a few cases the date of composition has been difficult to establish, and I discuss those texts accordingly, both briefly within the relevant chapters, and also in greater depth in Appendix 2.

---

[23]   Brian Stock, *Listening for the Text: On the Uses of the Past* (Philadelphia, 1990), p. 17.

[24]   Bull, "Views of Muslims and of Jerusalem," p. 21.

[25]   Also known as Caffaro "of Genoa," see Richard D. Face, "Secular History in Twelfth-Century Italy: Caffaro of Genoa," *Journal of Medieval History*, 6 (1980): 169–84.

Readers familiar with the contentions surrounding the definition of a crusade in the twelfth century will have already recognized that I side in general with the pluralists: I agree that the origins and characteristics of any given campaign were what defined it as a crusade for medieval contemporaries.[26] But to be most accurate, my position is that of a moderate (or modified) pluralist.[27] An extremely strict pluralist might say that until a campaign was authorized by the pope, it was not a crusade—and that any discourse related to the campaign was, by implication, not crusading discourse. To my mind, this would artificially distort the historical record, and would ignore the gradual accumulation of rhetoric and positioning that frequently accompanied the lead-up to official authorization. To give just one example, the Albigensian Crusade was officially proclaimed in 1208, but this was preceded by decades of textual references to Church-approved violent action—and the need to take violent action—against the Cathars. To say that such references only "count" after 1208 would be misleading.

What relationship existed between the concepts of crusading and vengeance, and what accounted for that relationship? Drawing upon not only narrative histories of the twelfth-century crusades, but also upon related letters, legends, *chansons*, and theology of the period, I have mapped the course of the idea of crusading as vengeance from the First Crusade until the end of Pope Innocent III's papacy in 1216. My research demonstrates that the general assumption previously advocated regarding the idea of crusading as vengeance must be revised. The concept of crusading as vengeance was no anomaly, and crusading was conceived as an act of vengeance not only through the application of "secular" values, but also through values inherent in twelfth-century Christianity.

---

[26]   For those unfamiliar with the debate on how to define a crusade, a good starting point is Norman Housley, *Contesting the Crusades* (Oxford, 2006), pp. 1–23.

[27]   Ibid., pp. 20–23.

Chapter One

The Meanings of *Vindicta, Ultio* and *Venjance*

Like other scholars, I have translated the terms *vindicta, ultio,* and *venjance* as "vengeance." But using this modern word is a convenience and an approximation, and does not really clarify the precise concepts lying behind the medieval Latin and vernacular vocabulary. What *did* the medieval terms mean?

Turning to great medieval dictionaries like those constructed by Charles Du Cange, Jan Niermeyer, and Alexandre Greimas is only moderately helpful, at best. From their works, we discover that *ultio* and related terms bear some relation to the idea of wounds and violent punishment, while *vindicta* and its family of vocabulary can be translated as some variation of vengeance, feud, justice, and criminal punishment.[1] The range of meaning accorded to these terms in the dictionaries suggests that medieval usage varied broadly, which will come as no surprise to anyone who has read medieval sources at some length. The dictionary entries also suggest we are on the right track—translating these terms into "vengeance" is not capricious—but above all they emphasize that the meanings of the medieval terms were various and depended on circumstances.

In this chapter I clarify how *vindicta, ultio,* and *venjance* were used by writers to represent individual and group interactions in my sources. These anecdotal

---

[1]   Du Cange did not include *ultio* in his dictionary as an entry, and only noted that *ultatus* meant "wounded" (Charles Du Cange, *Glossarium Mediae et Infimae Latinitatis* (7 vols, Paris, 1840–50), vol. 6, p. 863). Niermeyer went further, giving two potential meanings of *ultio*: "punishment, penalty" and "punishment inflicted by God" (Jan F. Niermeyer, *Mediae Latinitatis Lexicon Minus* (Leiden, 1997), p. 1050). For Du Cange, *vindicta* was "to give in vengeance ... that is, to give to justice, so that a worthy penalty may be exacted." He subdivided this into *vindicta sanguinis*, "high, or supreme, justice," and *vindicta* "as, it would seem, a beating." *Vindicatio* was "*jus* ... through which someone can avenge for himself something stolen or lost." *Vindicare* was simply "to have the use of something (*usum habere*)" (Du Cange, *Glossarium*, vol. 6, p. 838). Niermeyer defined *vindicalis* as "vengeful." *Vindicare* was "to acknowledge as true, to affirm ... to attest ... to hold a plea," while *vindicta* was a noun with multiple meanings including "feud," "wergeld," "the right of hearing and trying a criminal cause," and "infliction of capital punishment" (Niermeyer, *Lexicon*, p. 1108–9). Greimas, meanwhile, simply defined the Old French verb *vengier* as "to avenge" (Alexander J. Greimas, *Dictionnaire de l'Ancien Français* (Paris, 1999), p. 613).

examples of "ordinary" vengeance highlight the social conventions (or lack thereof) that governed the idea of vengeance in action, illustrate how the vocabulary of vengeance was used at the time, and enable us to begin to evaluate modern theories about vengeance in human societies within the specific context of medieval western Europe.[2]

It is clear that the vocabulary of vengeance was very much a part of everyday life for the crusaders and those who wrote about them. *Vindicta*, *ultio*, and *venjance* were not presented as exceptional or esoteric. Many authors used the vocabulary of vengeance without any further comment or elaboration, implying that the meaning was commonly understood and self-explanatory. Fortunately for the historian, other authors surrounded the vocabulary of vengeance with commentary on the meaning or moral value of events, presumably in an attempt to link events with the words they chose to describe them, or to otherwise serve their own narrative purpose. Although these authors were not concerned with providing "definitions" of their chosen vocabulary, nevertheless it is in their attempts to explain events that we can begin to reason backwards and try to deduce what the terms may have meant.

At the risk of spoiling the surprise, what seems to me the best working definition of the medieval concept underlying *vindicta*, *ultio*, and *venjance* (and perhaps other terms as well) is:

> violence (both physical and nonphysical) driven by a sense of moral authority, and in certain cases divine approbation, against those who are believed to question that authority and/or approbation.

This working definition is compatible with the associations shown below between *vindicta/ultio/venjance* and *iustitia*, *caritas*, *auxilium*, and *zelus*. Above all, it is compatible with the strong link that I will demonstrate existed between Christianity and *vindicta/ultio/venjance* in the twelfth-century texts.[3]

---

2   Of course, we are limited to analyzing the evidence given to us by the sources. And the sources often had their own narrative purposes for relating vengeance episodes, a point made firmly by Thomas Roche, "The Way Vengeance Comes: Rancorous Deeds and Words in the World of Orderic Vitalis," in S. Throop and P. R. Hyams (eds), *Vengeance in the Middle Ages: Emotion, Religion and Feud* (Aldershot, 2010), pp. 115–36. We are still at arm's length from everyday vengeance.

3   François Bougard recently attempted to clarify the relationships between *vindicta*, *ultio*, and *faida*. He concluded that although the three words were used interchangeably, *ultio* signified the vengeance of the state or deity roused by just anger, while *vindicta* was associated with the judiciary and the generic idea of chastisement or punishment ("Les Mots de la Vengeance," in D. Barthélemy, F. Bougard, and R. Le Jan (eds), *La Vengeance 400–1200* (Rome, 2006), pp. 1–6). In the same volume, Nira Pancer distinguished between *ultio* and

Vengeance and justice

Vengeance was always provoked by an *injuria*, an "injury."[4] This injury was a personal betrayal, a broken agreement, a physical injury or killing—as Hyams has argued based on the Norman *Summa de legibus*, simply "unwarranted harm" of one sort or another.[5] The injury may have been done directly to the one seeking vengeance, or indirectly to a family member or other closely allied associate of the avenger—at the most basic level, a friend (*amicus*) rather than an enemy (*inimicus*).[6]

Because it was a reaction to a prior event (real or imagined), vengeance was always embedded in a chronological context. An act of vengeance was never the beginning of the story, it always followed upon at least one other event. To describe an act as vengeance was to suggest the question, "vengeance for what?" The answer to that question would obviously vary quite a bit, depending upon whom you asked. However, an act could not be seen as vengeance, unless the act that preceded it was seen as unwarranted and harmful by the individual describing the act. Thus there was an inherent ethical value to vengeance— vengeance could be disputed or denied, but it was never morally neutral.

In our own times, for the most part we see a very keen distinction between private vengeance and public justice, but it was not the same in the Middle Ages.[7]

---

ulcisci, suggesting that the first corresponds to vengeance taken by a divinity or authority, while the latter corresponds to what we would deem private revenge ("La Vengeance Féminine Revisitée: Le Cas de Grégoire de Tours," in *La Vengeance 400–1200*, pp. 307–24, esp. p. 311). The sources I have looked at do not support the notion that writers were aware of these subtle distinctions, regardless of whether or not the distinctions existed, but certainly there are many common notes sounded by the work of Bougard and Pancer, and my working definition presented here.

[4] Also noted by Stephen D. White, "Un Imaginaire Faidal: La Representation de la Guerre dans quelques Chansons de Geste," in D. Barthélemy, F. Bougard and R. Le Jan (eds), *La Vengeance 400–1200* (Rome, 2006), p. 175.

[5] Paul Hyams, *Rancor and Reconciliation in Medieval England* (Ithaca NY, 2003), pp. 145–50.

[6] Medieval terms highlighted by Hyams, *Rancor and Reconciliation*, pp. 203–13; and previously by Daniel L. Smail, "Hatred as a Social Institution in Late-Medieval Society," *Speculum*, 76 (2001): 90–126.

[7] Clarification of when and why this distinction arose is greatly needed. One potentially significant development was in 1764 when the Milanese nobleman Cesar Beccaria wrote *On Crimes and Punishments*. Beccaria emphasized that punishment was only justified as a deterrent, and was never justified as revenge (Sasha Abramsky, *American Furies: Crime, Punishment, and Vengeance in the Age of Mass Imprisonment* (Boston, 2007), p. 17). In the fifteenth century, Christine de Pizan, working from Honore Bouvet's *Arbre des Batailles*, stated that it was wrong to seek violent retribution for an injury if the assailant had fled,

Ultio and *vindicta* were not viewed as opposed to justice (*iustitia*). Instead, the meaning of the Latin terms for vengeance and justice seem to have been closely related, if not exactly identical. After all, the event that sparked vengeance was always an "injury"—an *injuria*, translated literally, an unjust action.

An example of the overlap between justice and vengeance, occurs in a melodramatic scene in an account of the First Crusade. A dispute between the crusader Tancred and Arnulf of Chocques was heard before the *proceres* who were responsible for Arnulf's election as patriarch of Jerusalem. Arnulf felt that he had been slighted by Tancred. Since Arnulf was the "minister of God's house" and since the Holy Land could be said to be the *domus Dei*, Tancred had sinned against the minister of the Lord. Thus, Arnulf argued, Tancred was ultimately injuring both God and the *proceres* by wronging him, their minister. Reminding the *proceres* of his own loyalty, Arnulf exhorted them to seek vengeance on his/their/God's behalf: "therefore we uphold your law, O noblest princes; we avenge your injury (*injuria*), [now] punish the unjust (*injurius*)."[8] Otherwise, they would be ignoring the personal injury committed by Tancred to themselves and the law of God: "how could you not spurn one who spurns God?"[9] The passage's clever play on the words *injuria* (injury) and *injurius* (unjust man) suggests that vengeance and justice were analogous, in the rhetoric at least; both terms centered on the sense that a wrong had been committed and the right state of affairs (*ius*) had been breached.

The synonymity between the vocabulary of vengeance and judicial punishment was also evident in Odo of Deuil's criticism of Constantinople during the Second Crusade: "[there] a criminal has neither fear nor shame, and crime is not avenged by law, nor does it come openly to light."[10] From Odo's perspective, the lack of justice in Constantinople was evident in the fact that crimes were not avenged; the vocabulary of vengeance was applied to crime, an injury to society. Similarly, towards the beginning of his account of the First Crusade, Baldric of Bourgueil described the virtues of the crusading army. Among their praiseworthy attributes was their ability to discipline each other: "for if anyone was convicted of any dishonor, either having been censured he was upbraided to his face, or vengeance was gravely taken upon him, in order that

---

which she posited lay somewhere between self-defense, which was justifiable, and vengeance, which was not (*The Book of Deeds of Arms and of Chivalry*, ed. C. C. Willard, trans. S. Willard (University Park PA, 1999), pp. 161–2).

   [8]   Ralph of Caen, *Gesta Tancredi in Expeditione Hierosolymitana*, in RHCOc. 3 (Paris, 1866), p. 699.

   [9]   Ibid., p. 700.

  [10]   Odo of Deuil, *De Profectione Ludovici VII in Orientem*, ed. V. G. Berry (New York, 1965), p. 64.

fear might be excited in others."[11] Crimes were not punished, but avenged—or more precisely, the line we currently perceive between "vengeance" and "judicial punishment" was not in evidence.

These examples suggest that the vocabulary of vengeance was used in the Middle Ages not only to describe feuds and other events we are likely to consider "private," but also in much the same way as we today might use the term *punishment*, based upon Emile Durkheim's conception of punishment as violence visited on an individual by the authority of the group.[12]

Medieval writers did, however, express a distinction between vengeance (that is, punishment) and the concept of war. For instance, Ralph of Caen rhetorically questioned whether the First Crusade was vengeance or war. In one battle with the Muslims on the First Crusade, many Christians were slaughtered or deserted. Nevertheless, despite all odds Tancred and his brother William fought on. Describing their determination to see the battle through, Ralph of Caen wrote "this was certainly not judged a battle by them, but punishment: nor [did it seem] a conflict against enemies, but as if [it was] vengeance taken up concerning those condemned for capital offences."[13] In this passage, a "conflict against enemies" (external conflict) was contrasted with "vengeance..concerning those condemned for capital offences" (internal punishment). Modern theorists such as Raymond Verdier have suggested that the difference between punishment, vengeance, and war lies in our perception of our opponent (ally, adversary or enemy).[14] The passage from Ralph of Caen suggests that while medieval contemporaries of the First Crusade also saw a distinction between war against an enemy and punishment for wrongdoing within one's jurisdiction, surprisingly, to some degree, the First Crusade was perceived as an action more akin to vengeance (punishment) than to war.

---

[11]   Baldric of Bourgueil, *Historia Jerosolimitana*, in RHCOc. 4 (Paris, 1879), p. 28.

[12]   At the very end of the nineteenth century, sociologists such as Emile Durkheim focused on the human desire to conserve group solidarity. When Durkheim and others did pay attention to vengeance, they distinguished it from punishment, since they observed that, while acts of vengeance tended to give rise to negotiation between individuals, punishment was instead the action of a group against one of its members (Emile Durkheim, "Review of E. Kulischer 'Untersuchungen über das primitive strafrecht,'" trans. W. D. Halls, in A. Giddens (ed.), *Durkheim on Politics and the State* (Stanford, 1986), pp. 167–70).

[13]   Ralph of Caen, *Gesta Tancredi*, p. 623.

[14]   Verdier suggested that the terminology and concepts that define human modes of violence depend upon our view of "the other": if seen as an equal who commits a wrong, punishment ensues; if as an adversary, vengeance follows; and if as a completely alien enemy, war is the result (Raymond Verdier, "Le Système Vindicatoire," in R. Verdier (ed.), *La Vengeance: Études d'Ethnologie, d'Histoire et de Philosophie* (4 vols, Paris, 1980–84), vol. 1, pp. 13–42).

This conceptual overlap may not have been specific to the context of the First Crusade. General writers on sin and penance such as Thomas of Chobham drew explicit parallels between just vengeance (punishment) and just war: "it should be noted that just as it is necessary for princes to kill evildoers through just judgment, thus it is necessary to kill through just war."[15] Indeed, many thinkers, following Augustine of Hippo, agreed that one factor that made a war just was the avenging of injuries: "just wars ought to be defined as those which avenge injuries."[16]

Justice itself, in the abstract, was perceived as retributive: as William of Tyre reported himself saying, "justice is to pay back good for good, and evil for evil."[17] Justice was to get what you deserved—literally. Anecdotes from crusading texts reveal this principle expressed in action with vivid detail. In Robert of Clari's account of the Fourth Crusade, when Baldwin IV of Flanders, by then Latin emperor of Constantinople, was faced with his captured adversary, Emperor Alexius V, there was debate as to what fate suited his crimes.[18] The Doge of Venice, Henry Dandolo, said "for a 'high' [*haute*] man..I would advise you to take high justice."[19] Consequently Alexius was taken to the top of a tall column and thrown down to his death: "[thus] vengeance was taken on Mourtzouphlos the traitor."[20] The very means of execution were symbolically retributive, and were recognized to be such by those present, as evidenced by the Doge's speech.

Similarly, in one of James of Vitry's *exempla*, a traveling entertainer sought hospitality from a wealthy, but miserly, monastery, only to be given nothing but black bread, beans without salt, water, and a hard bed.[21] On his way the next morning, the entertainer was wondering how he could take vengeance on the stingy procurator who had treated him so badly, when he fortuitously met the abbot returning to the monastery. The entertainer falsely told the abbot

---

[15]   Thomas of Chobham, *Summa Confessorum*, ed. F. Broomfield (Paris, 1968), p. 430.

[16]   Augustine of Hippo, *Quaestionum in Heptateuchum Liber* 6.10 (cited by H. E. J. Cowdrey, "Christianity and the Morality of Warfare during the First Century of Crusading," in Marcus Bull and Norman Housley (eds), *The Experience of Crusading 1: Western Approaches* (Cambridge, 2003), p. 177).

[17]   William of Tyre, *Chronicon*, ed. R. B. C. Huygens, CCCM 63 (Turnholt, 1986), p. 868.

[18]   Alexius V, formerly Alexius Dukas Mourtzouphlos, had overthrown Alexius IV (placed on the throne by the crusaders) and demanded that the crusading armies leave Constantinople, resulting in the crusader assault on the city in 1204 and the subsequent crowning of Baldwin IV of Flanders as emperor.

[19]   Robert of Clari, *La Conquête de Constantinople*, ed. P. Lauer, CFM 40 (Paris, 1924), p. 104.

[20]   Ibid., p. 104.

[21]   James of Vitry, *The Exempla*, ed. T. F. Crane (London, 1890), p. 28.

(who was equally as stingy as his procurator) that he had enjoyed extravagant hospitality at the abbey, and "hearing this, the abbot, very angry, fiercely reprimanded [the procurator] for this grave crime and took away his office [as procurator] ... and thus the entertainer avenged himself on that vilest dog."[22] Again, the punishment fit the crime: the sin of miserliness was repaid with false "accusations" of generosity.

The moral argument connecting vengeance and justice was not that all acts described as vengeance were just, but that vengeance could be, and sometimes necessarily was just, for instance in the case of war or other common injury. Of course "could be" and "sometimes" left plenty of grey area, meaning that interpreting motives and events accurately was decisive when evaluating whether a specific act of vengeance was just—or not. Thomas of Chobham summarized the complicated position taken by the Church on vengeance, noting that "it is permitted for the laity to seek to regain their belongings from criminals through judgment and to demand the death penalty if they are evildoers and murderers, as long as they do this with a zeal for justice and not a vengeful desire (*libido*)."[23] Here Thomas did not distinguish between actions per se, but rather between the emotional sentiment behind those acts, approving of a "zeal for justice" and condemning "vengeful desire."[24] But a few pages on, Thomas qualified his earlier statement, implying that in some cases even "vengeful desire" was appropriate: "for it is one thing to avenge one's own injury, and another to avenge a common injury."[25] For Thomas of Chobham there was licit and illicit vengeance by the laity, although the ways in which the moral value of retributive actions was to be judged was complicated, and hinged upon both internal motivations and whether the injury was considered to be personal or communal.

Another factor that served to confirm or deny the justice of vengeful actions was implicit divine sanction. Gratian integrated the views of Augustine and Isidore of Seville into his corpus of canon law, arguing that just wars were those that avenged injuries and, moreover, those which God had commanded, "in which war the leader of the army or the people itself should not be judged so much the author of the war as the minister."[26] Christ himself was depicted as

---

[22]   Ibid., pp. 28–9.

[23]   Thomas of Chobham, *Summa Confessorum*, p. 436.

[24]   Chapter Five below will demonstrate that other writers of the period within the Church seem to have depicted the two motivations as synonymous, referring to a "zeal for vengeance" as well as a "zeal for justice."

[25]   Thomas of Chobham, *Summa Confessorum*, p. 440.

[26]   Gratian, *Corpus Iuris Canonici*, ed. A. E. Richteri (2nd edn, 2 vols, Lipsiae, 1879), vol. 1, cols 894–5.

judge and avenger, so it is little surprise that wars of vengeance authorized/administered by God were considered doubly just.[27]

Since there was canonical agreement (again following Augustine) that a war of vengeance was just, and that a war commanded by God, the ultimate judge and avenger, was undoubtedly just, it is not surprising that the crusading texts revealed this integration of justice, vengeance, war, and divine authority. Bernard of Clairvaux used this concept of a just war as one taking vengeance and also, crucially, authorized by God, to help to explain the failure of the Second Crusade to Pope Eugenius III. Going back to the Old Testament for an example of a war of vengeance undertaken without divine command, Bernard used Judges 20 to prove his point: "Benjamin sinned: the remnants of the tribes girded on their swords for vengeance, but without the nod of God ... But how terrible is God in his counsels upon the sons of men!"[28] To fight for vengeance was all well and good—as long as with "the nod" of divine consent. When that consent was withheld, disaster followed.

The construction of medieval Christian justice as fundamentally retributive may seem to contradict the Christian Gospels and their emphasis on mercy and forgiveness.[29] But mercy, *misericordia*, was not necessarily seen as a component of justice: justice and mercy were two distinct, and opposed, concepts. To put it another way, mercy was often in fact the denial of justice for the sake of some other motive—pity, charity, and so on. Justice and mercy complemented each other, and each had a place in Christian society—but it would be difficult indeed for an individual to be both just and merciful at the same time. The term "justice" implied the punitive side of law alone: "for justice alone condemns. But he is made worthy by mercy who seeks grace through spiritual labor."[30] Thus, when the First Crusaders were attacked by Greek mercenaries on the way

---

[27] For example see Orderic Vitalis, *Historia Aecclesiastica*, ed. M. Chibnall (6 vols, Oxford, 1969–80), vol. 5, pp. 284–6, where in a vision the Church (a "shining virgin") begs Christ for vengeance to be taken on William Rufus for the many injuries she has endured. Examples of *Christ ultor* have also been spotted in medieval Icelandic sagas (David Clark, "Revenge and Moderation: The Church and Vengeance in Medieval Iceland," *Leeds Studies in English*, new series, 36 (2005), pp. 145 and 147).

[28] Bernard of Clairvaux, *De Consideratione ad Eugenium Papam*, ed. J. Leclerq and H. M. Rochais, SBO 3 (Rome, 1963), p. 412.

[29] The concept of retributive justice, which is completely compatible with a society based on vengeance as a means of social control, dates back at least to the classical period in the West (Robert C. Solomon, *A Passion for Justice: Emotions and the Origin of the Social Contract* (London, 1995), p. 9; and Susan Jacoby, *Wild Justice: The Evolution of Revenge* (New York, 1983), p. 27).

[30] Pseudo-Augustine, *De Vera et Falsa Poenitentia*, ed. J.-P. Migne, PL 40 (Paris, 1845), col. 1122.

to Constantinople and Bohemond of Taranto ostentatiously declined to take vengeance when they were captured (as would have been just), Robert of Rheims described Bohemond as "moved by the spirit of mercy."[31]

The decision to be just or merciful in a given context was a decision to be made by the proper authority: God or his minister. Thus, as several scholars have noted, these concepts of justice and mercy were perceived as personal prerogatives, full of "the uneasy ambiguity of will."[32] *Iustitia* was the action of one in power, and *misericordia* was likewise the decision made by one in power to change his or her own rules and suspend vengeance. This placed great pressure on the one making the decision: "you will not be innocent, whether you punish him who by chance should be spared, or spare him who should be punished."[33] This may relate in part to the fact already noted that the ultimate test of the justness of acts of vengeance was divine sanction: in one sense, the personal prerogative of the ultimate moral authority.

One more point should be made here about justice and vengeance. By the early thirteenth century, a specific phrase highlighting the connection between justice and vengeance appeared in the writings of Robert of Auxerre: *vindicat ius*. At least twice, both times when discussing a dispute over inheritance, Robert of Auxerre wrote that not an individual human agent but *ius* avenged the injured party.[34] Was this a sign of the growing role of an impersonal concept of law and justice? Perhaps, but it depends on how we translate *ius*, since these passages also might be reinforcing the conceptual link between the general idea of moral right and vengeance, with *ius* signifying above all justice as a personal characteristic of the divine. In any event, Robert's phrasing is intriguing.

Vengeance, emotions, and power

As hinted above, vengeance was closely associated with those individuals capable of wielding power and moral authority. Ruling individuals needed to be seen taking vengeance if they wished to remain in power; at least, writers took care that they were presented in this way.[35] For example, Caffaro of Caschifelone

---

[31]   Robert of Rheims, *Historia Iherosolimitana*, in RHCOc 3 (Paris, 1866), p. 746.

[32]   Thomas Bisson, "Medieval Lordship," *Speculum*, 70 (1995), p. 759; see also Solomon, *A Passion for Justice*, p. 273.

[33]   Bernard of Clairvaux, *De Consideratione*, p. 428.

[34]   Robert of Auxerre, *Chronicon*, in MGHSS 26 (Hanover, 1882).

[35]   Stephen D. White "The Politics of Anger," in B. H. Rosenwein (ed.), *Anger's Past: The Social Uses of an Emotion in the Middle Ages* (Ithaca NY, 1998), p. 137.

praised Godfrey of Bouillon for his desire for vengeance.[36] Similarly, William of Tyre attributed Raymond of St. Gilles's reluctant alliance with Emperor Alexius I on the First Crusade to his attitude towards vengeance: "for it is said that he was a bold man, and perpetually mindful of the many injuries that, in his view, abounded."[37] Again, William of Tyre noted that Godfrey of Bouillon urged his men to take vengeance "as he was an active man, most prompt to take up arms."[38] Richard of Devizes likewise described King Richard I of England as one who "judges every man his own, no remnant of injuries are left unavenged. Whence ... he has the name of a lion."[39] Robert of Auxerre described King Henry I of England as "a fighter for equity among princes and a singular avenger of crimes."[40] The public character of those in power included the pursuit of vengeance.

It was not only secular leaders who needed to display their ability to take vengeance. In Bernard of Clairvaux's advice to Pope Eugenius III, he repeatedly advised him to display his authority by taking vengeance. The four virtues Bernard suggested for papal meditation were justice, prudence, fortitude, and temperance: "justice inquires, prudence discovers, fortitude, takes vengeance, and temperance holds fast."[41] The pope was urged to be like the prophets and apostles: "they were strong in war, not effeminate in silks. And you are the son of the Apostles and Prophets, do you the same."[42]

Are these examples simply evidence of writers adding drama and personality to their accounts, rather than a realistic depiction of the state of affairs in everyday medieval life? Did rulers really need to be seen to take vengeance? The texts argued explicitly that it was crucial that those with power be seen to take vengeance because doing so maintained their power. As the prior of Hereford reportedly said to King Richard I of England in April 1192, "unless like a mature man you listen to counsel and return to your homeland and take vengeance for your injuries ... these false lies will increase, and you will be unable to revive your rule in any way without the contest of war."[43] These sorts of passages

---

[36]   Caffaro of Caschifelone, *De Liberatione Civitatum Orientis*, ed. L. T. Belgrano, *Annali Genovensi di Caffaro e de'suoi continuatori* 1 (Genoa, 1890), pp. 99–100.

[37]   William of Tyre, *Chronicon*, p. 188.

[38]   Ibid., p. 276.

[39]   Richard of Devizes, *Cronicon de Tempore Regis Richardi Primi*, ed. J. T. Appleby (London, 1963), p. 17.

[40]   Robert of Auxerre, *Chronicon*, p. 233.

[41]   Bernard of Clairvaux, *De Consideratione*, p. 407.

[42]   Ibid., p. 420.

[43]   *Itinerarium Peregrinorum et Gesta Regis Ricardi*, ed. W. Stubbs, RS 38:1 (London, 1864), p. 334. This episode in the *Itinerarium Peregrinorum* originated in the Old French account of Ambroise, who wrote:

admittedly do not fully answer the second question, but they do suggest that talk of vengeance was not (simply) high drama—it was founded on, and seen to be founded on, extremely practical socio-political reasoning.

Nor was it only the laity who discussed this sort of practical reasoning. Gervase of Canterbury explained that neglecting the duty to take vengeance could open the floodgates to further weakness and lack of control within the ecclesiastical domain as well:

> for this abuse could become greater within the Church of God, because the archbishop is not strong enough to bring any vengeance to bear upon any criminals, and he will see priests and clerics flogged by monks or the laity, churches polluted with homicide or flagrant injury and murderers enraged, and adulterers and all criminals will multiply, since he cannot avenge the injuries of God in his city.[44]

No matter how flowery the language, these examples have the smell of hard political truth, even in our own day and age. Vengeance maintained power for both Church and secular leaders.[45] To pursue it was the duty as well as the prerogative of those in power.

The need for rulers to visibly pursue vengeance was surely intimately related to the virtuous *ira regis* of the earlier Middle Ages, and the lordly anger of the central Middle Ages, which were in turn connected with the duty to provide justice. Medieval writers described leaders as quick to become angry and take vengeance, and needing to display openly this kind of personality in order to convince their subordinates to follow their lead. This was what White has

---

"Good sire, for this reason it is required of you,"
said the prior, "that you return
to your land and avenge yourself
on those who have deserved this from you;
when these men increase, then they will offend even more:
in this land where they have taken this tax,
You will not enter again without a battle."

(Ambroise, *The History of the Holy War: Ambroise's Estoire de la Guerre Sainte*, ed. M. Ailes and M. Barber (2 vols, Woodbridge, 2003), vol. 1, p. 138)

[44]   Gervase of Canterbury, *Chronica*, in RS 73:1 (London, 1879), p. 78.

[45]   It is worth noting the contrast between this apparent state of affairs, and Hannah Arendt's classic assertion that "violence can destroy power; it is utterly incapable of creating it" (*On Violence*, cited by Samuel Peleg, *Zealotry and Vengeance: Quest of a Religious Identity Group* (Lanham MD, 2002), p. 125).

called a "script" for lordly anger: injury provoked shame and anger, anger led to vengeance, and the successful act of vengeance caused joy.[46]

Examples of this "script" in action frequently appeared in the crusading sources. When Emperor Henry IV was threatened by the anti-king Rudolf of Rheinfelden, one source claimed he had to rally his men to his cause:

> The emperor, moved by these injuries, acted to call together all the imperial princes to himself. To whom gathered before him he disclosed the injury, though it was known to all, and invited them to vengeance, but all of them, fervently indignant for the glory of the empire and considering no less grievous the enormous crime of the Swabians, placed themselves beside him with certainty, promising him men, asserting that such a deceit against the Roman empire could not be, and decreeing that the crime should be taken up by the deadly avenging sword of his majesty.[47]

Far from rushing to take vengeance alone in an emotional state, Henry was described coolly calling his men together and "revealing" the horrible crime that had been committed. Then his men, apparently emotionally inflamed in an instant despite the fact that they had already known about the offense, "insisted" that he take vengeance. A similar scenario reportedly took place in the camp of Muslim leader Nur al-Din when a military ally had been captured:

> Nur al-Din, however, upset at such a sinister event, was inflamed with anger, and having assumed the garb of confusion and fear, seeking to abolish the infamy by avenging the injury done to him and his, he solicited his friends and associates, all the princes of the east, now with a curse, now as a begging suppliant. He invited them, he revived his men, and collected military pledges.[48]

The language of emotion and injury was used in a terribly staged way—"Men, you won't believe what horrible injury has been done to me!" "My lord, that is outrageous and you must seek vengeance!"—but the reality was surely one of careful political planning and strategy, indicated by our author with careful parenthetical remarks like "though it was known to all" and "having assumed the garb of confusion and fear." It is possible that these scenarios described by William of Tyre illustrate a sort of ritual associated with vengeance, expected

---

[46]   White, "The Politics of Anger," pp. 142–5. The link between anger and vengeance goes back at least as far as Aristotle (Barbara H. Rosenwein, "Les Émotions des la Vengeance," in D. Barthélemy, F. Bougard, and R. Le Jan (eds), *La Vengeance 400–1200* (Rome, 2006), p. 237).

[47]   William of Tyre, *Chronicon*, p. 429.

[48]   Ibid., p. 874.

behavior on behalf of both those in power and those beneath them before violence ensued. The powerful one announces the injury to a gathering of his men, his men express outrage and loyalty, and the quest for vengeance ensues.

In addition to anger, another emotion prominently connected with the concept of vengeance in the twelfth-century crusading texts, and similarly used to poke and prod others towards vengeance, was shame.[49] Although the nature of an injury could vary widely, from an insult to a killing, one factor seems to have been universal: an injury evoked a feeling of shame in its recipient. Social scientists have noted that the phrase "painful injury" is sometimes used even today as a euphemistic label for the traumatic emotional experience of shame, especially in situations involving personal betrayal or public humiliation.[50]

Furthermore, to fail to take vengeance when one was shamed by an injury was to be doubly shamed, because one was clearly impotent and cowardly. Vengeance that was demanded by a certain situation but failed to materialize deserved the scorn and contempt of all, and the anger of the just.[51] Baldric of Bourgueil described the crusaders who fled from battle without avenging their comrades as "most shameful men," "betrayers of their own," "unmindful of the state of their brothers."[52] He went on to wreak his own vengeance upon them as best he could, by listing their names for all to see: "for they who fled from the battle, abandoning their companions, are known as the protectors of their companions, and for the most part ... vengeance should be taken on them."[53]

Albert of Aachen, for one, even tried to preempt criticism of the crusaders by offering explanations for occasions when vengeance was not immediately sought. For example, after the death of Roger of Barneville outside the walls of Antioch, "no one among the pilgrims dared to go forth from the city to the aid of Roger, who was killed and decapitated."[54] Faced with this embarrassment, Albert was quick to explain to his readers that Roger's unavenged demise was not

---

[49] Of course, shame as a spur to vengeance has been noted outside crusading literature as well, for example, in the romance of *King Horn* (Hyams, *Rancor and Reconciliation*, p. 65n).

[50] Thomas Scheff, *Bloody Revenge: Emotions, Nationalism and War* (Boulder, 1994).

[51] One notable exception was, of course, when the injury was chastisement from God.

[52] Baldric of Bourgueil, *Historia Jerosolimitana*, p. 64.

[53] Ibid., p. 64. That it was shameful to fail to take vengeance is indicated by the fact that failure to take vengeance placed one outside the pale, outside the boundaries of civilized behavior. When some crusaders retreated from battle on St. James's Day 1190, they were "inhuman and impious, who watched their brothers cut to the heart, but did not devote themselves to the task [of vengeance]" (*Itinerarium Peregrinorum*, p. 91).

[54] Albert of Aachen, *Historia Ierosolimitana*, ed. S. Edgington (Oxford, 2007), p. 288.

due to cowardice, but to a very reasonable lack of transportation: "this should not seem amazing to anyone, nor should anyone think that the shocked Gauls had become soft through a weakness of mind, or through fear of the oncoming multitude, and therefore were slow to aid and avenge their *confrere* ... for scarcely a hundred and fifty horses remained to the Gauls."[55]

The accusation of failing to take vengeance was used as a great insult among powerful men, one that the poet Raimbaut of Vaqueiras directed at his adversary, the Marquis Albert Malaspina:

> you are not as valiant as Roland, it seems to me,
> because Piacenza does not leave you Castagnero:
> she destroys all that land and yet you do not take vengeance.[56]

Moreover, to show mercy or even mere indifference to one enemy was, in some contexts, to risk earning the contempt of all the rest. King Richard I of England exhorted his men in Cyprus:

> We aim to fight Turks and Arabs, we aim to be a cause of alarm for the most unconquered nations, we want our right hand to make a way for us even to the ends of the earth following the cross of Christ, we would restore the kingdom of Israel, but yet we are going to show our backs to the vile and effeminate Griffons? I beg you for your honor, I say to you, I again say, if you will now go away unavenged, the vile story of your flight will precede you.[57]

Those in power, or who wished to be so, had to take vengeance, because to do otherwise was to open the floodgates to further injury, further shame, and presumably, eventual loss of power.

What if you were a powerful man, but could not expect unquestioning support for your vengeance, no matter how angry you appeared in public? One option was to offer reasonable, rational arguments for vengeance, as when Henry Dandolo, the Doge of Venice, sought help from the Fourth Crusaders to attack the Hungarian city of Zadar (then Zara) in 1201:

---

[55]   Ibid., pp. 288–90. Fortunately the crusaders were given another opportunity for vengeance at a later date and Albert was able to report that Tancred returned to the city "in great glory and happiness," carrying the heads of the Muslims killed to avenge Roger (ibid., p. 296).

[56]   Raimbaut of Vaqueiras, *The Poems of the Troubadour Raimbaut de Vaqueiras*, ed. J. Linskill (The Hague, 1964), p. 110.

[57]   Richard of Devizes, *Cronicon*, p. 21.

It is now winter, we cannot now go overseas ... But we can do a good thing! ... There is a city near here, Zara is its name. Those of that city have done wrong to me, and I and my men would like to avenge ourselves, if we can ... And the city of Zara is very fine and very full of all good things![58]

In this example, the Doge invokes two arguments for vengeance in addition to the moral appeal of righting a wrong: it is winter and they are unable to go to the Holy Land, and besides, Zara offers the opportunity for rich looting.

Sometimes, the opportunity to take vengeance could even serve as an enticing way to gain new allies in order to pursue one's *own* vengeance. Geoffrey of Villehardouin described how between March and July 1207 there were many "battles in Europe and Asia." In one such conflict, Theodore Lascaris (the son-in-law of Isaac II Angelus) sought an alliance with the Bulgarian emperor Johannitsa, who had been attacked by the emperor Henry of Flanders. Theodore sent messengers to Johannitsa, explaining the reasons why he should ally himself with Theodore, dangling the prospect of vengeance before Johannitsa like a carrot: "all the emperor's men were far from him ... and the emperor was in Constantinople with few men; so now he [Johannitsa] could avenge himself [on the emperor]."[59] Johannitsa's vengeance would be Theodore's vengeance too—in his case, vengeance for the overthrow of his kinsman, Isaac Angelus.

Sometimes, however, neither strong emotion, the ritual action of seeking counsel and aid, rational argument, or even the most enticing carrots were enough (or were unavailable) to convince either subordinates or peers to support the drive for vengeance. In these situations, powerful individuals relied on the threat of violence. According to one author, when Godfrey of Bouillon sought to rouse his army to "avenge the blood of their brothers" who had been attacked at Port St. Symeon during the First Crusade, he had to threaten his men "with penalty of death, lest anyone should dare to subtract himself at such a necessary time."[60] This example of recourse to threats of violence underlines a well-known difficulty with tit-for-tat social systems, often labeled "reciprocal altruism" in the natural sciences: there will always be those who seek to cheat the system by giving less support in time of conflict than they themselves receive from others.[61]

The responsibility and prerogative of great men to take vengeance was also evident in one voice from the early thirteenth century who strove to display

---

[58]   Robert of Clari, *La Conquête de Constantinople*, p. 12.

[59]   Geoffrey of Villehardouin, *La Conquête de Constantinople*, ed. E. Faral (2 vols, Paris, 1938), vol. 2, p. 274.

[60]   William of Tyre, *Chronicon*, p. 276.

[61]   Frans de Waal, *Good Natured: The Origins of Right and Wrong in Humans and Other Animals* (Cambridge MA, 1996), p. 159.

kings and emperors displaying very different virtues. Several times Arnold of Lübeck described situations in which powerful men considered vengeance but ultimately rejected it, and still apparently retained their honor (at least according to Arnold). Arnold even went to the trouble of "recording" speeches for these powerful men, explaining why they did not choose to take vengeance, perhaps to clarify that their actions were not cowardly or shameful. For example, when in 1181 Emperor Frederick I had besieged Lübeck, the bishop of Lübeck was sent out by the townspeople to speak with Frederick and endeavor to end the siege. The bishop was successful, and eventually Frederick remarked to him:

> since it is more necessary for us, through the censure of justice, to exhibit patience rather than vengeance to all [people], behold we consent to them even in this matter, so that, just as they have proposed, they may go to their lord and confer with him about his position, knowing one thing: if when returning they do not open the city to us, they will be sentenced to the gravest vengeance for this delay.[62]

Again, when in 1190 Emperor Henry VI sought greater power in the Holy Roman Empire, "nevertheless he released [some adversaries he had] besieged, whom he had held, in accordance with this: *Vengeance is mine, I will take retribution, says the Lord.*"[63] Arnold of Lübeck attempted, at least a few times, to depict secular powers leaving vengeance to God. However, his attempt appears to have been singular among its peers in its emphasis on imperial patience. Moreover, he only did so in certain passages; elsewhere in the account, as shown below, Arnold presented the taking of vengeance in a morally neutral, or even positive, light.[64]

We have seen that both secular and ecclesiastical powers were perceived as a source of vengeance. This basic political truth was further justified and enforced by the idea that the powerful were dispensing vengeance not (only) for themselves, but for God. This line of justification was especially important since Gratian had stressed that it was right to avenge injuries to God and one's neighbors, but wrong to avenge injuries to the self.[65] Not surprisingly, this line of thought encouraged the tendency to interpret actions against powerful individuals as actions against God, particularly within the Church. Gervase of

---

62   Arnold of Lübeck, *Chronica*, in MGHSS 21 (Hanover, 1869), p. 140.

63   Ibid., p. 174. Reference to Romans 12:1.

64   Pages 30 and 119–22 below.

65   Stanley Chodorow, *Christian Political Theory and Church Politics in the Mid-Twelfth Century: The Ecclesiology of Gratian's Decretum* (Los Angeles, 1972), p. 233. See also Thomas of Chobham, *Summa Confessorum*, p. 440, discussed above on page 17.

Canterbury described Thomas Becket speaking confidently before his murder in 1170, saying "I am right, and the lord Pope will avenge my injuries and those of the Church of God."[66] But secular leaders chose this approach to reinforce their right to vengeance, too. After all, the sanction to avenge injuries in the name of God was surely connected to the traditional duty of kings to protect the property of the Church within their realms. King Philip II of France certainly saw it as his duty to protect (that is, avenge) the Burgundian Church in 1186, issuing the ultimatum that "if the duke did not wish to restore the money [he had wrongly taken] to the churches, he would most gravely take vengeance upon him."[67] And at times secular and ecclesiastical powers worked in concert, averring that to disobey each other's mandates was a wrong against God and would be punished by violent vengeance. For example, William of Tyre wrote that Daimbert, the first Latin Patriarch of Jerusalem, said that "it is sacrilege to violate the commands of the highest princes, and either you will comply with this injunction, or it will be necessary for you to succumb to their avenging swords."[68]

It should be noted that lesser magnates also used this theme of acting on behalf of God to justify violence amongst themselves. Orderic Vitalis related that when Count Helias of Maine faced the ambitions of King William II of England he claimed:

> I wished to fight against the pagans in the name of the Lord, but now behold, I find a battle closer to home against the enemies of Christ. For any who resists truth and justice proves himself an enemy of God, who is truth itself and the sun of justice. He [God] has condescended to commend to me the stewardship of Maine, which I ought not to relinquish foolishly for any light cause, lest the people of God should be given over to predators, like sheep without a shepherd given over to wolves.[69]

On the battlefield with Stephen of Blois, the Earl of Gloucester reportedly told his men to "take hold of your spirits, and with all your strength, confident in justice from God, know that vengeance is being delivered by God [through us] on these villains."[70]

---

[66]   Gervase of Canterbury, *Chronica*, p. 225.

[67]   Rigord, *Gesta Philippi Augusti*, in *Rigord: Histoire de Philippe Auguste*, ed. E. Carpentier, G. Pon, and Y. Chauvin, Sources D'Histoire Médiévale 33 (Paris, 2006), p. 188.

[68]   William of Tyre, *Chronicon*, p. 443.

[69]   Orderic Vitalis, *Historia Aecclesiastica*, vol. 5, p. 230.

[70]   Gervase of Canterbury, *Chronica*, pp. 114–15.

By framing the powerful as agents of God, their vengeance was sanctified and injuries against them were deemed sacrilege—a way of interpreting events and violence that was a highly effective form of social control within both the Church and the rest of society. Indeed, the role of vengeance as social control was explicitly noted by Gervase of Canterbury when he theorized that there were three main weapons against crime: prohibition, precept, and example.[71] In his view, example was the most effective because "when [people] read or hear of someone's penalty for contempt, they will flee evil in terrified fear, lest they undergo a similar vengeance."[72]

So where did all this leave the less powerful who had suffered an injury? It is difficult to say conclusively due to the nature of the sources, but those without power and authority seem to have been discouraged from seeking personal vengeance, in part by stories of "vengeance gone wrong." For example, Guibert of Nogent presented his readers with the story of a "certain knight" who made a pact with the devil in order to take vengeance on his brother's murderer, who was his social superior. The knight could find no spiritual peace until he confessed (on crusade) that he had sinned in making a deal with the devil. The sin that demanded confession was his deal with the devil, not his desire for vengeance, but nevertheless the tale could be read as a warning against the dangers of seeking vengeance against superiors.[73] It was not for such men as this "certain knight" to seek vengeance on the powerful, and to persist in doing so could lead to devilish bargains that threatened eternal punishment.

Certainly less powerful individuals often attempted to conceal their injuries and their desire for vengeance due to political expediency. William of Tyre described the leaders of the First Crusade at Constantinople:

> coming together at [the emperor's] summons, although what had happened
> displeased many of them, nevertheless, seeing that it was not the opportunity for
> vengeance, they admonished [Raymond of St. Gilles] concerning his interests and
> exhorted him with frank arguments that he should wish to dissemble the injury
> that they held in common.[74]

---

[71]   Ibid., p. 85.

[72]   Ibid., p. 86.

[73]   Guibert of Nogent, *Dei Gesta per Francos*, ed. R. B. C. Huygens, CCCM 127A (Turnholt, 1996), pp. 323–4.

[74]   William of Tyre, *Chronicon*, pp. 188–9.

Richard of Devizes described the Duke of Austria insulted at Acre by the trampling of his banner: "savagely raging against the King ... he failed to dissemble the injury" as he should have done.[75]

Often the desire for vengeance was only suppressed until the balance of power had shifted and action could be taken. Concerning the 1136 war between the Welsh and the English, Gervase of Canterbury wrote that "the Welsh, remembering the evils which King Henry [I of England] had done to them and desiring to avenge their injuries, made a great slaughter of men, destroying churches, towns and the suburbs."[76] Similarly, Otto of St. Blasien wrote that, when the Germans under Emperor Henry VI were at a disadvantage in Sicily in 1197, they found themselves facing an angry populace "mindful of the injuries which they had sustained from the Emperor Henry, they were most inflamed with hatred towards the German people and avenged themselves for their injury as much as they could."[77]

Alternatively, well-connected individuals could use the rituals of lordly anger and vengeance to promote their own causes. When imperial legates encountered difficulties at Milan in 1158, they "returned to the emperor, told him about the Milan rebellion and the injury done to himself, and incited him to take vengeance immediately."[78] Similarly, one could take part in a broader conflict in order to satisfy a personal desire for vengeance. In the *Chanson de la Croisade Albigeoise* one knight explained that he fought for Toulouse's cause only to avenge the death of his own lord, King Peter II of Aragon.[79]

In addition, there was always the chance that a powerful man might court popularity by turning public enemies over to the people for vengeance, as when in 1191 Emperor Henry VI gave a Tuscan town to its Roman enemies who subsequently destroyed it "in vengeance."[80] Robert of Clari described with greater dramatic detail the death of the former emperor of Constantinople, Andronicus I Comnenus, at the hands of the people in 1185. Andronicus was put on a camel with his hands tied and sent from village to village; the people, as expected, seized the opportunity:

> "You hung my father, and you took my wife from me by force!" And the women
> whose daughters he had taken by force seized him by his moustache, and did to

---

[75] Richard of Devizes, *Cronicon*, p. 47.

[76] Gervase of Canterbury, *Chronica*, pp. 95–6.

[77] Otto of St. Blasien, *Chronici ab Ottone Frisingensi episcopo conscripti continuatio auctore ... Ottone Sancti Blasii monacho*, in MGHSS 20 (Hanover, 1868), p. 328.

[78] Ibid., p. 309.

[79] *La Chanson de la Croisade Albigeoise*, ed. M. Zink (Paris, 1989), p. 402.

[80] Otto of St. Blasien, *Chronici*, p. 320.

him such a thing of pure shame that when he arrived at the next village, there was not one bit of flesh left on his body, so they took his bones, and threw them on a midden heap. In such manner vengeance was taken on that traitor.[81]

And of course, one could also take a risk, hope that public sentiment and sympathy would go your way, and embark on acts of vengeance that seemed more likely to be universally approved, or at least tolerated. For example, Arnold of Lübeck described the men of Horneburg fighting to free their lord, the Bishop of Horneburg, who had been imprisoned: "the men of the Bishop of Horneburg were zealous concerning the injuries of their lord, and frequently made attacks on the Duke's men and running through his land laid waste the surrounding villages with fire."[82] Arnold neither praises nor blames the bishop's men for their acts of vengeance. Likewise, when Duke Welf was hanged by Hugh of Tübingen in 1164, his son, the younger Welf "was moved, he got on his horse with greatest indignation, and with fire and sword he avenged the injury he had received."[83] It would seem that to avenge one's lord or one's father did not excite disapproving comment. (Although I think we can safely assume that an author from the household of Hugh of Tübingen may have viewed Welf Junior's vengeance in a more negative light.)

In any event, subordinates were keenly aware of the dangers to themselves of ongoing vengeance amongst the powerful, and although they incited great men to action when it suited them, when they stood to suffer from such action they instead tried to quell the desire for vengeance. When King Henry II of England and Thomas Becket were at odds, the earls of Leicester and Cornwall mediated between them, "fearing for themselves lest because of this uproar more bitter vengeance would rage against them."[84] The powerful also recognized the destructive effects of ongoing conflict, and pressured each other to limit their acts of personal vengeance. In 1204, Henry Dandolo and others sought to effect peace between Baldwin of Flanders and Boniface of Montferrat, pleading with Baldwin "that they would not destroy Christianity ... you know that it commands you not to engage in war without end."[85]

Because of the terrible threat of vengeance from those in power, sometimes the threat of vengeance was vengeance enough. When Emperor Manuel I Comnenus visited Raymond of Antioch he (Raymond) "fearing his coming, lest by chance [the emperor], having been excited by the querulous voices of the

81   Robert of Clari, *La Conquête*, p. 28.
82   Arnold of Lübeck, *Chronica*, p. 136.
83   Otto of St. Blasien, *Chronici*, p. 311.
84   Gervase of Canterbury, *Chronica*, p. 177.
85   Geoffrey of Villehardouin, *La Conquête*, vol. 2, p. 102.

aforesaid clamor, was descending [upon him] to avenge their injuries, anxiously sought to deliberate ... how he could be reconciled with the imperial family for such an offense."[86] The writer of the *Itinerarium peregrinorum* remarked that King Richard I of England forgave his brother John, "judging it sufficient that he [Richard] was able to take vengeance."[87] In a political sense it must have been so. There is even today little more humiliating than being considered beneath contempt and fear, and the shame of humiliation is still recognized by moral philosophers as a key component of punishment.[88]

Vengeance and religious identity

Arnold of Lübeck's descriptions of powerful individuals seeking alternatives to vengeance emphasizes a fundamental question: in regards to vengeance, was there always a sharp ideological contrast between the ethos and behavior of churchmen and that of the laity, as Hyams and others have posited?[89] Do crusading texts from the twelfth-century demonstrate a fundamental conflict between Christianity and the concept of vengeance? How did the factor of religious belief affect the habits of vengeance?

Text after text suggests that it would be inaccurate to envision a heavy ideological dividing line separating a pro-vengeance laity from an anti-vengeance Church.[90] Vengeance and Christianity were ideologically compatible; *ultio* and *vindicta* were depicted as the actions of a Christian, actions worthy of emulation—even the actions of a pope. To a great degree this has already been demonstrated above in the multitude of examples discussing vengeance and justice, and vengeance and power, but there are a few additional passages worth examining in detail.

In Albert of Aachen's account, the Muslim Prince of Apamea was killed by his associate, Botherus. The two sons of the dead prince fled to Damascus, and Tancred besieged Apamea. Hearing of Tancred's siege, "[the sons] sent

---

86   William of Tyre, *Chronicon*, p. 845.

87   *Itinerarium Peregrinorum*, p. 449.

88   Solomon, *A Passion for Justice*, p. 258.

89   Hyams, *Rancor and Reconciliation*, p. 43.

90   David Clark comes to a similar conclusion looking at medieval Iceland ("Revenge and Moderation: The Church and Vengeance in Medieval Iceland"). Kimberly Rivers has noted that the fear of divine vengeance was even used as a mnemonic device by monastics ("The Fear of Divine Vengeance: Mnemonic Images as a Guide to Conscience in the Late Middle Ages," in A. Scott and C. Kosso (eds), *Fear and Its Representations in the Middle Ages and Renaissance* (Turnholt, 2002), pp. 66–91).

messengers to Tancred, [saying] that they would come to him in order to help
and take vengeance for the blood of their father, if it would seem useful and
acceptable to him and his men."[91] Tancred formed an alliance with them, which
the three men affirmed in person, *dextris datis*. Eventually the city surrendered to
Tancred, and in return he allowed the murderer Botherus to go free. The sons of
the murdered prince protested, but Tancred ruled that it would be unchristian to
break the agreement he had already made with Botherus (which had resulted in
the surrender of the city). However, Tancred told his two allies that "[Botherus']
accomplices, to whom we did not grant [anything], may be taken in your hand
either to be killed or allowed to live, in vengeance for the blood of your father."[92]
The reason why it was immoral to kill Botherus was not that vengeance itself
was unchristian, but rather that it was unchristian to break a specific agreement
already made. Vengeance could be lawfully (and, it is implied, piously) taken on
others with whom no such agreement had been made. In this passage, Tancred
made a rational, informed moral judgment based on what he considered to be
Christian values. Not all members of the Church may have agreed with him,
but to label this decision ignorant or unchristian for that reason alone would be
mistaken.[93]

Indeed, it was not only lay leaders like Tancred who expressed an
understanding that vengeance in the right circumstances was perfectly Christian.
After all, similar moral weighing took place before the Fourth Crusaders stormed
Constantinople. The crusaders were concerned about the morality of the assault,
and asked the bishops of the crusading army whether it would be a sin to attack
the city. According to Robert of Clari, the bishops replied "that it would not
be at all a sin, moreover it would be a great good deed, for they who had been
disinherited [the Latin inhabitants of Constantinople] would have the right to
inherit, and they [the crusaders] could well help them [the Latin inhabitants] to
conquer their right and avenge themselves on their enemies."[94] In this case, the
laity expressed moral concern, and were reassured by members of the Church
hierarchy that it would be right to attack Constantinople, not *despite* the
connotations of vengeance, but in fact *because* they would be taking vengeance
and thus participating in a just war. It is worth repeating that, although not all
Christians at that time may have agreed that these were Christian opinions,
nevertheless, clearly Christian values mattered to the crusaders; and equally

---

[91]   Albert of Aachen, *Historia Ierosolimitana*, p. 738.

[92]   Ibid., p. 740.

[93]   This closely parallels the argument made by Raymond Schmandt about the Fourth
Crusade (Raymond H. Schmandt, "The Fourth Crusade and the Just-War Theory," *Catholic
Historical Review*, 61 (1975): 191–221).

[94]   Robert of Clari, *La Conquête*, p. 40.

clearly, for some who considered themselves Christian, lay and cleric alike, vengeance was compatible with those values.

This is further confirmed by the fact that powerful men within the Church used the vocabulary of vengeance repeatedly in their letters and treatises—not just when corresponding with the laity, but also in reference to domestic Church matters. Bernard of Clairvaux used the vocabulary of vengeance when dealing with a variety of affairs, and did so in correspondence intended for a number of different individuals. For example, in 1142 he wrote to Pope Innocent II concerning Raoul of Vermandois, who had repudiated his wife and taken another against the counsel of the bishops: "many cry out to you from their whole heart, that you might avenge the injury of your sons and the oppression of the Church with worthy punishment."[95] Suger of St. Denis' letters revealed the same trend. Circa 1148–49 Suger wrote to Pope Eugenius III against the canons of St. Genève: "therefore on these men, who disregard apostolic reverence with these kinds of injuries to God and his saints, for contempt, for disobedience, for sacrilege, they have decided on ecclesiastical vengeance, which retribution they deserve to receive according to the rigor of justice."[96]

Peter the Venerable also used the vocabulary of vengeance in his correspondence about European matters that concerned him. In 1134, he wrote to Matthew, Cardinal-Bishop of Albano, about a number of monks who had been wrongfully expelled from the monastery of St. Paul's in Vermandois: "if such an injury remains unavenged, it will allow the laughter of the enemies of the monastic order."[97] Later, Peter wrote to a number of his contemporaries about the threat posed by the heretic Peter of Bruys: "through the grave of Peter of Bruys at St. Gilles the zeal of the faithful of the lord's cross avenged [God] ... afterwards clearly that impious man made the eternal journey from fire to [hell]fire."[98]

Vengeance was presented by many as a Christian activity, at times almost a Christian virtue. On the battlefield, churchmen were depicted urging the laity

---

[95]   Bernard of Clairvaux, *Epistolae*, ed. J. Leclerq and H. M. Rochais, SBO 7–8 (Rome, 1974–77), vol. 8, p. 77. Similarly, in 1143 Bernard wrote to the bishop of Soissons: "greater zeal for avenging the injuries of Christ and the Church is required" (ibid., vol. 8, p. 89). See also pages 19–20 above.

[96]   Suger of St. Denis, *Epistolae*, in RHGF 15 (Paris, 1878), p. 506. Suger also warned Raoul of Vermandois: "those who burn with zeal will most shamefully punish those who are found to side with you ... therefore those living with you have fled from vengeance" (ibid., p. 528).

[97]   Peter the Venerable, *The Letters of Peter the Venerable*, ed. G. Constable (2 vols, Cambridge MA, 1967), vol. 1, p. 145.

[98]   Peter the Venerable, "Epistola ad archiepiscopos Arelatensem et Ebredunensem, Diensem et Wapincensem episcopos," in RHGF 15 (Paris, 1878), p. 640.

to take violent vengeance. William of Tyre noted that on the First Crusade members of the clergy "exhorted princes to ... avenge the blood of the dead."[99] But Church thinkers and leaders used the vocabulary of vengeance amongst themselves also; they did not simply resort to the concept of vengeance when communicating with the laity. As has been shown, justice, the power to judge and dispense punishment, was very closely affiliated with the vocabulary of vengeance in the period. The pope, and every member of the Church hierarchy below him, had a power and responsibility to maintain justice; they had the ability to bind and loose souls, thereby judging men's actions and calling them to account.[100] Not all within the Church agreed as to what powers exactly this granted to the Church, but some (including Pope Innocent III) judged that the pope had moral authority to dispense justice for all crimes, since all crimes were sins.[101] The Church's political responsibility and right to uphold justice linked Church doctrine with the vocabulary of vengeance, because the concepts of vengeance and justice were so co-dependent.[102]

Perhaps both because of its political nature and relationship with contemporary perceptions of Christian values, the vengeance of the powerful in the Church was a flexible system of response that need not always take the form of bloodshed. When ecclesiastical authorities needed to take direct vengeance themselves, they sometimes did so without resorting to violence, relying instead on the shame caused by traditional actions such as excommunication and deposition. For example, at Christmas 1186 Archbishop Baldwin "withdrew his presence from Canterbury as though in vengeance, and celebrated the Lord's Birth in a little town in Otteford."[103] The Archbishop of Rouen took vengeance on William Longchamp (Bishop of Ely, then Chancellor) for his excommunication of the English exchequer officials: "in vengeance for that presumptuous excommunication of the treasurers, he order[ed] [the interdict] to be announced throughout Normandy."[104] The *Chronique d'Ernoul* also described excommunication as vengeance in the case of Emperor Otto IV in 1210: "when the Pope knew that [Otto's armies] had taken his castles and had

---

[99]   William of Tyre, *Chronicon*, p. 216.
[100]   John A. Watt, *The Theory of Papal Monarchy in the Thirteenth Century* (London, 1965), p. 15.
[101]   Ibid., pp. 52–3.
[102]   I discuss this at greater length below, pages 88–96.
[103]   Gervase of Canterbury, *Chronica*, pp. 345–6.
[104]   Richard of Devizes, *Cronicon*, p. 54.

fought against him..he was very upset. And he could do no other thing than take vengeance by excommunicating Otto."[105]

There were those in the Church who counseled caution when seeking vengeance. In several of his *exempla* James of Vitry illustrated the dangers of taking vengeance hastily or carelessly. In his fable of the body and the stomach, James described all the members of the body ganging up against the stomach because of its apparent sloth: "for whatever the hands acquired through work, and the feet through walking, and the other members through working, that greedy collector (that is, the stomach) consumed, and because of his eating.. they were fatigued with various labors." The rest of the body decided to punish the stomach by not giving it anything to eat, but "when they had gone hungry for one day, in order to avenge themselves on the stomach, they began to grow a little weak."[106] One moral of the story was that vengeance on another could come back and harm the perpetrators.

Similarly, in another *exemplum* James told of a young man who was living on his own as a hermit. One day his father set out to visit the young hermit. A demon, seeing the father on his way, appeared to the hermit looking like an angel and "warned" him: "protect yourself from the Devil, for he himself seeks subtly to deceive you. Right now he is coming to you in the guise of your father, so take vengeance on him: have a hatchet ready so that when he comes, you may strongly strike him so that he does not presume to come near you."[107] Predictably, the gullible young hermit did as advised, only to discover too late that the man truly was his father, and that the true demon was the "angel" who had incited him to violence. It would seem that the main moral of this story was to be wary of those who incite vengeance: "behold how wretchedly that one was deceived who ought to have questioned the spirit and not easily acquiesced."[108] James of Vitry and his contemporaries rarely condemned vengeance outright and often used the vocabulary of vengeance themselves, but they did advise caution and reliance on the proper moral authority—especially when they were addressing the lower echelons of society. It is worth wondering whether James would have been so precautionary in an audience with a king or pope, or if, like Bernard of Clairvaux, he would have advised a clear demonstration of power and authority.[109]

---

[105]   *Chronique d'Ernoul et de Bernard le Trésorier*, ed. M. L. de Las Matrie (Paris, 1871), pp. 397–8.

[106]   James of Vitry, *The Exempla*, p. 33.

[107]   Ibid., p. 34.

[108]   Ibid., p. 35.

[109]   See above pages 19–20 and 33.

Was vengeance against or between Muslims presented differently than "Christian" vengeance? After all, in some cultures, one of them ancient Israel, a distinction was made between actions taken against those outside the group and actions against group members.[110] Interestingly, no linguistic distinction appears to have been made in the Western crusading texts between actions against or by Christians and actions against or by Muslims—*vindicta* and *ultio* were used to describe both types of situation. Indeed, writers frequently depicted Muslims pursuing the same types of vengeance as Christians, suggesting that, for these medieval authors, the social rules governing vengeance were not perceived as specifically "Christian"; or, perhaps, that they did not (or could not) imagine that other people had dramatically different conventions for vengeance. This is not to say that Christian writers did not imagine a particularly "Muslim" approach to vengeance, but rather that when they did so, and even when they imagined Muslims talking about Muslim ideas of vengeance, the imagined "Muslim" approach looked an awful lot like a western Christian approach. For example, Baldric of Bourgueil characterized the crusaders as "most avid avengers of the blood shed by their own," and similarly characterized the Muslims who besieged Antioch after its fall to the Christians: "[the Muslims] said that they [themselves] were inglorious ... unless they avenged the blood of their own shed at the hands of their enemies."[111] According to Robert of Rheims, Peter the Hermit barely escaped violent retribution for his failure to show due respect to Kerbogha: "when the Turks saw this [injury], they endured it with difficulty; and if [Peter and others] had not been messengers, [the Muslims] would have avenged the dishonor of [such] proud indifference."[112] Given the similarities that are so blatant to modern eyes, it is ironic that at least one medieval writer characterized the desire for vengeance within Islamic society as a specific consequence of the Islamic religion: "[my fellow Muslims] fear this more than dying ... that they should die unavenged. They do this not from obstinacy, but from the religion of our faith. For we [Muslims] believe that the shades of the unavenged wander forever."[113]

According to the sources, the conventions governing vengeance sometimes called for Christians to take vengeance on other Christians for wrongs done to Muslims that contradicted the laws of war. Following the capture of Jerusalem in 1099, Tancred granted quarter to a group of Muslims within the city. In his absence, they were all killed by the other crusaders. Tancred was furious, and

---

[110]   Andre Lemaire, "Vengeance et Justice dans l'Ancien Israel," in R. Verdier (ed.), *La Vengeance: Études d'Ethnologie, d'Histoire et de Philosophie* (4 vols, Paris, 1980–84), vol. 3, pp. 14–15.

[111]   Baldric of Bourgueil, *Historia Jerosolimitana*, pp. 50 and 59.

[112]   Robert of Rheims, *Historia Iherosolimitana*, in RHCOc. 3 (Paris, 1866), p. 825.

[113]   Richard of Devizes, *Cronicon*, pp. 77–8.

the leaders of the crusade were able to persuade him that the slaughter was right only with difficulty: "Tancred, the glorious knight, was incensed with violent anger concerning this underhanded injury to him; nor could his fury be quieted without discord and great vengeance, until the counsel and judgment of the great and prudent men had tempered his mind with words."[114] What is most intriguing about this passage is that a Christian crusader was prepared to take vengeance upon other Christian crusaders for the death of Muslims whom he felt should not have been killed, because he had personally granted them quarter. The injury had been done to Tancred's honor, and so Tancred was in truth avenging himself not the Muslims, but the fact that the parties who had been killed were Muslim in no way alleviated that injury in his mind.

This mentality was echoed during the reign of King Baldwin I of Jerusalem, when men from Pisa "unjustly" killed Muslims with whom an agreement had been made. The slaughter of these Muslims awoke the anger of the King:

> When this unjust treachery had completely ceased, the King was vehemently indignant concerning this injury done to himself by the Pisans and the Genoese on account of his oath. And therefore, lest in sorrow it should be believed that his faith and pact were false with his consent, having admonished his companions and his household, he wished to avenge this crime gravely.[115]

Both Tancred and Baldwin I perceived the killing of Muslims with whom they had entered into an agreement, in accordance with the laws of war, as an injury to themselves. They desired to avenge that injury just as they would have done if their associates had been Christian; the religious identity of the allied party did not seem to affect their reaction. It would seem that the behavior of the crusaders towards the Muslims followed the same social rules of conduct that moderated their behavior among themselves. What dictated their behavior was not the identity of the other party, but their own identity.

Gender, ethnicity, and vengeance

As shown, many writers used the same vocabulary to describe similar conventions of vengeance among Christians and Muslims, as if there were no other possible way of behaving.[116] On the other hand, some sources—often exactly the same

---

[114]   Albert of Aachen, *Historia Ierosolimitana*, p. 440.

[115]   Ibid., pp. 607–8.

[116]   James of Vitry even took it a step further and made the desire for vengeance for dead kin a characteristic of the animal world, describing how a monkey mourning its dead

ones, in different places—suggested that the desire to take vengeance did indeed vary due to ethnicity or gender.

Sometimes, writers portrayed the propensity for vengeance as a national characteristic, one which even extended to a nation's saints: "just as the Spanish nation and the Welsh nation, before other peoples more precipitate in anger, are known to be prone in life towards vengeance, so in living death the saints of these lands seem to be more vengeful in spirit than others."[117]

The desire to take vengeance was attributed to women as well as men, and some suggested that women were even more vengeful than their male counterparts.[118] Gerald of Wales related the story of Bernard of Newmarch and his wife Nesta, who, according to Gerald, injured her husband by committing adultery. Bernard sought to take vengeance by poisoning her, but she in turn "vomited forth the poison in vengeance. Therefore going to Henry the First, King of the English, [Bernard] asserted [his son's illegitimacy], more as a vengeful assertion than as a true one."[119] Nesta, Gerald concluded, "in order that her vengeful anger could be satisfied ... with one and the same crime [of adultery] had deprived her son of his patrimony, and herself of her honor." Gerald concluded somberly that Juvenal was right: "no one rejoices in vengeance more than a woman."[120]

The *Chanson de Jérusalem* would seem to agree with this prognosis, stating that at Antioch

> the women cried out, they who had gone there with the host of God
> to conquer the city where God was resurrected—
> he who well avenged [God] would have their love all his days.[121]

---

child "began to think how it could avenge itself" on the bear that had killed the infant (*The Exempla*, p. 64).

[117]   Gerald of Wales, *Itinerarium Kambriae*, ed. J. F. Dimock, RS 21.6 (London, 1868), p. 130. Those interested in the question of saintly vengeance and the stereotype of the "vengeful Irish" may wish to look at Máire Johnson's work on Irish saints: "'Vengeance is Mine': Saintly Retribution in Medieval Ireland," in S. Throop and P. Hyams (eds), *Vengeance in the Middle Ages: Emotion, Religion and Feud* (Aldershot, 2010), pp. 5–50.

[118]   Nira Pancer and Isabel Alfonso have also noted the presence of both feminine and masculine vengeance, but neither encountered the stereotypical "overly vengeful woman," as I have (Pancer, "La Vengeance Féminine Revisitée"; and Alfonso, "Vengeance, Justice et Lutte Politique dans l'Historiographie Castillane du Moyen Âge," in D. Barthélemy, F. Bougard, and R. Le Jan (eds), *La Vengeance 400–1200* (Rome, 2006), pp. 383–419).

[119]   Gerald of Wales, *Itinerarium Kambriae*, p. 29.

[120]   Ibid., p. 30.

[121]   *La Chanson de Jérusalem*, ed. N. R. Thorp, OFCC 6 (Tuscaloosa, 1992), p. 115.

The *Chronique d'Ernoul* likewise described vengeful women in Constantinople tearing the body of Emperor Andronicus I to pieces and eating the pieces: "and they said that all those who had eaten of him would be saved, because they had helped to avenge the evil that he had done."[122] Whether enacting violent vengeance themselves or inciting men to take vengeance, the women in these passages avidly desired vengeance and went to great lengths to procure it.

A slightly different example of female vengeance was put forth in one of the *exempla* of James of Vitry. A woman whose husband was committing adultery "frequently prayed to the image of the blessed Mary, the blessed Virgin, [saying] that she was overcome by the whore who had carried off her husband."[123] One night Mary appeared to the wife in a dream and said, "I cannot avenge you on that woman, for that sinner bends her knees a hundred times every day before me saying: Hail Mary." Completely frustrated and infuriated, the wife visited the mistress in person, saying to her rival:

> O vilest whore, because you have seduced my man and taken him away from me,
> I was even defeated by you when I invoked the blessed Virgin. Because you salute
> her with your filthy mouth a hundred times each day, she does not wish to give me
> justice concerning you, but told me that she cannot avenge me, because you bend
> your knees a hundred times a day. But I will complain about you to the son of him
> who justly ought to be mine, and he will take vengeance on you.

The mistress, feeling pangs of guilt that the Virgin was unable to take right vengeance because of her prayers, fell at the wife's feet and promised that she would not sin with the husband any more. And thus "the blessed Virgin made peace between those women and was satisfied with the best kind of female vengeance."[124] This example of "vengeance" between women was presented in an approving manner by James of Vitry, as opposed to examples of women taking vengeance on men, which he most definitely censured.[125] The evidence is limited in the crusading sources, but it would seem that for women, as for

---

[122]   *Chronique d'Ernoul*, p. 94. The suggested parallel between this act of cannibalism and the consumption of the eucharist ("they said that all those who had eaten of him would be saved") is striking and surely worth further investigation. For another episode of cannibalism as female vengeance, see Marina Brownlee, "Verbal and Physical Violence in the *Historie of Aurelio et Isabell*," in S. Throop and P. Hyams (eds), *Vengeance in the Middle Ages: Emotion, Religion and Feud* (Aldershot, 2010), pp. 137–50.

[123]   James of Vitry, *The Exempla*, pp. 92–3.

[124]   James does not even consider the possibility that the mistress was swayed not by piety, but by the threat of physical vengeance from her rival's son.

[125]   Ibid., p. 99 — the story made famous by Molière in *Le Médécin malgré lui*.

men, there were both appropriate and inappropriate forms of vengeance and times to seek vengeance. Hopefully, in time scholars will more fully flesh out our understanding of vengeance and gender in the Middle Ages.

*   *   *

Although crusading texts are a selective group of sources for twelfth-century Europe, they provide evidence on how vengeance in general functioned in society. Any *injuria*—a physical injury, betrayal, broken agreement, or other act that engendered shame in the recipient—demanded vengeance. The social emotion of shame was a critical component of medieval vengeance, as many would argue it still is today. Not only did the shame of an injury demand vengeance, but failure to take vengeance when expected only increased the shame of the injured party.

During this period vengeance was a concept closely related to justice. A crime, as an injury against God, those in power, and the victim, was as much an *injuria* as a brawl that we might consider to be "private." In the twelfth-century crusading texts there was limited sign of a Christian distaste for vengeance; on the contrary, vengeful behavior was generally held up as that of a model Christian who possessed the right authority. The vocabulary of vengeance was used forcefully by members of the Church in reference to internal affairs, and was an acceptable component of religious rhetoric on topics including, but not limited to, the crusades. The mores of vengeance did not alter when Christians interacted with Muslims.

Some medieval contemporaries assumed that a predisposition for vengeance varied from group to group—women, certain nationalities, and figures of authority were especially discussed—while at the same time they presented vengeance as a universally experienced and understood phenomenon. The representation of authorities as vengeful corresponded with the idea of the virtuous anger of the king and other powerful men. Both Church and secular leaders further justified their entitlement to take vengeance by claiming to take vengeance for God himself.

I have argued that the prerogative to take vengeance was used to consolidate power and exercise social control. One study of another culture has suggested that a system based solely on immediate personal vengeance within a society of true equals cannot evolve into factional power politics, but in later twelfth-century crusading texts the vocabulary of vengeance *was* merging with a new political hierarchy, most likely because twelfth-century Europe decidedly was *not* an egalitarian society.[126] As elsewhere, in western Europe it seems that the personal vengeance of powerful individuals and factions transformed over time into vengeance as a means of consolidating "official" power.[127]

---

[126]   Robert M. Glasse, "Revenge and Redress among the Huli: A Preliminary Account," *Mankind*, 5 (April 1959), p. 289.

[127]   Ronald Cohen, "Warfare and State Formation: Wars Make States and States Make Wars," in R. B. Ferguson (ed.), *Warfare, Culture, and Environment* (London, 1984), p. 340.

Chapter Two

Early Years: Crusading as Vengeance, 1095–1137

In 1095 Pope Urban II did something rather unusual.[1] He embarked on a papal preaching tour through France, making his way with due pomp and circumstance through villages and rural regions, where it is likely most people had never dreamed of seeing a real pope in the flesh. On the way he delivered a singular message, known to historians now as the sermon he gave at the Council of Clermont: Christians should embark on an armed pilgrimage to Jerusalem, to liberate the city and eastern Christians in general from the abusive tyranny of the Muslims. Because of the necessary hardships involved, this armed pilgrimage would serve as an act of penance, earning for participants remission of their sins.

The resultant expedition that launched in two waves in 1096 is generally referred to now as the First Crusade. The second wave of the crusade was unexpectedly successful, conquering major cities like Nicaea and Antioch in 1097 and 1098, and taking Jerusalem itself in 1099. This success, viewed as nothing short of miraculous by contemporaries, encouraged a number of less successful expeditions eastward in 1100, 1101, and 1102. It also resulted in the production of an extraordinary number of written commemorations of the 1096 expedition.

This chapter examines the idea of crusading as an act of vengeance in the crucial period surrounding the First Crusade, from 1095 through 1137, assessing the assertion made by Jonathan Riley-Smith and others that the idea of crusading as vengeance was predominant among the laity and faded after the taking of Jerusalem in 1099. The uniqueness, and significance, of this period has led me to adopt a slightly different approach for this chapter. While in the other chapters the sources for a given period are discussed together, for the period 1095–1137 they are discussed in terms of the participation of the authors in the First Crusade—eyewitness accounts and non-participant accounts. The eyewitness accounts were for the most part not written earlier than the non-participant accounts, but they were written by people who (as far as we

---

[1]   Unusual but not entirely unprecedented, since Pope Leo IX had done similarly in 1049.

can tell) witnessed the events that they describe. These authors were not only reporting the opinions or ideas of others, at least potentially they were reporting their own ideas and actions as part of a larger group. Their distinctiveness, and my treatment of the sources for the period, is supported by the evidence they provide.[2]

Assessing the earliest crusading sources

There are a very limited number of documentary sources that can be safely considered contemporary with the late 1090s—various letters associated with the First Crusade and another, disputed source, the forged document known as the Encyclical of Sergius IV.[3] The limited number of sources necessarily makes it difficult to definitively prove or disprove the idea that crusading as vengeance was a lay idea of great popularity in 1095. However, despite the difficulties of the evidence for the mid to late 1090s, it at least provides a counterpoint for the many accounts written after 1100.

Only two letters of the First Crusade (of those collected by Heinrich Hagenmeyer) contained a reference to vengeance. In one, sent by the lay leaders of the crusade to Pope Urban II from Antioch in September 1098, the crusaders claimed "we the *Hierosolymitani* of Jesus Christ have avenged the injury [done to] the highest God."[4] The second letter, written by Pope Paschal II to the Pisan consuls in 1100, stated that "the Christian people ... most strenuously avenged [Jerusalem] for the tyranny and yoke of the barbarians and, with God helping, restored those regions, sanctified by the blood and presence of Jesus Christ, to their former refinement and majesty with adornment and veneration."[5] These two letters show the presence of the idea of crusading as vengeance at the cusp between the eleventh and twelfth centuries, but to a limited degree, since the vast majority of the letters made no connection between the First Crusade and vengeance. In addition, the two letters differ in their assumption of what constituted the injury that deserved vengeance. While the letter from the lay leaders of the First Crusade simply stated that they had avenged an unspecified

---

[2]   Similarly, later texts do not show the same division of evidence that led me to discuss eyewitness accounts and non-participant accounts separately in this chapter.

[3]   For a discussion of the historiography of the Encyclical, see below pages 194–5. As discussed there, I follow Alexander Gieszytor on dating, who argues that the document dates to the very late eleventh century.

[4]   *Epistulae et Chartae ad Historiam Primi Belli Sacri Spectantes*, ed. H. Hagenmeyer (New York, 1973), p. 164.

[5]   Ibid., p. 180.

injury done to God, the letter from Paschal II made it clear that the injury in question was the prior seizure of Jerusalem by the Muslims.

The forged Encyclical of Sergius IV presents us with more problematic evidence.[6] And yet, faced with the fact that someone deemed its contents important enough to forge, and also facing a scarcity of sources for the period leading up to 1095, historians certainly cannot disregard the Encyclical.

The purpose of the Encyclical, in its own words, was "to make known to all Christians that ... the Holy Sepulchre of our Lord Redeemer Jesus Christ has been destroyed by the impious hands of pagans."[7] The document further stated: "certainly it is our burden, however, to avenge this for the Lord at this time ... thus let us fight against the enemies of God, so that we may be worthy to rejoice in heaven with him. It seems right ... that we should avenge the Redeemer and his tomb."[8] Moreover, the text drew parallels between the legend of the Roman destruction of Jerusalem and the proposed medieval expedition to Jerusalem:

> just as it was in the days of Titus and Vespasian, who avenged the death of God's Son ... and for their sins received forgiveness (*indulgentia*). And if we do similarly, without doubt we will abide in eternal life. We make known to you..[that there are many who] are greatly concerned with avenging the Holy Sepulchre.[9]

This Encyclical is tantalizing yet mitigated evidence for the idea of the First Crusade as an act of vengeance in the late eleventh century. Although the text did describe a crusade-like expedition as vengeance, it primarily stressed the motivating desire for eternal life: "he who loses his present life for Christ ... will find a future [life]."[10] The audience was exhorted to "recollect the day of judgment, when you will possess all joys from Christ, if you do well. Come, sons, defend God and acquire an eternal kingdom."[11] The author also wished to "make known to you ... [that there are many who] just as the Evangelist tells, desire to take up [their cross]."[12] In short, the Encyclical was an amalgam of different motivating

---

[6]   As I discuss below at pages 194–5.

[7]   *Encyclical of Sergius IV*, ed. H. M. Schaller, "Zur Kreuzzugsenzyklika Papst Sergius' IV," in H. Mordek (ed.), *Papsttum, Kirche und Recht im Mittelalter* (Tübingen, 1991), pp. 150–51.

[8]   Ibid., p. 151.

[9]   Ibid., p. 151–2.

[10]   Ibid., p. 151.

[11]   Ibid., p. 151.

[12]   Ibid., p. 152.

factors (as were most crusading accounts), and, perhaps more importantly, it was not in fact widely disseminated.[13]

Nevertheless, the Encyclical of Sergius IV, taken together with the two First Crusade letters discussed above, demonstrates that the idea of crusading (or something like crusading) as vengeance was in existence in the late eleventh century. It also signals the significance of the legend of the destruction of Jerusalem in 70 C.E. that would inform the later text known as *La Venjance de Nostre Seigneur* by the end of the twelfth century. But the Encyclical and the letters alone are not overwhelming evidence for a widespread and dominant desire for vengeance that supposedly thrived in the armies of the First Crusade as they left Europe, and then subsequently faded. The evidence suggests only that the idea of crusading as vengeance was circulating at the time, and that some of the themes emphasized in later texts were already in existence—the "injury" of the Islamic occupation of Jerusalem, and the connection between the crusades and the legendary destruction of Jerusalem.

Let us turn to the eyewitness accounts of the First Crusade. These are, of course, the traditional starting point for the study of the First Crusade. Next to the letters, they represent the most directly available evidence concerning the opinions and actions of the crusaders themselves while on crusade. There is no certainty that they reflect the reality of the First Crusade experience with complete accuracy, but compared with the accounts of non-participants, they are more likely to do so.

The five most commonly examined eyewitness accounts in Latin are the anonymous *Gesta Francorum*, Fulcher of Chartres's *Historia Iherosolymitana*, Peter Tudebode's *Historia de Hierosolymitano Itinere*, Ekkehard of Aura's *Hierosolymita*, and Raymond of Aguiler's *Liber*.[14] In four of these eyewitness accounts, there were absolutely zero references to the idea of crusading as vengeance, and, indeed, almost no references to vengeance of any kind; even descriptions of everyday "he hit me so I hit him" vengeance were uncommon.

In the accounts of Fulcher of Chartres, Peter Tudebode, and the *Gesta Francorum* there were only five references altogether to vengeance of any kind, and three of the references strongly emphasized that God, not man, takes vengeance.[15] The final two references were unremarkable: Peter Tudebode remarked that Raymond of St. Gilles was so incensed by Emperor Alexius I that

---

[13]   Alexander Gieysztor, "The Genesis of the Crusades: The Encyclical of Sergius IV (1009–1012)," *Medievalia et Humanistica*, 5 and 6 (1948), vol. 6, p. 30.

[14]   For a description of these sources, see below pages 193.

[15]   *Gesta Francorum et Aliorum Hierosolimitanorum*, ed. R. Hill (Oxford, 1962), pp. 17 and 54. Fulcher of Chartres, *Historia Hierosolimitana*, ed. H. Hagenmeyer (Heidelberg, 1913), p. 166.

"he meditated on how he could take vengeance on the army of the emperor," and Fulcher of Chartres included in his account the letter written in 1098 from the crusaders to Pope Urban II discussed above.[16] These were quite literally the only references to vengeance of any kind in these three accounts—and none of them can be construed as an original reference to the idea of crusading as a whole as an act of vengeance. Meanwhile, Ekkehard of Aura did not refer to any actual deeds of vengeance in his text.

The one eyewitness account that did yield more evidence for the idea of crusading as vengeance was the *Liber* of Raymond of Aguilers, where the idea of crusading as vengeance surfaced twice. The English went forth because they "heard the name of the Lord of vengeance (*audito nomine ulcionis Domini*) on those who unworthily occupied the land of Jesus Christ's birth and of his apostles."[17] Likewise, the taking of Jerusalem was when "the sons of apostles avenged the city and the fatherland for God and the fathers."[18] Like Pope Paschal II in his letter of 1100 and like the Encyclical, Raymond of Aguilers suggested that vengeance was owed for the Islamic occupation of Jerusalem.[19]

When we consider the eyewitness accounts alongside the letters and the Encyclical, two things are clear. First, the idea of crusading as vengeance was in circulation at the time of the First Crusade. This is not surprising in the least; the idea of holy war as vengeance for God in fact dates back before the crusade, making it likely that the understanding of the First Crusade as vengeance was an adaptation of a previous trend, and not an entirely new ideology specific to the crusades.[20] Second, nevertheless, the understanding of crusading as vengeance at the time of the First Crusade does not seem to have been as widespread as previous historians have thought—at the least, it was not recorded by the majority of those who kept written accounts. Even Raymond of Aguilers, who twice described the crusade as vengeance, also explicitly noted two occasions when restraint was shown by the crusaders, claiming specifically that the

---

[16]　Peter Tudebode, *Historia de Hierosolymitano Itinere*, ed. J. H. Hill and L. L. Hill, DHC 12 (Paris, 1977), pp. 95 and 47. Fulcher of Chartres, *Historia Hierosolymitana*, p. 261.

[17]　Raymond of Aguilers, *Liber*, ed. J. H. Hill and L. L. Hill, DHC 9 (Paris, 1969), p. 134.

[18]　Ibid., p. 151.

[19]　*Epistulae et Chartae*, p. 180. Full text given above at page 44.

[20]　Jean Flori, *Croisade et Chevalerie* (Brussels, 1998), p. 189. This raises the following questions: what exactly was the previous trend, how did the idea of war as vengeance come to be adopted for crusading, and did it change in the process? These questions are beyond the scope of this book, but I hope other scholars will pursue them in the future.

crusaders did not want vengeance—their minds were fixed on the journey ahead of them rather than on the desire for vengeance.[21]

On the whole, the eyewitness accounts favored the concepts of the crusade as pilgrimage and of the crusaders as pious, quasi-monastic martyrs. According to the anonymous *Gesta Francorum*, the crusaders were instructed by Pope Urban II at Clermont concerning their future ordeals. "Brothers, it is necessary for you to suffer many things for Christ's name, namely wretchedness, poverty, nakedness, persecution, want, sickness, hunger, thirst and other things of this kind, just as the Lord said to his disciples: *it is necessary that you suffer many things for my name.*"[22] And the example of the virtuous crusader *par excellence* for Peter Tudebode and the author of the *Gesta Francorum* was Bohemond, who mercifully "allowed [the Byzantine agents] to leave without any punishment."[23]

Similarly, the eyewitness accounts emphasized the glory of martyrdom, not the glory of vengeance. Raymond of Aguilers described one of Peter Bartholomew's visions, in which Christ divided the Christians into five graded orders. The first and most important order of men were crusaders who had been killed on crusade. "They die for me, and I died for them. And I am in them, and they are in me. Truly when such as these perish, they are gathered by the right hand of God, where, ascending into heaven after the Resurrection, I sat."[24] Peter Tudebode described the captured knight Rainald Porcet peacefully refusing to convert to Islam and choosing his own death instead, "humbly beseeching God that he might come to him, and might take up his soul honorably into Abraham's bosom."[25] This early characterization of Rainald markedly contrasts with that of the late twelfth-century *Chanson d'Antioche*, in which Rainald insults his Muslim captors and insists that Christians will avenge his death.[26]

The earliest documents as a whole do not provide overwhelming evidence for the dominance of the idea of crusading as vengeance in the late eleventh and very early twelfth century. Some might argue that this was because the idea circulated among the lower laity who of course were illiterate; but, while the highest lay leaders of the Crusade touched upon the idea in their letter to Pope Urban II, as did Raymond of Aguilers (a knight who was only ordained during the crusade), other "lay" texts such as the *Gesta Francorum* ignored it, and at least one pope (Paschal II) included the idea in his correspondence. So far, the evidence as we have it simply does not allow for the ideological separation of

---

21   Raymond of Aguilers, *Liber*, p. 38.

22   *Gesta Francorum*, pp. 1–2. Reference to Acts 9:16.

23   Peter Tudebode, *Historia*, p. 42.

24   Raymond of Aguilers, *Liber*, pp. 113–14.

25   Peter Tudebode, *Historia*, p. 80.

26   *La Chanson d'Antioche*, ed. J. Nelson, OFCC 4 (Tuscaloosa, 2003), p. 197.

the laity and the religious, or of those of low and high rank—nor for a popular, widespread belief that the crusade was an act of vengeance in the late eleventh century.

The question remains of the contended decline of the significance of vengeance in the early years of the twelfth century. According to this hypothesis, the laity seized upon the idea of crusading as vengeance during the course of the First Crusade, but subsequently discarded it in the early twelfth century as their fervor died down and monastic revisionists addressed themselves to the task of shaping crusade ideology. Is there a visible de-emphasis on the idea of crusade as vengeance in the second-generation Church histories, as opposed to the accounts of the eyewitnesses?

Quite simply, and rather surprisingly, the opposite is true. It is in the twelfth-century histories of the First Crusade written by non-participants, both monastic and otherwise, that the idea of crusade as vengeance is discernable, although the idea of crusading as vengeance was not the only theme, or even the predominant one, presented in them.[27] On the whole, the position that monastic historians viewed the crusaders as though they were members of a vast, itinerant monastery is accurate.[28] The non-participant writers did not confine themselves to one theme, and certainly not to the one theme of vengeance. Much of the rhetoric concerning martyrdom, pilgrimage, and the imitation of Christ was alive and well in these accounts. The important point is that the non-participant accounts emphasized vengeance more than the eyewitness accounts did, however limited their treatment of vengeance was. Moreover, as we shall see, the non-participant texts suggest that the idea of crusade as vengeance was rooted not simply in the immediate emotional appeal of violence against an enemy in lay minds, but also in the intellectual, religious, and social frameworks of thought that members of the Church used to glorify and justify the First Crusade after the fact.

In general, non-participant writers portrayed the Christians enacting divine vengeance for the Islamic occupation of Jerusalem and the purported sufferings of Christians at the hands of the Muslims. For Albert of Aachen, when Peter the Hermit saw the conditions in Jerusalem that drove him to return to Rome to beg Pope Urban II for an armed expedition, "he called on God himself to be

---

[27]   For this study, I analyzed the histories of Albert of Aachen, Baldric of Bourgueil, Guibert of Nogent, Robert of Rheims, Ralph of Caen, and Orderic Vitalis. For more on these sources, see page 193 below.

[28]   Jonathan Riley-Smith, *The Crusades: A History* (2nd edn, New Haven, 2005), pp. 14–15.

the avenger of the injuries he had seen."[29] Orderic Vitalis summarized the events surrounding the First Crusade as follows:

> The detestable Saracens, permitted by divine justice, had crossed the borders of the Christians and invaded the holy places; they murdered the Christian inhabitants, and polluted the holy objects abominably with their filth, but after many years they rightly endured the vengeance they deserved from the arms of the northern peoples.[30]

Robert of Rheims depicted Pope Urban II saying at Clermont "by whom therefore will these things be avenged, to whom does the labor of recapture fall, unless to you, to whom before other peoples God has given the worthy sign of his love?"[31] In this example, the crusaders were acting out the will of God by taking vengeance for an unspecified injury on the Muslims, although the Islamic occupation of Jerusalem was highlighted.[32]

For Orderic, even the Muslims themselves understood that the crusaders had come to avenge the deaths of Christians in the East.[33] Both Robert of Rheims and Guibert of Nogent also made it seem as though some among the Muslims were aware that the crusaders were seeking vengeance, expanding upon the dialogue between Kerbogha and his mother seen in the eyewitness accounts. Robert of Rheims attributed the following speech to Kerbogha's mother:

> of their invincible God the prophets say: *I kill, and I give life; I strike, and I heal; and there is no one who can escape my hand. Thus I will sharpen my sword as lightning, and my hand will snatch justice, I will return vengeance on my enemies, and retribution on those who hate me* ... This God is angry at our people, because we do not hear his voice, nor do we do his will.[34]

In essence, this passage implies that vengeance was deserved by the Muslims' lack of faith in the Christian God, their failure to "hear his voice" and "do his

---

[29]   Albert of Aachen, *Historia Ierosolimitana*, ed. S. Edgington (Oxford, 2007), p. 4.

[30]   Orderic Vitalis, *Historia Aecclesiastica*, ed. M. Chibnall (6 vols, Oxford, 1969–1980), vol. 5, p. 4.

[31]   Robert of Rheims, *Historia Iherosolimitana*, in RHCOc. 3 (Paris, 1866), p. 728.

[32]   According to Orderic Vitalis, in response to Urban's speech "arms were bought, with which divine vengeance would be exercised on the lovers of dirt (*allophilos*)" (*Historia Aecclesiastica*, vol. 5, p. 16).

[33]   Orderic Vitalis, *Historia Aecclesiastica*, vol. 5, p. 40.

[34]   Robert of Rheims, *Historia Iherosolimitana*, p. 812. Reference to Deuteronomy 32:39–42.

will." In Guibert of Nogent's account, his mother warned Kerbogha that "their [the Christians'] God does not avenge the crime on the perpetrator right away, but even while he allows that crime the penalty on the criminals is deferred," suggesting that the Christian attack on the East had been a long time coming.[35]

Guibert of Nogent also applied the words of Zechariah 12:6 to the First Crusade, explaining that "therefore *they devoured all the people to the right and to the left in a circle* [means that] while over here the elect, whom the right hand signifies, are incorporated into the piety of Christianity, over there the reprobate, who are known to pertain to the left, are devastated with deserved vengeance of slaughter."[36] For Guibert, vengeance was deserved by the Muslims not for one specific action but rather because they were "reprobate."

Descriptions of specific key battles often evoked references to the idea of crusading as vengeance. Robert of Rheims commemorated the fall of Antioch to the Christians with a succinct verse on the matter:

> Divine vengeance thus wished to be avenged
> on the dog-like people, and thus it was pleased.[37]

In Baldric of Bourgueil's account, before the crusaders assaulted Jerusalem an inspiring sermon was preached on the theme of vengeance:

> I say to fathers and sons and brothers and nephews: for if some stranger struck one of your own, would you not avenge your blood [relation]? How much more should you avenge your God, your father, your brother, whom you see blamed, proscribed, crucified; whom you hear crying out and forsaken and begging for aid: *alone I am trampled in the winepress* ...[38]

In this example, the crusaders were to avenge Christ himself, their father and brother, who, it was suggested, was suffering the Passion at that very moment in time. Orderic Vitalis imagined a similarly encouraging (though notably abbreviated) speech delivered by King Baldwin I of Jerusalem at Jaffa: "brave men, take up arms, and go forth with distinction against the enemies of all good men. Let us take up arms to avenge God manfully."[39]

---

35 Guibert of Nogent, *Dei Gesta per Francos*, ed. R. B. C. Huygens, CCCM 127A (Turnholt, 1996), pp. 213–14.

36 Ibid., p. 304.

37 Robert of Rheims, *Historia Iherosolimitana*, p. 805.

38 Baldric of Bourgueil, *Historia Jerosolimitana*, in RHCOc. 4 (Paris, 1879), p. 101. Reference to Isaiah 63:3.

39 Orderic Vitalis, *Historia Aecclesiastica*, vol. 5, p. 348.

In terms of quantity there were more references to the idea of crusading as vengeance, or indeed to vengeance of any kind, in the non-participant accounts than there were in the letters and eyewitness accounts. However, the question is not simply one of a sheer number of references. What was truly noteworthy about the accounts of non-participants was the connection they drew between the idea of crusading as vengeance, on one hand, and other ideological structures and cultural themes, on the other. The letters, the Encyclical, and the eyewitness accounts, even taken together, provide limited explanations for the concept of crusading as vengeance. In contrast, the later, non-participant accounts outline discernible patterns of thought that led their authors to connect the concept of vengeance with the First Crusade. It is to these patterns of thought that we now turn.

God's vengeance on the unfaithful

Throughout the non-participant histories of the First Crusade, a certain preoccupation with sin and its due is evident. This is hardly surprising; the Church's views on sin, guilt and punishment were shifting. The simpler model of confession, satisfaction and reconciliation was gradually expanding to include the conviction that acts of penance could not satisfactorily repay the debt owed to God for any specific sin. Certainly eternal punishment might be avoided, but by the end of the eleventh century it became harder to be certain of fully remitted temporal punishment at the time of death; even the theology explaining the crusade indulgence in detail only truly emerged in the twelfth century, after the First Crusade. Despite—or perhaps because of—this uncertainty, the desire for the remission of sins was a powerful motivating factor. For one scholar, it was the motivation for the First Crusade that "put all the others in the shade."[40]

Looking at sources related to the First Crusade, it is easy to see that issues of sin and the remission of sins concerned people in the late eleventh and early twelfth centuries. Time and again, authors referred to the judgments of God upon the Christians, often drawing upon the formulaic medieval explanation *peccatis exigentibus hominum*.[41] Examples of this explanation for military failure abounded in the sources of the period. To give one example, in a battle following the capture of Jerusalem, the Christians suffered heavy losses. Albert of Aachen explained this as the judgment of God against the Christians: "the Christian knights, impeded by the weight of their sins, were given over by divine judgment

---

[40]   Hans E. Mayer, *The Crusades*, trans. J. Gillingham (2nd edn, Oxford, 1988), p. 23.

[41]   For more on the subject and its relation to crusading see Elizabeth Siberry, *Criticism of Crusading, 1095–1274* (Oxford, 1985), p. 72.

to unbelieving and impious men for punishment."[42] Likewise, according to Baldric of Bourgueil, the army of Peter the Hermit bewailed the sins that had brought divine wrath upon the Christians: "we remember that we gravely offend him and irritate [God], we who have inexplicably rioted in greed for the goods of [our] brothers and in destruction of churches."[43]

The First Crusade letters also showed a Christian preoccupation with God's punishment. There are two surviving letters from crusaders in which they remarked upon God's chastisement of the Christians at Antioch. One noted: "*God, who scourges all his sons, in whom he delights*, thus far chastised us, with the result that scarcely 700 horses could be found in our army."[44] The other stated: "God..detained us there for nine months and humiliated us in a siege outside, while our swollen pride quickly gave way to humility."[45] The fact that the First Crusade was a war supposedly authorized by God would have served only to intensify an already present anxiety about God's judgment.[46] If the First Crusade were to fail, surely it would be because the sins of the crusaders had made them unworthy.

In Baldric of Bourgueil's version of the speech addressed to Kerbogha by his mother, she noted that "the Franks' God is omnipotent, [and] unless they were to previously offend him seriously, he always grants them victory."[47] The "unless" clause is key—God was not always and unequivocally on the side of the Christians; there was the potential for them to lose his favor by offending him. If they did so, they could expect his judgment to be severe. Orderic Vitalis recorded one of Stephen of Valence's visions in the following terms:

> The Lord Jesus Christ appeared with his company of saints to a certain priest, while he spent the night in the basilica of the Holy Mary, and prayed for the afflicted people of God; and [Christ] complained about certain fornications committed by the Christian troops with both foreign and Christian whores, proclaiming stern threats against the rabble who frequented brothels. ... Then the blessed Mary, Mother of mercy, and St. Peter, chief of the apostles, fell at the feet of the redeeming Lord and with their pious supplications for the sufferings of the Christians they softened the wrath of he [Christ] who was admonishing [the priest]; and they lamented the pagans who were shamefully defiling the holy house of God with their filth. [Christ] gave way to the concluded supplications of

---

42   Albert of Aachen, *Historia Ierosolimitana*, p. 610.

43   Baldric of Bourgueil, *Historia Jerosolimitana*, p. 19.

44   *Epistulae et Chartae*, p. 157.

45   Ibid., p. 169.

46   Siberry, *Criticism of Crusading*, p. 72.

47   Baldric of Bourgueil, *Historia Jerosolimitana*, p. 63.

his Mother and the apostle ... and with a happier expression he ordered the priest to castigate all the people publicly and invite them to repent all [their sins].[48]

This evocation of a stern divinity harshly judging his followers, never mind those who did not even attempt to adhere to his will, corresponded to the Christian concept of punishment as correction. As Baldric of Bourgueil explained at the beginning of his text, "[God] corrects the pious, that he might advance them; he punishes the impious, that he might set them straight."[49] Both those who heeded God and those who did not could expect to feel his judgment upon them, either as a function of his love or of his anger.[50]

Just as vengeance was a function of human justice in the histories of the First Crusade, it was the primary expression of God's judgmental punishment.[51] Albert of Aachen recounted an episode in the prophetic dream of a certain knight named Hezelus, following the capture of Antioch. This dream concerned the further progress of the crusade: "all hardships were changed into prosperity; nor was there anything that could impede the way, or any things which adversity could harm, except when iniquity was found in crimes and transgressions; but when iniquity was found, out of the true justice of God followed vengeance, which is sanctified law."[52] In this text, God's vengeance was *the* expression of "true justice," "sanctified law." This equation of divine vengeance and divine justice reinforced the connection between human vengeance and justice, which, in turn, was often represented as being divinely inspired or supervised.[53] It is not surprising that the perception of God as a holy and just avenger punishing the wrongdoer was echoed in the way the non-participant historians characterized leaders of the crusade such as Raymond of St. Gilles. Ralph of Caen described

---

[48]   Orderic Vitalis, *Historia Aecclesiastica*, vol. 5, pp. 98 and 100.

[49]   Baldric of Bourgueil, *Historia Jerosolimitana*, p. 9.

[50]   Anne-Marie Helvétius has suggested that the notion of God's mercy gained ground at the end of the Carolingian era, and that the idea of a vengeful God "se transforme peu à peu en bon pasteur, soucieux du salut de toutes les âmes. Il ne s'agit donc plus de détruire les pécheurs, maix de corriger les péchés; la *vindicta* est devenue synonyme de *correctio*." In my opinion, these conclusions are not borne out by the evidence in the twelfth-century crusade sources I have looked at, suggesting that perhaps these ideas shifted again between the ninth and twelfth centuries, for an as yet unidentified reason, or else that crusading sources are materially different in this regard ("Le Récit de Vengeance des Saints dans l'Hagiographie Franque (VIe–IXe siècle)," in D. Barthélemy, F. Bougard and R. Le Jan (eds), *La Vengeance 400–1200* (Rome, 2006), p. 448).

[51]   See above pages 13–19.

[52]   Albert of Aachen, *Historia Ierosolimitana*, p. 448.

[53]   See above pages 17–18.

the count as "a cultivator of fairness, an avenger of iniquity ... a lamb towards the timid, a lion towards the proud."[54]

This imagery was reminiscent of the zealous God of the Old Testament, a loving father to those who obeyed his precepts justly and a wrathful persecutor of those who did not. Robert of Rheims stated that Godfrey of Bouillon "did not lust after chests, or pots, or gold, or silver, or any other spoils..he desired to avenge the mockery and wounds the [Christian] pilgrims had endured."[55] Robert contrasted the sinful lust for wealth with a commendable desire for vengeance for injuries done to the common good, bringing to mind the admonitions of Thomas of Chobham earlier discussed.[56] Raymond of St. Gilles and Godfrey of Bouillon did not avenge personal injuries, they avenged sin, especially sin committed against Christians.

From this perspective, divine vengeance was necessarily expressed through human agents, aside from lightning bolts and earthquakes. Thus, divine vengeance was by its definition exacted by the pious and elect of God upon the wrongdoers in their midst, and this ideology of divine vengeance was applied to the First Crusade. Towards the end of his account, Guibert of Nogent embarked upon a lengthy explication and gloss of the Old Testament Book of Zechariah.[57] Guibert was specifically referring to the First Crusade. When events were interpreted in light of Zechariah 12:6, the crusaders had embodied the elect in the West, and "laid waste with proper vengeance of slaughter the reprobate" in the East.

Like Guibert of Nogent, Baldric of Bourgueil referred to the correction of the pious and the punishment of the impious near the beginning of his account, when he was still expounding upon the significance and meaning of the First Crusade. In effect he gave a description of the very nature of the Crusade: "*[God] changes kings and times*: he corrects the pious, that he might advance them; he punishes the impious, that he might set them straight."[58] Three pages later Baldric made it even more clear that, in his mind, the Muslims deservedly experienced the punishment of God executed by the crusaders: "and thus [the Muslims] provoked God against themselves, they who abominably dishonored God ... therefore [God] decreed a divine counsel to chastise them."[59] God's chastisement and punishments were to be felt by all and Biblical verses that distinguished

---

54 Ralph of Caen, *Gesta Tancredi in Expeditione Hierosolymitana*, in RHCOc. 3 (Paris, 1866), p. 617.

55 Robert of Rheims, *Historia Iherosolimitana*, p. 868.

56 See above page 17.

57 Full text given above at page 51.

58 Baldric of Bourgueil, *Historia Jerosolimitana*, p. 9.

59 Ibid., p. 12.

between the righteous and the criminal were applied to distinguish between Christians and Muslims respectively.

All of these passages point to a mindset that classified the Christians and the Muslims as subordinate to the same divinity, and subject to his discipline, whether for their instruction or their punishment. The two religious groups were presented as though part of one large community, both subject to punishment if they offended God.[60] From a broad perspective, in the crusading texts of this period the Muslims were not *the others*, but rather *those of us who are doing wrong.* It was not so much that they were "other" in the sense of unknown and alien; rather, they were portrayed as deviant and criminal, and legitimately subject to punishment.[61] This was no new trend, although crusading itself was a new kind of enterprise. When Christians had faced for the first time an emerging Islam centuries before, a verse from the New Testament that had previously been used to discuss heresy was used to discuss Islam:

> every spirit that confesses that Jesus Christ has come in the flesh is of God, and every spirit that does not confess Jesus is not of God. This is the spirit of Antichrist, of which you heard that it was coming, and now it is in the world already.[62]

The just punishment of God was also known as the vengeance of God, *ultio Dei*, largely thanks to Biblical terminology. In a very direct sense what the Muslims experienced during the First Crusade was vengeance, and it should come as no surprise that medieval writers used the terms *vindicta* and *ultio*. Like Orderic Vitalis, Baldric of Bourgueil, Guibert of Nogent, and others, Ralph of Caen suggested that those who were killed in Jerusalem had brought this retribution upon themselves: "[Each crusader was a] shedder of unclean blood, pouring out guilty blood: you who tore Christ to pieces in all his limbs, accept in [your own] members the recompense of Christ they now give you."[63] In a nice combination

---

[60]   A point also made by Dominique Iogna-Prat who, writing about the Cluniac Church in the mid twelfth-century, states they "envisaged eventual inclusion of the universe and all mankind on earth" (*Order and Exclusion: Cluny and Christendom Face Heresy, Judaism and Islam, 1000–1150*, trans. G. R. Edwards (Ithaca NY, 2002), p. 360).

[61]   A point also made by John V. Tolan, *Saracens: Islam in the Medieval European Imagination* (New York, 2002), p. 165, and by Jonathan Riley-Smith, "The Military Orders and the Orient, 1150–1291," unpublished (n.d.), p. 4. To a certain degree there is evidence for a similar mindset in the eyewitness accounts. Fulcher of Chartres in particular applied the vocabulary of chastisement to Muslim defeat. However, he did not connect the language of chastisement with the vocabulary of vengeance.

[62]   1 John 4:2–3. Hugh Goddard, *A History of Christian–Muslim Relations* (Edinburgh, 2000), p. 10.

[63]   Ralph of Caen, *Gesta Tancredi*, p. 697.

of the image of the crucifixion with the understanding that Christians were the body of Christ, the non-Christians had "torn Christ to pieces in all his limbs," and they had to accept what was done to their own bodies in return. The First Crusade was divine vengeance and the *ius talionis* in action.

The non-participant histories of the First Crusade evinced a preoccupation with sin and the ever-present judgment and punishment of God. God was perceived as the chastiser and punisher of his people, which included both the Christians and the Muslims. Due to the presence and usage of Biblical terminology of vengeance as divine justice, God's punishment was described with the vocabulary of vengeance. The incorporation of both Christians and Muslims into this picture, the subjection in Christian minds of both groups to the same religious standards, allowed for the application of Biblical passages concerning divine vengeance on the erring sinner to the First Crusade. The Book of Zechariah did not say explicitly that God would wreak *digna ultio* on the Muslims, but it did say that he would do so on the *reprobi*, and given this mindset, "Muslim" and "*reprobi*" were read equivalently. This is not evidence that all and sundry viewed the First Crusade as vengeance, but it is evidence for a Christian perspective that would have permitted contemporaries to insert the Muslims into a Biblical framework of punishment that was frequently described with the vocabulary of vengeance.

Military obligation and social relationships

The second pattern of thought that led to the idea of crusading as vengeance was rooted in the social obligations owed to both the living and the dead. In the early twelfth-century crusading texts, *vindicta* and *ultio* often appeared side by side with *auxilium*, the term signifying the military support owed to lords, family members and others perceived as part of one's social group (*amici*).[64] Appropriately for a Christian society, this notion of vengeance as *auxilium* was also linguistically connected with *caritas*, Christian love for one's neighbor, another concept frequently invoked in crusading rhetoric. The double obligation to provide *auxilium* and express *caritas* meant that in certain situations vengeance was required two times over—not because of an obligation to punish, but because of a positive obligation to help and express love.[65]

---

[64] For more on the term *amici*, family, and vengeance see David Herlihy, "Family," *American Historical Review*, 96 (1991): 1–16; and Paul Hyams, *Rancor and Reconciliation in Medieval England* (Ithaca NY, 2003).

[65] Phillipe Buc has noted that Haymon d'Auxerre depicted saints themselves taking vengeance "for charity." ("La Vengeance de Dieu: De l'Exégèse Patristique à la Réforme

How did a social demand for vengeance translate to the idea of crusading as vengeance? The key is the way in which crusaders and their historians categorized themselves. Writers strongly stressed group solidarity, and they employed the language of family and of lordship to great effect. Crusaders were friends and brothers, *amici* and *fratres*. Their father was God; they were to be "powerful sons," according to Baldric of Bourgueil.[66] In another common metaphor, the crusaders were sons of their mother, Jerusalem: "the holy city was besieged, our mother Jerusalem, whom the offspring of adultery had invaded and denied to her legitimate sons."[67]

But God was not only their father, he was also their lord, their "strong warrior, duke and protector."[68] Direct parallels were drawn between the crusaders' relationship with God, and their relationship with their human lords. Robert of Rheims depicted Bohemond saying to his men: "if anyone is the Lord's [man], let him be joined to me; O knights, now mine, be the Lord's."[69]

Verbal labels must have meant little without the emotional consent of those involved.[70] What bound the crusaders together were not words or metaphors, but rather their recognition and acknowledgment that there *was* a bond between them. It was their own awareness of belonging to a group that gave the group existence. This awareness was described in the crusading texts with many similar verbs (and their related adjectives and participles): *cognoscere, reminiscor, memorare.* The crusaders acknowledged and remembered who they were, what they were doing, and why they were doing it.

Memory was also invoked as a motivation for the crusade. In one account Pope Urban II exhorted the Franks: "remember, I pray you, the thousands of those who detestably perished, and go forth for the sake of the holy places."[71] Throughout the histories of the First Crusade, crusaders were valued according to their ability to remember their relationships, and to take appropriate action based on those remembered relationships. For example, Robert of Rheims

---

Ecclésiastique et à la Première Croisade," in D. Barthélemy, F. Bougard, and R. Le Jan (eds), *La Vengeance 400–1200* (Rome, 2006), p. 456.

[66]   Baldric of Bourgueil, *Historia Jerosolimitana*, p. 15.

[67]   Albert of Aachen, *Historia Ierosolimitana*, p. 410.

[68]   Robert of Rheims, *Historia Iherosolimitana*, p. 763.

[69]   Ibid., p. 741.

[70]   Brian Stock makes a similar point when he writes "The essential bond was forged by means of belief; its cement was faith in the reality of belonging" (*Listening for the Text: On the Uses of the Past* (Philadelphia, 1990), p. 37).

[71]   Guibert of Nogent, *Dei Gesta per Francos*, p. 116.

praised a certain young knight for being "unmindful (*immemor*) of himself, but mindful of his fellows."[72]

It was vital that crusaders remembered their social obligations on the battlefield, and in the texts they were described repeatedly as remembering and fighting at the same time. As noted above, Robert of Rheims paid tribute to the actions of that honest young knight during battle. Guibert of Nogent described the crusaders fighting "driven by sorrow for their killed brothers."[73]

Moreover, in battle crusaders did not simply remember their fellow crusaders, they also remembered Christ. According to Guibert of Nogent, the crusaders charged into battle outside Antioch with "suspending the son of God, crucified for them, before their eyes."[74] Stephen of Blois reported a similar phenomenon to his wife, writing that at Antioch the crusaders "incensed with anger at the sacrilegious Turks, ran together to die, for Christ and for sorrow for their brothers."[75] For Orderic Vitalis, the assault on Jerusalem took place "in the third hour when the Jews damned the Lord before Pilate, the Christians remembering his Passion ... began to fight."[76]

Memory was valued because those who remembered their social obligations took action. This violence on behalf of remembered social obligation was deemed vengeance on numerous occasions when one part of the crusading army was attacked, and the rest of the army rushed to assist. For example, when Godfrey of Bouillon led men to join the Battle of Dorylaeum, "each going as fast as he could pressed on the way to aid and avenge the Christians."[77] When Christians led by Bohemond were ambushed at Port St. Symeon, the other crusaders rushed to help: "in no way unmindful of the injuries of their brothers, the avengers were most eager to shed their own blood."[78] Orderic Vitalis noted that "the Franks thirsted to destroy the cruel beasts to avenge their brothers and secure victory."[79] The crusader who remembered his obligations sought vengeance.

Or, to put it another way, "the vengeful do not forget."[80] It seems that this statement could be applied to the broader biological family of which humanity

---

[72]   Robert of Rheims, *Historia Iherosolimitana*, p. 847.

[73]   Guibert of Nogent, *Dei Gesta per Francos*, p. 191.

[74]   Ibid., p. 240.

[75]   *Epistulae et Chartae*, p. 151.

[76]   Orderic Vitalis, *Historia Aecclesiastica*, vol. 5, p. 168.

[77]   Albert of Aachen, *Historia Ierosolimitana*, p. 132.

[78]   Baldric of Bourgeuil, *Historia Jerosolimitana*, p. 50. For a more cynical perspective, see above page 25.

[79]   Orderic Vitalis, *Historia Aecclesiastica*, vol. 5, p. 84.

[80]   Jonathan Riley-Smith, *The First Crusade and the Idea of Crusading* (London, 1986), p. 57.

is a member. Frans de Waal has drawn attention to the practical link between memory and the desire for revenge within the family of primates as a whole: "both reconciliation and its counterpart, revenge, require that the participants remember with whom they have had a fight."[81] It is plausible that the link between memory and vengeance in these accounts of the First Crusade was not merely a literary device employed to increase tension, but rather a fundamental component of human behavior.

Similarly, it is probable that the characterization of crusaders as brothers and friends was not simply a pleasing metaphor. Many noble families played a role in the First Crusade, and often in consecutive expeditions, leading to the development of family traditions of crusade participation.[82] Crusaders frequently traveled in the entourage of a more powerful and wealthy lord, and even regional confraternities, born from financial need and the familiarity of shared language and tradition, were not uncommon.[83] In these circumstances, it is not a great stretch to imagine brothers, cousins and comrades in arms taking the cross, and later fighting, together.[84] Additionally, from a medieval perspective, the idea of God as father must have been so entrenched that it seemed an established and heartfelt truth, not simply a handy rhetorical tool, as it can seem to modern readers. Using the language of family and friendship would affect most human beings regardless of context, but when we consider that many crusaders were living and dying side by side with their family, lords, vassals and comrades while on crusade, the appeals to the obligations owed to social relationships must have been even more moving.

The crusaders were not merely to take vengeance because they were aware of their social relationships with each other and other Christians—they were to take vengeance because they were mindful of their relationship with Christ. The most outstanding example of this was contained in a speech delivered to the crusaders outside the walls of Jerusalem, just prior to the assault on the city. According to Baldric of Bourgueil, the crusaders were exhorted to pay attention to Christ, "who until now today has been persecuted and crucified in this city."[85] The current occupants of Jerusalem were compared to the principal actors in the crucifixion: "just as much as these evil judges, accomplices of Herod and Pilate, mocked and tormented your brothers, they crucified Christ; just as much as they tortured and killed these people, they struck the side of Christ with a

---

[81]   Frans de Waal, *Peacemaking Among Primates* (Cambridge MA, 1989), p. 38.

[82]   Jonathan Riley-Smith, *The First Crusaders* (Cambridge, 1997).

[83]   Norman Housley, *Fighting for the Cross: Crusading to the Holy Land* (New Haven, 2008), p. 160.

[84]   Ibid., p. 47.

[85]   Baldric of Bourgueil, *Historia Jerosolimitana*, p. 101.

lance alongside Longinus." The crusaders were encouraged to think upon Christ as a member of their family, and to consider their probable actions if that were the case.[86] They were not supposed to think about Christ in order to imitate his patient suffering, as in some of the eyewitness accounts; they were meant to consider the crucifixion of Christ in order to become angry enough to slaughter those within Jerusalem's walls in vengeance for his death.

The crucifixion of Christ was written about in the present tense, as though it were just then happening, reminding historians of the emphasis on the actual presence of the body of Christ in the Eucharist in orthodox Catholic thought. In the eleventh century Lanfranc of Bec and Berengar of Tours had debated whether the Eucharist was a literal piece of Christ's body, and in a similar way, the crusading texts in the early twelfth century were not entirely clear about whether the crucifixion was simply being remembered by the crusaders, or was literally happening before their eyes. Whichever was the case, vengeance resulted from the conjunction of remembered group identity and remembered (as though they were current) injuries: "in the hour in which the Lord suffered because of the will of the Jews, the Christians, not unmindful of his Passion," attacked Jerusalem.[87]

The emotional and theological immediacy of the crucifixion, combined with the extremely strong emphasis on the parallels between family and lordship relationships and Christian relationships with God, brings us to the critical word *auxilium*. The sermon from Baldric of Bourgueil's account called for vengeance, but Christ himself was not portrayed in this passage directly asking for vengeance. Rather, he was *auxilium poscentem*, "begging for aid." The military support sometimes embodied in the term *auxilium* was connected to the social obligation to take vengeance, as we have seen.[88] In a sense, vengeance may have functioned as an extension of military obligation beyond the barrier of life and death—one helped a living ally if possible, and if not, one avenged their death. Reynolds has demonstrated that there was no fixed, universal system of military service for all of western Europe.[89] Nevertheless, there seems to have been a general relationship between the medieval concepts of vengeance and *auxilium*, and that relationship was invoked to describe the First Crusade.

But there was another reason for the connection between the remembrance of social identities and the ideology of crusading as vengeance. Since vengeance was a function of both divine and human justice, and had its place within the

---

[86] Ibid., p. 101. Full text above at page 41.

[87] Ibid., p. 102.

[88] Albert of Aachen, *Historia Ierosolimitana*, p. 248. Full text given above at page 59.

[89] Susan Reynolds, *Fiefs and Vassals: The Medieval Evidence Reinterpreted* (Oxford, 1994), p. 482.

Christian world of the twelfth century, it was also an expression of Christian *caritas.*

As Riley-Smith has already demonstrated, crusading was in many ways viewed as an act of love, since love would lead Christians to sacrifice themselves and defend their fellow Christians.[90] For example, Baldric of Bourgueil recorded Pope Urban II stating at Clermont that, although it was wrong to kill a Christian, it was a lesser evil to kill a Muslim, since in that situation one risked one's own life: "it is a horrible thing, brothers, it is a horrible thing, that you extend a rapacious hand towards Christians; it is a lesser evil to brandish your swords against Saracens; indeed, it is a good thing, since it is charity to lay down your lives for your brothers."[91] In 1096, Urban wrote of the crusaders "that they have committed their property and their persons [to the crusade] out of love for God and their neighbor."[92] In 1100, Pope Paschal II wrote to the crusaders: "we remember how many things you gave up for love of God, how many dangers you underwent for the well-being and salvation of your brothers."[93] As these passages illustrate, *caritas* led to self-sacrifice for the sake of others and thus was a key component of crusading ideology.

But *caritas* did not only lead to self-sacrifice. At least occasionally it carried with it the attendant obligation to take vengeance. In Albert of Aachen's account, in the fight for the city of Arsuf, a knight named Gerard was crucified by the Muslims and set up as bait for the Christians. The Muslims expected that the crusaders would swarm to the aid of their suffering comrade and thus forfeit the battle. Not surprisingly, Gerard begged Godfrey of Bouillon to be released from his martyrdom. Godfrey replied with a speech that was, in fact, theologically sound:

> Gerard, fiercest knight, by no means can I have mercy on you and avert all men
> of this city for the sake of avenging your injury. And therefore, [even] if you were
> my birth brother, as Eustace, you would not be liberated [if it meant] that the
> city would remain untaken. Certainly if you have to die, it is more useful that you
> alone should die than that our decree and oath should be violated and this city
> should always be held unsafe for pilgrims. For if you will die to the present life,
> you will have life with Christ in heaven.[94]

---

[90]   Jonathan Riley-Smith, "Crusading as an Act of Love," *History*, 65 (1980), p. 191. See also Riley-Smith, *The First Crusaders*, p. 41.

[91]   Baldric of Bourgueil, *Historia Jerosolimitana*, p. 15.

[92]   *Epistulae et Chartae*, p. 137.

[93]   Ibid., pp. 178–9.

[94]   Albert of Aachen, *Historia Ierosolimitana*, p. 488.

Albert remarked that then the Christians assailed the city, "forgetful of all piety and mercy."[95] Meanwhile, Gerard was struck with a spear in a manner reminiscent of Christ's death, and the Christians were taunted by the Muslims: "impious and cruel people, you who have no regard for sparing your brother and fellow Christian, but, having seen him and his torment, you fight the city and citizens more bitterly!"[96]

The assault was a complete failure, and many of the Christians were killed, wounded, or scattered. Arnulf of Chocques, Patriarch of Jerusalem, roundly condemned Godfrey and the other Christians, first for abandoning Gerard and another named Lambert to their fate, and then for failing to avenge their deaths. From his perspective, this abandonment and subsequent failure to take vengeance was a betrayal of the precepts of the Christian religion as well as a betrayal of personal honor: "[Arnulf] began to argue with the Duke and all men, great and small, concerning the treachery and hardheartedness with which they had sinned towards their brothers, Gerard and Lambert ... he admonished all of them concerning this impiety and this base filth of all crimes."[97] Granted, Arnulf did not specifically say that their crime was the abandonment of Gerard *without vengeance*. However, it is fairly clear from the text that Godfrey and everyone else involved (including the Muslims who set up the executions as bait) considered the choice to be between continued battle or the pursuit of vengeance for the injuries committed to Gerard and Lambert. In this case, the narrative made it known that vengeance should have been sought because it would have been an act of pious charity towards their brothers to rescue them from torment, or at least, to avenge their injuries.

These circumstances were unusual, but the one example of this perspective on vengeance is striking, and suggests that the ideology of crusading as vengeance was compatible with the well-documented ideology of crusading as an act of love. Riley-Smith has shown that to sacrifice one's own life for a fellow Christian on crusade was perceived as an act of love, leading some to view the desire to display Christian love as a motivating factor that drove people to go on crusade. Perhaps for some, to take vengeance for an unjust death was also perceived as an act of love in the right context, and thereby led some to view the desire to take vengeance as another aspect of the desire to display Christian love. From this perspective, both vengeance and self-sacrifice could coexist under the broader banner of Christian love. This suggests that, at least for some, to take vengeance and to display Christian love were not necessarily mutually exclusive or

---

95   Ibid.
96   Ibid.
97   Ibid., p. 492.

contradictory principles, and both contributed to the ideology of the crusading movement.

Anti-Jewish sentiment

There was one more pattern of thought connecting vengeance to the First Crusade in the non-participant histories of the early twelfth century: the relationship between the First Crusade and anti-Jewish sentiment. On their way through France and Germany towards the East, a few crusader armies attacked (and sometimes devastated) Jewish communities in Cologne, Trier, Speyer, Worms, Mainz, Metz, Prague, and perhaps Regensburg. Anti-Jewish violence also sometimes erupted right away when Christians took the cross, as in Rouen. These persecutions were attested to by Christian writers, including Ekkehard of Aura, Guibert of Nogent, Albert of Aachen, and (much later) Otto of Freising, but they were narrated in the most detail in three Hebrew accounts: the so-called *Mainz Anonymous* and the *Chronicles* of Solomon bar Simson and Eliezer bar Nathan.[98] The *Mainz Anonymous* was the only Hebrew account written within the time frame of this chapter, but in the past historians have linked all three of these accounts with other texts, such as the *Chanson d'Antioche* and the *Venjance de Nostre Seigneur*, as evidence for a very significant desire for vengeance at the beginning of the First Crusade.

Before any other texts are considered, the picture of the crusaders' purported thinking in attacking both the Jews and the Muslims in the *Mainz Anonymous* must be examined. Near the very beginning of the account, the Christians "said to each other: Look now, we are going to a distant country to make war against mighty kings and are endangering our lives to conquer the kingdoms which do not believe in the crucified one, when actually it is the Jews who murdered and crucified him."[99] This is a key passage used by historians to argue for the importance of vengeance at the beginning of the First Crusade. Significantly, the word for vengeance was not used in this passage, as it would be in the parallel passages in the two later Hebrew narratives that utilized the *Mainz Anonymous* as a source. Also, the crusaders were not described going east in order to take vengeance on the Muslims, as they were in the later Hebrew narratives. There is after all a moral distinction between killing Jews or Muslims because you perceive them as enemies and killing them because you desire to avenge an injury they have already committed. The attention paid to the crucifixion of Christ

---

[98]   For more on the Hebrew sources, see below pages 194 and 199.

[99]   *Mainz Anonymous*, trans. S. Eidelberg, *The Jews and the Crusaders* (Madison WI, 1977), p. 99.

probably aroused anger and a desire for vengeance in the First Crusaders, but the vocabulary of vengeance was not chosen for this passage in this earliest Hebrew account.

As the *Mainz Anonymous* continued, the Jews wrote to warn each other of the oncoming crusader armies, and there was a rumor that "whosoever kills a Jew will receive pardon for all his sins."[100] The first violence occurred in Speyer, and was relatively mild, if homicide can ever be said to be mild. Eleven Jewish men were killed, Bishop John of Speyer protected the other Jews, and no more bloodshed occurred in that city. It was in Worms that violence really erupted. A rumor arose that the Jews had poisoned the water with the boiled corpse of a Christian. After reporting this rumor the report made its first reference to vengeance: "when the errant ones and the burghers heard this, they cried out. They all assembled ... and declared: Behold, the time has come to avenge him who was nailed to the wood, whom their forefathers slew."[101] Some members of the Jewish community were hiding at that time in the bishop's chambers. Eventually the Christians decided that their vengeance should encompass the hidden Jews as well: "let us also take vengeance against those who have remained in the courtyard and chambers of the bishop."[102] In describing events at Mainz, the vocabulary of vengeance was again used. The townspeople opened the doors to the crusading army under Emicho, which the crusaders interpreted as divine intercession: "look, the gate has opened by itself; this the crucified one has done for us in order that we may avenge his blood on the Jews."[103]

The *Mainz Anonymous* suggests that the idea of vengeance for the crucifixion of Christ served to motivate some of those who attacked the Jews prior to the First Crusade. But the evidence deserves a close examination. First of all, the references to vengeance in this account were nowhere near as frequent or as detailed as those contained in the other two Hebrew narratives that were composed later in the mid-twelfth century. And in the *Mainz Anonymous*, the cry for vengeance for the crucifixion arose only after the Jews were accused of attempting to poison the city of Worms. In other words, the lone cry for vengeance seems to have been a response to an immediate injury: the poisoning of a well. Above all, the *Mainz Anonymous* did not claim that the crusaders were heading east to take vengeance on the Muslims.

Moreover, in the Hebrew narrative the desire to convert the Jews to Christianity frequently took precedence over the desire to take vengeance. The *Mainz Anonymous* recounted numerous examples of Jews who were accosted,

---

[100]   Ibid., p. 100.
[101]   Ibid., p. 102.
[102]   Ibid., p. 103.
[103]   Ibid., p. 108.

asked and even begged to convert, and then killed only when they refused to do so. In the case of David ben Netanel in Mainz, a priest begged him to convert "so that you may be saved—you, your money, and your entire household—from the errant ones." David feigned a willingness to convert, but when the Christians came "rejoic[ing] greatly," he condemned their beliefs. "Upon hearing the words of the pious man, [the Christians] flew into a rage. They raised their banners and encamped around the house and began to cry out and shout in the name of the crucified one. They advanced toward him and slew him..and his entire household and kin."[104] According to this account, the Christians did not show up in a mood of murderous rage; violence occurred after David actively renounced Christianity. It seems fair to state that David and his family were killed at least partly in retaliation for his vocal rejection of Christianity.

What can be concluded from the *Mainz Anonymous*, keeping in mind its singularity as a source? First, in the minds of the Christian aggressors there was some connection between violence against Muslims and violence against Jews, but the account did not offer a clear explanation for the link. Second, the violence against the Jews was at times depicted as vengeance for the crucifixion of Christ. Third, the desire for vengeance for the crucifixion seems to have blended with a number of other desires: a desire for vengeance for present injuries, a general desire to fight God's enemies, the desire to convert, and greed. Moreover, these elements conjoined to spark significant violence only in certain crusading armies.[105] Did the crusaders seek vengeance upon the Jews because of the crucifixion, their refusal to convert, or rumors of well-poisoning? And is the fact that the concept of vengeance was used to motivate anti-Jewish violence evidence for the idea of crusading as vengeance, let alone evidence for an overriding concern with vengeance within the armies of the First Crusade at the end of the eleventh century?

There are no immediate answers within the *Mainz Anonymous*, and regrettably only three Latin historians of the First Crusade referred to these persecutions. Ekkehard of Aura's description of the events was brief: "[Emicho and his men] fully undertook an accursed slaughter of Jews, [seeking] wherever their people were found, either to completely eliminate them, or even to compel them into the fold of the Church, being devoted to the zeal of Christianity

---

104   Ibid., p. 114.

105   Robert Chazan, *God, Humanity, and History: The Hebrew First Crusade Narratives* (London, 2000), p. 134. For which armies were involved, see Jonathan Riley-Smith, "The First Crusade and the Persecution of the Jews" in W. J. Sheils (ed.), *Persecution and Tolerance* (Oxford, 1984), pp. 57–72.

even in this matter."[106] Ekkehard clearly did not approve of these activities, and likewise condemned the killing of Christians in Hungary. To some degree he equated the two actions as the result of zeal: "thus the men of our people have the zeal of God, but not according to the knowledge of God ... [they] soon began to persecute other Christians, repressing divine mercy with fraternal blood."[107] Ekkehard shed no light onto the motivations of the crusaders, beyond noting that they were driven by religious zeal and tried to convert the Jews.

Albert of Aachen most definitely did not approve of the massacres or of the forced conversions, and referred to them as "the cruelest slaughter." He gave two explanations for the crusaders' behavior. First of all, he wrote that the crusaders asserted "that this was the beginning of their expedition and service against the enemies of the Christian faith."[108] From that perspective, the Jews counted equally as enemies of the Christian faith alongside the Muslims. Second, after the Christians suffered death themselves, Albert explained that:

> This is believed to be the hand of the Lord against the pilgrims, who with great dirtiness and in fornicating beds sinned in his sight, and destroyed the exiled Jews with grave slaughter, more with greed for money than for the justice of God, since although they were contrary to Christ, God is a just judge, and he would not order that anyone should come to the yoke of the Catholic faith unwilling or forced.[109]

In other words, the Christians killed the Jews who refused to convert to Christianity, and God then punished the Christians for their sins. Nowhere did Albert state that the Jews were killed in vengeance for the crucifixion. This is an important point, since Albert constantly described the crusaders taking vengeance upon not only Muslims, but also other Christians, in the East. But, like the initial passage in the *Mainz Anonymous*, he simply stated that the Jews were perceived as enemies. Perhaps he had a personal reason for not connecting the anti-Jewish violence with anti-Muslim violence, but it is more probable that he, like Ekkehard, had not heard (or did not believe) that the anti-Jewish violence was motivated by a desire for vengeance.

---

[106] Ekkehard of Aura, *Hierosolymita*, in RHCOc. 5 (Paris, 1895), p. 20. Later in the century Otto of Freising used similar language to describe events—"vel delere vel ecclesiae incorporare" (*Chronica sive Historia de Duabus Divitatibus*, ed. A. Schmidt, AQDGM 16 (Darmstadt, 1961), p. 502).

[107] Ekkehard of Aura, *Hierosolymita*, p. 21.

[108] Albert of Aachen, *Historia Ierosolimitana*, p. 50.

[109] Ibid., p. 56–8.

Guibert of Nogent did not refer to the massacres of the Jews in his *Dei Gesta per Francos*, but he did do so in his *De Vita Sua*. There he reported crusaders in Rouen saying "we desire to attack the enemies of God in the East, after having crossed vast tracts of land. The undertaking is preposterous, when before our eyes are the Jews, [compared] to whom no people more unfriendly to God exist."[110] Again, Guibert's version was very similar to that given by Albert of Aachen and the *Mainz Anonymous*, and did not report any references to vengeance per se.

According to the Latin and early Hebrew accounts of the Jewish massacres, the crusaders attacked the Jews because they were seen as enemies of God, as were the Muslims. This view was also advanced by Orderic Vitalis, who claimed that "these pilgrims held all Jews, heretics, and Saracens equally detestable, whom they all called enemies of God."[111] The accounts also hinted at various other motivations including revenge for the crucifixion, anger at the Jews' refusal to convert, and rumors of Jewish attempts to sabotage the Christian community. Nowhere was the idea of crusading as an act of vengeance referred to explicitly, and it is of interest that the Latin historians who did acknowledge the massacres steered clear of the terminology of vengeance in relation to the destruction of the Jews, but not that of the Muslims.

Historians have viewed the *Mainz Anonymous* and the Jewish persecutions in general as evidence for a preoccupation with vengeance in the late eleventh century that later evaporated. In part, they have viewed the *Mainz Anonymous* in this way in light of the existence of several other texts that provide a link between anti-Jewish violence as vengeance for the crucifixion upon the Jews and crusading as an act of vengeance against the Muslims. These texts are the *Chanson d'Antioche*, the *Venjance de Nostre Seigneur*, and the Encyclical of Sergius IV. We must consider whether it is reasonable to use these texts to bolster the argument for the dominance of the idea of crusading as vengeance at the time of the First Crusade.

The *Chanson d'Antioche* was compiled and partially composed in 1180 by one "Graindor of Douai." There may or may not have been a certain "Richard the Pilgrim" whose eyewitness account was supposedly the foundation of the *chanson*. In my opinion Cook has offered the most logical and straightforward approach to the dating of the first three poems of the Crusade Cycle.[112] In the

---

[110]   Guibert of Nogent, *De Vita Sua*, ed. E.-R. Labande (Paris, 1981), pp. 246 and 248.

[111]   Orderic Vitalis, *Historia Aecclesiastica*, vol. 5, p. 44.

[112]   Robert F. Cook *"Chanson d'Antioche," Chanson de Geste: Le Cycle de la Croisade est-il Epique?* (Amsterdam, 1980). Likewise, see Geert H. M. Claassens, "The Cycle de la Croisade: Vernacular Historiography," in B. Besamusca, W. P. Gerritsen, C. Hogetoorn, and O. S. H. Lie (eds), *Cyclification: The Development of Narrative Cycles in the Chansons de Geste*

past it was convenient to group these vengeful passages with similar references in the *Solomon bar Simson Chronicle*, but since the relevant passages in the *Chanson d'Antioche* would seem to have originated circa 1180, and since the applicable parts of the *Solomon bar Simson Chronicle* have been dated to the mid-twelfth century, such a comparison appears invalid for any discussion of the time of the First Crusade and directly thereafter.[113]

La Venjance de Nostre Seigneur first appeared as a written epic poem right around the year 1200; among other evidence for that dating, it contained references to the cities of Barletta and Acre in a manner indicative of Third Crusade accounts such as that of Ambroise, written in 1196.[114] The broader legend of the *Vindicta Salvatoris* had been gathering momentum from the time of Josephus, but there is no way to determine accurately what parts of the circa 1200 textual version date to the earlier Middle Ages, and which had their origins in the later twelfth century. Because of the late appearance of the written version of this legend and the difficulties in attempting to subdivide the text chronologically, it is inadvisable to use it to support arguments about the late eleventh century.

That leaves the Encyclical of Sergius IV, a forged text that also referred to the legend of the destruction of Jerusalem by the Romans as vengeance on the Jews for the crucifixion.[115] If Gieyzstor's dating is in fact correct, then the legend of the *Vindicta Salvatoris* was used to promote the idea of crusading as vengeance in the late eleventh century, and the Encyclical of Sergius IV can be used alongside the *Mainz Anonymous*.

Nevertheless, on the whole we have scanty and ambiguous evidence for the connection between anti-Jewish sentiment and the idea of crusading as vengeance at the end of the eleventh century and the beginning of the twelfth. The certain knowledge that crusading armies on their way east were motivated

---

and the Arthurian Romances (Amsterdam, 1994), pp. 184–8. Cook argued that hypotheses of more ancient versions of the poems of the Cycle should not logically affect the discussion and analysis of the actual extant texts available to modern scholars (Cook, p. 10). To date, no one has been able to prove the actual existence of Richard and Graindor. Moreover, even if (as Susan Edgington has argued) Albert of Aachen had been drawing upon an early *Chanson d'Antioche*, he nevertheless incorporated none of its prominent insistence upon the crusade as an act of vengeance for the crucifixion; this alone strongly suggests that at least those passages were composed in the later twelfth century. For more on why I concur with Cook, see below pages 198–9.

[113] *Solomon bar Simson Chronicle*, trans. S. Eidelberg, *The Jews and the Crusaders* (Madison WI, 1977), pp. 22 and 25–7.

[114] Loyal A. T. Gryting, "Introduction," in *The Oldest Version of the Twelfth-Century Poem La Venjance de Nostre Seigneur* (Ann Arbor, 1952), p. 31.

[115] See also above pages 45–6 and below pages 194–5.

to attack Jewish communities in Europe suggests some connection between crusading ideology and anti-Jewish sentiment. The *Mainz Anonymous* offered as explanations for the crusaders' attacks on the Jews their belief in the Jews as enemies of Christ, the desire to take vengeance on the Jews for the crucifixion, anger at Jewish refusal to convert, and rumors of Jewish crimes. The Latin accounts of the First Crusade attacks on European Jews likewise suggested that the crusaders believed themselves to be attacking the enemies of Christ and were angry at Jewish refusals to convert. The Encyclical of Sergius IV suggested that the First Crusade was promoted as vengeance for God, just as the Roman destruction of Jerusalem and the Jewish diaspora was vengeance for Christ. Again and again the sources suggest a link between crusading and anti-Jewish violence, and again and again the ideas of vengeance and the crucifixion crop up; but it is nevertheless impossible to state concretely, based upon the sources for this period, that the Jews were attacked in 1096 because the First Crusaders saw the overall crusade as an act of vengeance.

So what can be concluded? First, in the minds of the Christian aggressors there was some connection between violence against Muslims and violence against Jews. Second, the violence against the Jews was at times depicted as vengeance for the crucifixion of Christ. Third, some at the time saw the First Crusade against Muslims as vengeance, and some compared it to the vengeful destruction of Jerusalem in 70 C.E. Fourth, the texts of the *Chanson d'Antioche* and the *Venjance de Nostre Seigneur* should not be used as evidence for the late eleventh century. In short—there was a relationship between anti-Jewish sentiment, vengeance, and the First Crusade at that time, but the texts for the period do not make that relationship explicit.

*   *   *

The idea of crusading as vengeance *was* in limited existence at the end of the eleventh century, as evidenced by the Encyclical of Sergius IV and two crusading letters written in 1098 and 1100. However, the vast majority of evidence for the idea of crusading as vengeance comes from documents written almost exclusively in Latin by non-participants in the early twelfth century. In their accounts, three major patterns of thought contributed to the ideological relationship between vengeance and crusading: a concentration on the justice and punishment of God, perceived in Biblical terminology as the *ultio Dei*; vengeance as a component of the social obligation to provide *auxilium* and *caritas*, hinging on the social importance of memory and the identification of crusaders as friends and brothers, Jerusalem as mother, and God as both father and lord; and a tie between anti-Jewish sentiment, vengeance, and crusading.

The evidence demonstrates that, although there was some emphasis on vengeance from 1095 through 1137, the previous model advanced by Riley-Smith and others that described a peak in the emphasis on vengeance at the beginning of the First Crusade, and a subsequent drop in attention to the idea, should be revised. As I will show in the following chapters, the connections between vengeance and crusading increased through the twelfth century, culminating in later texts such as the *Chanson d'Antioche* and the *Venjance de Nostre Seigneur*. As these ideological connections increased, the rationale behind the idea of crusading as vengeance, and the relationship between anti-Jewish sentiment and crusading, became clearer.

Chapter Three

A Growing Appeal: Crusading as Vengeance, 1138–1197

The period from 1138 to 1197 witnessed a number of disastrous events in the Frankish Levant, as well as notable failures when western Christians attempted to crusade. On Christmas Eve 1144, the Muslim leader Zengi took the city of Edessa out of Christian hands. A year later, in December 1145, Pope Eugenius III launched the letter *Quantum praedecessores*, hoping to motivate the Franks to aid their "brothers" in the East. Although King Louis VII responded with enthusiasm, his court did not. In an attempt to rouse public opinion, in 1146 Bernard, Abbot of Clairvaux, undertook a dramatic preaching tour, Eugenius reissued *Quantum praedecessores*, and popular enthusiasm finally responded. Indeed, in some cases, all too well—unauthorized preaching led to anti-Jewish violence in the Rhineland.

Eventually, Eugenius III authorized Christians to fight on three fronts: Louis VII of France and Conrad III of Germany in the Holy Land, Alfonso VII of Castile in Iberia, and the Saxons against the Wends in northern Europe. Overall, the results from these expeditions, known collectively as the Second Crusade, were uninspiring. At this point in time, the Saxons were only moderately successful against the Wends. Despite some triumphs in Iberia (especially the conquest of Lisbon and Almeria in 1147), there were no dramatic gains. In addition, the armies of Louis and Conrad were decidedly unsuccessful in the East, and returned home humiliated after failing to take Damascus in 1148. Not surprisingly, there was little impetus to launch another expedition to the Holy Land in the decades that followed.

That changed when the news of the catastrophic Battle of Hattin and the loss of Jerusalem to Salah al-Din reached Western ears in 1187. Pope Urban III was said to have dropped dead at the news, and his successor, Pope Gregory VIII, wasted no time in launching a crusade letter, *Audita tremendi*. During the winter of 1187–88 King Henry II of England and King Philip II of France took the cross, though neither was in a hurry to leave. Henry II died and was succeeded by his son, Richard I, who had previously rebelled against him with the help of Philip II. In 1190, under pressure to fulfill their vows, Richard and Philip mustered their troops and prepared to sail. Meanwhile, in 1188 the fervent

70-year-old Emperor Frederick I, who had accompanied Conrad III in 1147 and thus experienced the failure of the Second Crusade first-hand, had taken the cross. He and his army had departed for Jerusalem by the overland route in 1189.

After a variety of interesting developments—Frederick died whilst swimming in the river Göksu in 1190, Richard stopped to conquer and loot Sicily and Cyprus, picking up a wife for himself and a dowry for his sister on the way—the armies of Richard and Philip confronted Salah al-Din at Acre in 1191. They also confronted the convoluted nature of Frankish politics in the Kingdom of Jerusalem, as factions centered on Sibylla and Isabella, the two sisters of King Baldwin IV of Jerusalem, argued over the throne. After the fall of Acre, Philip returned home, leaving Richard to face Salah al-Din alone. In 1192, ill and worried about the state of his kingdom, Richard signed a truce with Salah al-Din for three years and eight months, leaving Jerusalem in Muslim hands, but guaranteeing free passage throughout Palestine for Christians and Muslims alike.

Meanwhile, back in Europe, writers continued to commemorate the First Crusade, even while recording events related to the Second and Third Crusades. The switch from Latin to vernacular writing had begun, and many of the earliest examples of entertainment literature—written redactions of what were originally orally delivered narratives—date from this time. Historians thus face a relative cornucopia of sources, dealing with a number of crusading enterprises, from the mid to late twelfth century.

In the previous chapter we saw that, although there was some evidence for a relationship between crusading and vengeance during the period from 1095 to 1137, it was limited in scope. Significantly, the idea of crusading as vengeance was emphasized more in the early twelfth-century histories of the First Crusade written by non-participants than it was in the eyewitness accounts. This evidence led me to suggest that the ideology of crusading as vengeance was utilized more frequently, and by a greater breadth of writers, throughout the twelfth century.[1] Implicit in this hypothesis, of course, is the notion that the three patterns of thought identified for the period 1095–1137 continued to evolve from 1138 to 1197.

Did, in fact, crusading texts composed between 1138 and 1197 promote the idea of crusading as vengeance more frequently than texts from earlier in the century? And was the relationship between crusading and vengeance in later twelfth-century texts based on the same themes as before—that is, was

---

[1]   Of course, alternative explanations include that traditional demon of medieval studies: that this apparent trend is a phantom produced by the nature of the sources that remain to us.

crusading perceived as an act of vengeance for the same reasons? In this chapter I demonstrate that texts from the mid to late twelfth century indeed utilize the idea of crusading as vengeance more frequently, and for similar, if not completely identical, reasons.

Three languages. One idea?

The period from 1138 to 1197 contains a large number of crusading sources in Latin, Hebrew, and Old French.[2] In most of the texts, regardless of language of composition, the vocabulary of vengeance *was* applied to crusading. Moreover, the moral value of vengeance in general was presented in a more unambiguously positive fashion (more on this below). The high proportion of texts referring to the ideology demonstrates convincingly that the idea of crusading as an act of vengeance was presented much more frequently in later twelfth-century crusading texts than in texts from the early twelfth century. It should be noted, however, that at the same time the ideology did *not* appear in a number of sources from the period. Not everyone presented crusading as vengeance, and this should caution against enthusiastic avowals that the idea was universally present and popular.

As already noted, in all of the sources the idea of crusading as an act of vengeance was discussed with less ambiguity. Many of the crusading texts written in the early twelfth century had explicitly referred to occasions when the crusaders did *not* seek out vengeance, implying that the pursuit of vengeance was inappropriate in those situations.[3] There were no references to such self-restraint in the texts from the period from 1138 to 1197. To give just one example, in Odo of Deuil's *De Profectione Ludovici VII in Orientem*, he repeatedly described the crusaders taking individual vengeance upon those attacking them (Greeks and Muslims). Unlike Raymond of Aguiler's First Crusaders, who declined to take vengeance, the Frankish leaders of the Second Crusade were depicted leaving battle "mourning that they were not able to avenge their injuries."[4] They were, however, able to take further action during another ambush: "all [the crusaders]

---

[2]   For details on these sources, see below pages 195–201.

[3]   Raymond of Aguilers, *Liber*, ed. J. H. Hill and L. L. Hill, DHC 9 (Paris, 1969), p. 38. Peter Tudebode, *Historia de Hierosolymitano Itinere*, ed. J. H. Hill and L. L. Hill, DHC 12 (Paris, 1977), p. 42.

[4]   Odo of Deuil, *De Profectione Ludovici VII in Orientem*, ed. V. G. Berry (New York, 1965), p. 138.

unanimously ran against them, and those whom they could, they killed, because of their own who had died and to avenge their own injuries."[5]

Of course, most of the time vengeance was presented as an understood social commonplace, with little moral commentary of any sort offered by the authors. But when vengeance was commented on explicitly in the 1138–97 sources, it was always discussed as a good thing. As Bernard of Clairvaux wrote to the Knights Templar, "a Christian glories in the death of a pagan, since Christ is glorified; in the death of a Christian, the generosity of the King is revealed, since the knight is led forth to be rewarded. Moreover a just man rejoices over [the former], since he sees vengeance [done]."[6]

Not only was the general idea of vengeance presented in a more consistently positive light, but the specific idea of crusading as vengeance appeared with much greater frequency in the sources for this period, necessitating a breakdown of the four main reasons for crusading as vengeance given in the texts. It should be noted that I have made distinctions between these four different strains of ideology for analytical purposes, not because they were always kept separate in the sources themselves. Indeed, in most of the texts different reasons for vengeance were presented side by side. For example, the anonymous author of the *Gesta Stephani* wrote regarding the Second Crusade:

> Therefore when the disgraceful news of such an intolerable expulsion had been made known to the pious ears of the mother Church, the lands were agitated, kingdoms were disrupted, the powers of the world were shaken, and the whole world joined together manfully to avenge the shame of this universal injury. And especially the strong youths of all England, all marked with the strength of a manly heart and a constant mind, came together for this most particular [act of] vengeance.[7]

The injuries that demanded vengeance in this passage were: (a) the Muslims were "hostile to [the Christian] religion," (b) they had seized Christian cities (including Edessa), (c) they had killed some Christians and taken others hostage, and (d) "what is a crime to say, they sought to abolish the temple, destroy the holy places, and delete the name of Christ."[8] These reasons are hardly unrelated, and yet at the same time the writer delineates each element—hostility, conquest,

---

[5]   Ibid., p. 126.

[6]   Bernard of Clairvaux, *Liber ad Milites Templi de Laude Novae Militiae*, ed. J. Leclerq and H. M. Rochais, SBO 3 (Rome, 1963), p. 217.

[7]   *Gesta Stephani Regis Anglorum*, ed. K. R. Potter (Oxford, 1976), p. 127.

[8]   Ibid., p. 127.

murder, desecration. Horrible crimes in and of themselves, they are pulled together with great effect, and all apparently deserved vengeance.

The first of the four main reasons for vengeance that writers emphasized was conquest—the past or present seizure of Christian lands in the East. The theme of vengeance for conquest is to be found especially after Salah al-Din had captured Jerusalem in 1187, although writers used this theme to discuss earlier expeditions as well. In a letter to King Louis VII of France in 1146, Peter the Venerable wrote that during the First Crusade "by the command of God [the crusaders] exterminated the profane people with warlike strength, and avenged the land for God and themselves."[9] Ambroise's account of the Third Crusade claimed that the land itself had not only been seized, but injured:

> The host of God ...
> turned all their wanderings towards Arsuf
> in order to seize the injured land
> where they went most chivalrously
> and avenged the great shame of God.[10]

The third stanza of the Old French crusading song *Pour lou peuple rescon forteir* stated:

> It is a very great sorrow when one loses
> the true sepulchre where God was placed
> and when the holy places are deserted.
> Do you know why God endures it?
> He wants to prove his friends,
> who have offered their service to him
> to take vengeance on his enemies.[11]

Similar passages can be found in both the *Chanson de Jérusalem* and the *Chanson d'Antioche.*[12]

Vengeance for the Holy Land was often connected to vengeance on behalf of the person of Christ. The *Gesta Regis Henrici Secundi* recorded a letter from

---

[9]   Peter the Venerable, *The Letters of Peter the Venerable*, ed. G. Constable (2 vols, Cambridge MA, 1967), vol. 1, p. 327.

[10]   Ambroise, *The History of the Holy War: Ambroise's Estoire de la Guerre Sainte*, ed. M. Ailes and M. Barber (2 vols, Woodbridge, 2003), vol. 1, p. 112.

[11]   *Les Chansons de Croisade*, ed. J. Bédier and P. Aubry (Paris, 1909), p. 79.

[12]   *La Chanson de Jérusalem*, ed. N. R. Thorp, OFCC 6 (Tuscaloosa, 1992), p. 149. *La Chanson d'Antioche*, ed. J. Nelson, OFCC 4 (Tuscaloosa, 2003), p. 50.

King Henry II of England to Aimery, Patriarch of Antioch in 1188, in which Henry wrote "anyone who is of the Lord now girds on his sword, and everyone judges himself blessed and faithful who leaves his father and mother and all people, in order that he may avenge the injuries [done to] Christ and the Holy Land."[13] Sometimes writers elaborated on the connection between injuries to Christ and injuries to the land by describing the East as Christ's inheritance. A link with Christ also related to the heavy emphasis on the Holy Sepulchre noted in the previous paragraph.

Second, alongside the need to avenge conquest, a few writers emphasized the need to avenge the physical injuries and deaths of Christians in the East. William, Archbishop of Tyre wrote that the preaching of the Second Crusade involved this particular sort of cry for vengeance:

> There were those who spread their words at this time far and wide among the people and the nations and solicited the provinces, slack from a long peace, to avenge such injuries. Lord Eugenius III ... directed the men most powerful in deed and sermon to diverse western regions, and they denounced the intolerable pressures on the princes, people, and tribes of their eastern brothers, and sought to animate them to go to avenge the injuries of fraternal blood.[14]

Roger of Howden recorded a song purportedly sung on the journey to Jerusalem in 1190:

> Therefore the God of the Hebrews took up
> the Christian princes, and their best men,
> namely to avenge the blood of the saints,
> to rescue them from the sons of the dead.[15]

The meaning of this song is open to interpretation, and phrases like "to avenge the blood of the saints ... /from the sons of the dead" are, to say the least, inflated with melodramatic metaphor, but the song nevertheless seems to be related to the theme of vengeance for Christians killed and conquered in the East.

---

[13]   *Gesta Regis Henrici Secundi*, ed. W. Stubbs, RS 49 (2 vols, London, 1867), vol. 2, p. 39. See also Roger of Howden, *Chronica*, ed. W. Stubbs, RS 51 (4 vols, London, 1868–71), vol. 2, p. 343. Similarly, see *La Chanson de Jérusalem*, p. 146.

[14]   William of Tyre, *Chronicon*, ed. R. B. C. Huygens, CCCM 63 (Turnholt, 1986), pp. 739–40.

[15]   Roger of Howden, *Chronica*, ed. W. Stubbs, RS 51 (4 vols, London, 1868–71), vol. 3, pp. 37–8.

Third, injuries to the cross required vengeance, perhaps due in part to the loss of the relic of the True Cross in the Battle of Hattin. The crusade song *Pour lou peuple rescon forteir* continued in stanza 5 with:

> What do the kings think?
> Would it not be a great wrong
> if they, the kings of France and of England,
> do not go to avenge the Lord and
> deliver his holy cross?[16]

The lament of Berter of Orleans in 1187 was cited in the *Gesta Regis Henrici Secundi* and the chronicle of Roger of Howden:

> Against which the prophet writes,
> that the Law will come forth from Zion,
> will the Law perish there?
>> Will it not have vengeance?
>> There where Christ drank
> the chalice of the Passion ...
>
> The one who despises the Cross burdens the cross
> from which faith mourns, oppressed;
> who does not howl for vengeance?
>> As many as value their faith
>> will redeem the cross,
> for certainly the cross redeems [them].[17]

Pope Celestine III wrote to the Archbishop of Canterbury in 1195: "[the people of God] will gird on the material sword to strike against the persecutors of the faith, so that they may swiftly avenge with vengeance the injury of the cross."[18]

Fourth, the overwhelming majority of references to crusading as vengeance called for vengeance for injuries done to Christ alone, without reference to any other factors. This hardly comes as a surprise after the way in which the other injuries calling for vengeance (the Islamic occupation of the Holy Land, the death of Christians in the East, and injuries to the cross) were in some way or

---

[16]   *Les Chansons de Croisade*, p. 80.

[17]   *Gesta Regis Henrici Secundi*, vol. 2, pp. 27–8. See also Roger of Howden, *Chronica*, vol. 2, pp. 330–31.

[18]   Celestine III, *Epistolae*, ed. J.-P. Migne, PL 206 (Paris, 1855), col. 1108 (*Misericors et miserator*).

another linked to the person of Christ. The theme was evident in many of the examples above, and is even more clearly demonstrated by the following body of evidence. According to Roger of Howden, in October 1191 King Richard I of England wrote to Garnier of Rochefort, Abbot of Clairvaux, that "the friends of the cross of Christ are flying forth ... to avenge the injuries of the Holy Christ."[19] Richard of Devizes ironically noted that Richard "left the English realm in the first year of his reign for Christ as though he would not return ... the devotion of this man was great, so quickly, so swiftly and fast he ran forth, no indeed flew forth, to avenge the injuries of Christ."[20]

Crucially, similar language about "injuries to Christ" was used to explain violence associated with the crusades against people other than the Muslims. According to the *Sefir Zekhirah* of Rabbi Ephraim of Bonn, Ralph the Cistercian incited anti-Jewish violence in 1146: "wherever he went, he spoke evil of the Jews of the land and incited the snake and the dogs against us, saying 'Avenge the Crucified One upon his enemies who stand before you; then go to war against the Ishmaelites.'"[21] The *Gesta Regis Henrici Secundi* described attacks against southern French heretics that preceded the official declaration of crusade as acts of vengeance in three separate passages, noting that "it is clear to the Christian princes that they are avenging the injuries of Christ."[22]

The vernacular song *Chevalier, mult estes guariz*, composed between December 1145 and June 1147, remarked that the Christian knights "went to serve [God] in his need ... in order to provide God with vengeance."[23] By interpreting the need for vengeance in terms of men fulfilling their lord's need to take vengeance, in effect the song eliminated the need for more specific justification. Similarly, the Occitan troubadour Marcabru wrote circa 1146–47: "since the son of God summons you to avenge him on the lineage of Pharaoh, you indeed ought to be joyful."[24] In another poem Marcabru wrote that vengeance was owed for injuries done to God throughout the world: "the Lord who knows all that is, and all that will be, and [all] that was, has promised us crowns and the name of emperor ...

---

[19]   Roger of Howden, *Chronica*, vol. 3, p. 130.

[20]   Richard of Devizes, *Cronicon de Tempore Regis Richardi Primi*, ed. J. T. Appleby (London, 1963), p. 5. Similarly, Roger of Howden reported that, in 1191, the pope wrote that Richard "had gone forth to avenge the injuries of our Redeemer" (*Chronica*, vol. 3, p. 151).

[21]   *Sefir Zekhirah*, trans. S. Eidelberg, in *The Jews and the Crusaders* (Madison WI, 1977), p. 122.

[22]   *Gesta Regis Henrici Secundi*, vol. 1, p. 220 (see also vol. 1, pp. 199 and 228).

[23]   *Les Chansons de Croisade*, p. 10.

[24]   Marcabru, *Marcabru: A Critical Edition*, ed. S. Gaunt, R. Harvey, and L. Paterson (Cambridge, 2000), p. 310.

as long as we take vengeance for the wrongs they do to God, both here and there towards Damascus."[25]

The Old French epics of the First Crusade also emphasized the wrongs done to the person of Christ. The *Chanson de Jérusalem* described the First Crusaders as "those who had come to avenge God," "to avenge the Lord," "who crossed the sea to avenge ... Lord Jesus," and those who asked God to "allow us to take vengeance on all [His] enemies."[26] The *Chanson d'Antioche* stated that the first crusaders were:

> they who came to avenge God on the servile slaves
> who wounded him and his holy name.[27]

They had gone to "avenge [Christ] on the lineage of the Antichrist" and "avenge God on his enemies."[28]

Moreover, a number of passages referred to the body of Christ and the crucifixion in a way that suggested that vengeance was owed specifically for the Passion. Peter of Blois, in his text *Conquestio de Dilatione Vie Ierosolimitane*, wrote that "the blood of Naboth cried out, the blood of Abel cried out from the ground for vengeance, and found vengeance. The blood of Christ clamors for aid, and does not find anyone to help."[29] The *Chanson de Jérusalem* more simply claimed that the crusaders "had passed over the sea to avenge [Christ's] body."[30] The *Chanson d'Antioche* described the crusaders as

> the noble barons who love God and hold him dear,
> [who] went over the sea to avenge his body.[31]

Further passages in the *Chanson d'Antioche* confirm that the references were meant literally: the First Crusaders were there to avenge the crucifixion. When the crusaders despaired inside the besieged Antioch, Adhémar bishop of Le Puy reminded them:

---

25   Ibid., p. 438.
26   *La Chanson de Jérusalem*, pp. 39, 65, 125 and 58.
27   *La Chanson d'Antioche*, p. 72.
28   Ibid., pp. 51 and 59.
29   Peter of Blois, *Conquestio de Dilatione vie Ierosolimitane*, ed. R. B. C. Huygens, CCCM 194 (Turnholt, 2002), p. 83.
30   *La Chanson de Jérusalem*, p. 90.
31   *La Chanson d'Antioche*, p. 49.

you have all well heard the commandments from God,
and we have the [holy] lance, that we know truly,
by which he [Christ] suffered for us death and torment,
when the criminal Jews cruelly killed him.
We are all his sons, and we will take vengeance.[32]

This characterization of the crusade as vengeance for the crucifixion was validated in the *chanson* by Christ himself, who told Anselm of Ribémont in a vision what Anselm later related to Godfrey of Bouillon:

the time has come that God named ...
and his sons will avenge him for his redeeming death.[33]

In fact, the *Chanson d'Antioche* directly linked the crucifixion, the prophecy of the destruction of Jerusalem, the subsequent actions of Titus and Vespasian, and the First Crusade. In laisse 8 Jesus and the two robbers spoke during the crucifixion. The robber on Christ's right said:

now it would be well if it happened that you are avenged
on these slavish Jews by whom you have been wounded.[34]

Jesus then prophesied vengeance and the destruction of Jerusalem:

Friend ... the people are not yet born
who will come to avenge me with sharp lances,
and will come to kill the faithless pagans
who have always refused my commandments.[35]

The robber on Christ's left then mocked the believing robber, who retorted:

... over the sea a new people will come
to take vengeance for the death of their father..
the Franks will have all the land through deliverance.[36]

---

[32] Ibid., p. 289.
[33] Ibid., p. 387.
[34] Ibid., p. 53.
[35] Ibid., p. 53.
[36] Ibid., p. 54.

The narrative of the *Chanson d'Antioche* went on to describe the destruction of Jerusalem by Titus and Vespasian as vengeance for Christ.[37]

In addition to these four main themes of vengeance for land, Christian deaths, injuries to the cross, and injuries to Christ, a few passages in the period expressed the need to take vengeance but simply did not clarify the nature of the injury requiring retribution. For example, Bernard of Clairvaux, writing to "the universal faithful" about the Second Crusade in March 1147, reminded his audience that during the First Crusade "God elevated the spirit of kings and princes to take vengeance on the nations and eradicate the enemies of the Christian name from the land."[38] Another annalist claimed that Bernard of Clairvaux invited people to go "make a pilgrimage and avenge Christianity."[39] When it came to describing the arm of the Second Crusade that attacked Lisbon, the generality of appeals for vengeance was marked. There was a sermon put into the mouth of Peter, Bishop of Oporto, by the author of the *De Expugnatione Lyxbonensi* in which crusading was referred to as "divine vengeance," "vengeance for the blood of [the Church's] sons," "vengeance taken upon the nations," and "deeds of vengeance."[40] By the end of the narrative, the author stated that the taking of Lisbon was "divine justice ... vengeance upon the evildoers."[41]

However, even these more ambiguous passages related to aspects of the ideology we have already explored. The passage from the *De Expugnatione Lyxbonensi* quoted above hinted at the need to avenge the Christian dead and suggested that vengeance was divine justice on those who had done evil. Similarly, Rigord attributed the following speech to King Philip II of France in 1190 upon taking the cross: "we, through the counsel of God, will take vengeance concerning this thing."[42] Rigord portrayed the king noting that it was vengeance with explicit divine consent, thus compatible with contemporary ideas of just war.[43] Gervase of Canterbury recorded that, in a 1177 letter to the Cistercian chapter, Count Raymond V of Toulouse wrote, "[I] will gird on my sword, and I declare that I will be an avenger of the anger of God and the minister of God in

---

[37]   Ibid., pp. 54–5.

[38]   Bernard of Clairvaux, *Epistolae*, ed. J. Leclerq and H. M. Rochais, SBO 7–8 (Rome, 1974–77), vol. 8, p. 432.

[39]   *Gesta Abbatum Lobbiensium*, in MGHSS 21 (Hanover, 1869), p. 329.

[40]   *De Expugnatione Lyxbonensi*, ed. C. W. David (New York, 1936), pp. 76, 78 and 80.

[41]   Ibid., p. 182.

[42]   Rigord, *Gesta Philippi Augusti*, in *Rigord: Histoire de Philippe Auguste*, ed. E. Carpentier, G. Pons, and Y. Chauvin, Sources D'Histoire Médiévale 33 (Paris, 2006), p. 278.

[43]   See above pages 17–18.

this matter [heresy in Languedoc]."[44] Although it is unclear what the injury was, the passage explicitly referred to Romans 13:4, linking the idea of crusading as vengeance with the concept of divine punishment of wrongdoers.

Similarly, the Hebrew accounts did not clearly state what injury was to be avenged through crusading, but the language used hinted at possible reasons for vengeance. As we saw in the previous chapter, at the beginning of the late eleventh-century *Mainz Anonymous* the crusaders were depicted saying: "look now, we are going to a distant country to make war against mighty kings and are endangering our lives to conquer the kingdoms which do not believe in the crucified one."[45] The account of Eliezer bar Nathan, written after 1140 and before 1146, changed that passage to:

> Look now, we are going to seek out our profanity and take vengeance on the Ishmaelites for our messiah, when here are the Jews who murdered and crucified him. Let us first avenge ourselves on them and exterminate them from among the nations so that the name of Israel will no longer be remembered, or let them adopt our faith and acknowledge the offspring of promiscuity.[46]

The compilation known as the *Solomon bar Simson Chronicle*, also dating to the 1140s, repeated a very similar version of the passage, again emphasizing the idea of crusading as vengeance.[47] The references to the "profanity" or "profane shrine" (in the *Solomon bar Simson Chronicle*) suggest, perhaps, vengeance for the Islamic occupation of the Holy Sepulchre in Jerusalem.

The absence of vengeance

There were also a relatively small number of sources for crusading during the period that did not incorporate the idea of crusading as vengeance. Pope Eugenius III (even in the well-known papal bull *Quantum praedecessores*), Pope Hadrian IV, Pope Alexander III, and Suger, Abbot of St. Denis, did not refer

---

[44]   Gervase of Canterbury, *Chronica*, in RS 73:1 (London, 1879), p. 270. Reference to Romans 13:4.

[45]   *Mainz Anonymous* trans. S. Eidelberg, in *The Jews and the Crusaders* (Madison WI, 1977), p. 99.

[46]   *Eliezer bar Nathan Chronicle*, trans. S. Eidelberg, in *The Jews and the Crusaders* (Madison WI, 1977), p. 80.

[47]   *Solomon bar Simson Chronicle*, trans. S. Eidelberg, in *The Jews and the Crusaders* (Madison WI, 1977), p. 22.

to the idea.[48] Caffaro of Caschifelone did not utilize the idea of crusading as vengeance at all, though he did discuss the desire for personal vengeance.[49] Henry of Huntingdon did not employ the specific vocabulary of vengeance to describe the First or Second Crusades.[50] Henry noted that the capture of Edessa led to the Second Crusade, but did not use the vocabulary of vengeance; the Christians simply went "to fight the pagans who had taken the city of Edessa."[51] Vincent of Prague was likewise succinct about the Second Crusade: "no small [number] of Christians were moved to defend Jerusalem against the king of Babylon."[52]

The *Annales Herbipolenses* described the beginning of the Second Crusade in 1147 with vitriolic language aimed at those who promoted the crusade rather than at its target: "for some pseudo-prophets, sons of Belial, witnesses (*testes*) to the Antichrist, who seduced Christians with inane words, compelled all kinds of men to go against the Saracens to liberate Jerusalem with vane sayings."[53] The fierce disapproval in the text may have been the result of the notorious failure of the Second Crusade, and certainly many writers of historical accounts of the Second Crusade concentrated on its disastrous outcome rather than the motivations that drove people on the Second Crusade.[54] Otto of Freising talked of vengeance taken on the Christians themselves by God, rather than vengeance taken through their actions.[55] It is certainly conceivable that the results of the Second Crusade suggested to some that an ideology such as vengeance, with its implicit emphasis on the pursuit of justice and divine punishment, might not have been appropriate.

Even when these writers did devote a line or two to the reasons for crusading, they did not use the vocabulary of vengeance. Helmold of Bosau recorded that Bernard of Clairvaux "exhorted princes and certain people of the faithful to march to Jerusalem to seize the barbarous nations of the east and subject them to Christian laws."[56] Odo of Deuil depicted the Bishop of Langres exciting people

---

[48]   It should be noted that Eugenius III did use the term *retributio*, though only to describe the rewards of crusading for those who took the cross.

[49]   See above page 20.

[50]   Henry of Huntingdon, *Historia Anglorum*, ed. T. Arnold, RS 74 (London, 1879), pp. 219–30 and 279.

[51]   Ibid., p. 279.

[52]   Vincent of Prague, *Annales*, in MGHSS 17 (Hanover, 1861), p. 662.

[53]   *Annales Herbipolenses*, in MGHSS 16 (Hanover, 1859), p. 3.

[54]   For more on this, see Elizabeth Siberry, *Criticism of Crusading, 1095–1274* (Oxford, 1985).

[55]   Otto of Freising, *Gesta Frederici seu rectius Cronica*, ed. F.-J. Schmale, AQDGM 17 (Darmstadt, 1965), p. 220.

[56]   Helmold of Bosau, *Chronica Slavorum*, ed. H. Stoob, AQDGM 19 (Berlin, 1963), p. 216.

at Bourges at Christmas 1145, "warning all of the depopulation and oppression of the Christians and the insolence of the pagans, so that with their king they would fight with Christian reverence for the King of all."[57] Otto of Freising even described the First Crusaders without the vocabulary of vengeance: "confident in the strength of the cross, with Godfrey as their leader, a journey to fight against the enemies of the cross in the East was announced."[58] These writers hit upon familiar themes: the centrality of Jerusalem, the need to conquer Islamic territory, the ill-treatment of Christians by the Muslims, the desire to fight against the enemies of the cross. But they did not use the vocabulary of vengeance.

So while in most of the sources for the period from 1138 to 1197 the idea of crusading as vengeance flourished, nevertheless seven historical narratives, one Hebrew account (the *Sefir Zekhirah*), and an assortment of ecclesiastical correspondence did not contain the idea of crusading as vengeance.[59] We saw a similar divide, between vengeance-rich and vengeance-free accounts, when looking at earlier texts in the previous chapter. In that case, the divide in the evidence for the period from 1095 to 1137 was apparently due to whether the writers of the texts were eyewitnesses or not.

This distinction does not suit the evidence from the texts in the period from 1138 to 1197, especially since some texts were discussing the First Crusade, some the Second Crusade, some the Third Crusade, and others all three expeditions. Nor does the divide in evidence correspond strictly to membership in the ecclesiastical hierarchy, genre, or language of composition. Moreover, regardless of whether the vocabulary of vengeance was used, the same motifs appeared in almost all of the texts from the period: the fall of Edessa, the loss of Jerusalem, the renewed Islamic presence in the East, the need to defend Christendom against its enemies. In other words, similar causes for Christian action were given in the sources, but while some specifically used the vocabulary of vengeance, others did not choose to do so with respect to crusading, even when (like Otto of Freising in his *Chronica*) they did not hesitate to employ the vocabulary to describe many other events, including some with religious significance.[60] This suggests that these writers did not disapprove of the terminology and concept of vengeance per se, but that they did not apply them to crusading.

Is it possible to infer why? The vocabulary of vengeance *was* used in texts written before the Second Crusade's failure became known, texts that dealt with

---

57   Odo of Deuil, *De Profectione*, p. 6.

58   Otto of Freising, *Chronica sive Historia de Duabus Divitatibus*, ed. A. Schmidt, AQDGM 16 (Darmstadt, 1961), p. 502.

59   For more details on the specific sources, see pages 195–201 below.

60   So these sources differ from the eyewitness accounts of the First Crusade, which barely used the terminology at all, even to describe day-to-day human behavior.

the success in Lisbon rather than the failure in the East, and texts dating to much later in the twelfth century. As already stated above, it is certainly possible that the failure of the Second Crusade in the East, understood as God's punishment *peccatis exigentibus hominum*, led some to avoid the language of vengeance with all its overtones of moral superiority, at least those writing in the immediate aftermath of the crusade. Since vengeance was strongly tied to the concept of justice, the failure of the crusade could have been said to have demonstrated that it was not just, because it was not in agreement with God's will.

However, this argument cannot completely account for the evidence, since Pope Eugenius III, writing well before the Second Crusade reached its tragic end, nevertheless did not use the idea, and some who did talk about vengeance, like the author of the *Gesta Stephani*, wrote after the Christian failure. Moreover, by the time Jerusalem fell to Salah al-Din in 1187 the vast majority of writers were again using the idea of crusading as an act of vengeance unreservedly. There must have been other factors at work, though at the moment they are unclear.

Negative evidence is troublesome in virtually any academic discipline. When studying medieval history, it becomes particularly problematic due to the constant question of how many sources are simply lost to us altogether. Despite the uncertainty, the fact that the evidence is inevitably incomplete reminds us that twelfth-century writers *chose* to use the idea of crusading as an act of vengeance and that their choice involved deliberation and analysis of the situation—conscious or subconscious. We are not dealing with a black-and-white world, where some advocated crusading as vengeance and others despised it. Some talked about the fall of Edessa, some did not. Some utilized the idea of vengeance, some did not. And, while some surely cared deeply what ideas they incorporated into their accounts and deliberated at length about which words to use, others almost equally surely did not, but used whatever ideas or clichés first sprang to mind. Moreover, if the writers, the literate, present such a continuum of evidence, then it seems fairly safe to assume that the culture itself, from top to bottom, contained an at least equally broad set of ideas about crusading.

After all, even among those who wrote about *ultio* and *vindicta*, the context ranged from very specific events to a broad, general sense of wrong. Some texts emphasized certain, specific circumstances that demanded vengeance. Peter the Venerable claimed that the First Crusaders were avenging the Islamic occupation of the Holy Land, and the *Gesta Stephani* listed the destruction wrought by the Muslims in the East and their disruption of Latin kingdoms there.[61] At the same time, other texts used the vocabulary of vengeance obscurely, employing

---

[61]　These same themes, Islamic occupation and destruction, were echoed, though not with the vocabulary of vengeance, by Henry of Huntingdon and Odo of Deuil.

phrases that suggested general religious hostility towards what they perceived as a blasphemous religion that threatened Christianity: "enemies of the Christian name," "injury done to the Christian religion," "vengeance upon the evildoers," "vengeance for the wrongs they do to God."[62]

The specific need to avenge Edessa and Jerusalem is easily understandable in the context of Augustine's definition of a just war as one that avenges injuries. But that does not address the indefinite references to vengeance that hinged on an amorphous sense of religious hostility, nor those that called for vengeance for injuries done to Christ. What does account for this range of evidence? What was all the vengeance *for*?

God's vengeance, papal power, and the nature of Islamic injuries

I argued in the previous chapter that one of the major patterns of thought responsible for the construction of crusading as vengeance was belief in God's vengeance on the wrongdoer, and certainly the *Deus ultionis* continued to figure prominently in crusading texts from 1138 to 1197. Using both Old and New Testament references and language, writers depicted God (and his human agent) as a wrathful avenger of wrongs, and portrayed the circumstances around crusading as worthy of vengeance for God. Peter of Blois drew explicit parallels between crusading and Biblical events, comparing, as we have seen, the avenged deaths of Naboth and Abel with the as yet unavenged death of Christ.[63] Roger of Howden, like many of his contemporaries, pictured the crusading armies following in the footsteps of the Israelites and thus taking vengeance.[64] Gervase of Canterbury recorded a letter to a Cistercian chapter which employed a key verse from the New Testament Epistle to the Romans to epitomize the role of the crusader as the avenging minister of God.[65]

As before, one fundamental belief underlying crusading as vengeance was that God actively sought vengeance for human sin. The *Gesta Regis Henrici Secundi* noted that, in 1184, a lay brother at Worcester went into a trance and recited the following prophetic poem, which aptly illustrates the nature of the *Deus ultionis* in contemporary Christian minds:

---

[62]   Bernard of Clairvaux, *Epistolae*, vol. 8 p. 432. *Gesta Abbatum Lobbiensium*, p. 329. *De Expugnatione Lyxbonensi*, p. 182. Marcabru, *Marcabru*, p. 438.

[63]   Peter of Blois, *Conquestio*, p. 84.

[64]   Roger of Howden, *Chronica*, vol. 3, pp. 37–8.

[65]   Gervase of Canterbury, *Chronica*, p. 270. Reference to Romans 13:4.

For with the sword of death the proper vengeance of God
will expiate the sins of the people; miserable me! What can I do?
Behold! The sword shines, that will contort the whole world.
Behold! The hand of the Lord! Where can a wretched man escape it?
Behold the fury of the Lord; where can I flee or hide?[66]

As William of Tyre reminded his readers, God was believed to have said "I will not give my glory to the proud, but my vengeance, I will take retribution, I will strike and I will heal and I will give life and there is no one who can escape my hand."[67] Indeed, this characterization of God as avenger had seemed so well-known to earlier writers of crusading texts that they placed the same verse from Deuteronomy that William of Tyre used in the mouth of an Islamic noblewoman.[68]

From this perspective, which also underpinned the familiar phrase *peccatis exigentibus hominum*, God struck out with vengeance when faced with sin and impiety. Christians approved of this vengeance, despite being aware of their own vulnerability. Addressing God, Peter of Blois wrote "to me as a sinner it seems best that you should eliminate all sinners from the face of the earth, rather than allow the sons of perdition among us who proudly and audaciously inflict shame upon your name."[69] But, at the same time, Peter's approval was tempered by anxiety that God's vengeance might be directed at the Christian community:

a local proverb says *a wrong is badly avenged by he who cuts off his own nose*. Do not thus punish your impious servant Lord ... We have sinned, but with a contrite and humble heart we beg for mercy after your anger: *vengeance for the blood of your servants that was shed enters your face.*[70]

This anxiety—and the tendency to cry "take vengeance, but not on us!"—may well have resulted from the impossibility of completely comprehending God's judgments. It was not always clear to human bystanders why some received justice (vengeance) and others mercy. In the *Passio Raginaldi*, Peter of Blois used the Old Testament to emphasize his despair and uncertainty after the battle of Hattin:

---

[66]   *Gesta Regis Henrici Secundi*, vol. 1, p. 326.
[67]   William of Tyre, *Chronicon*, p. 622. References to Romans 12:19 and Deuteronomy 32:39–42.
[68]   See above page 50.
[69]   Peter of Blois, *Conquestio*, p. 78.
[70]   Ibid., *Conquestio*, p. 78. Reference to Psalms 78:10–11.

> O God of inexhaustible and ineffable mercy, why do you humiliate and confound
> the heart of your people, and why do you permit injuries to your name and shame
> to the Christian faith to be proclaimed with the horns of your enemies? The cry
> of Jeremiah is *wherefore do the ways of the impious prosper?* Even Job complains and
> says *why do the impious live?*[71]

Living with this anxiety and uncertainty, it was in the Christians' own best
interest to punish the wrongdoers in their midst before God punished them all
collectively. All humanity bore responsibility to God and should obey his law.
It would seem therefore that between 1138 and 1197 contemporaries were still
viewing the Muslims within a Biblical framework of divine punishment that was
frequently described with the vocabulary of vengeance.

For some, this meant that Christians who did not wish to take vengeance
for God on the Muslims would suffer divine vengeance themselves. Gerald of
Wales noted two occasions when men who did not immediately respond to the
call to crusade were struck by God's wrath. On one occasion the young members
of a certain family in Wales failed to respond to a crusading sermon, but "divine
vengeance followed, since the youths insisted on pursuing plunderers of their
land with many others; they were immediately killed by the robbers and set to
flight, with one and another of them lethally wounded, the cross that before
they had spurned they now affixed on their own flesh."[72] When the crusade was
preached at St. Dogmael's, one woman did not want her husband to go. That
night she heard a voice in her sleep saying, "You have taken my servant from me;
on this account that which you love more will be taken away from you." The next
day "a little son, whom she had with her in the maternal bed more from love than
from carefulness, was crushed ... And immediately the man, reporting the vision
as well as the vengeance to the bishop, took up the cross."[73]

How do we get from a vengeful God to the idea of crusading as vengeance?
We have seen that there was a close relationship between the concepts of
vengeance and justice, and that ecclesiastical as well as secular leaders needed to
display their ability to take vengeance.[74] Theoretically, this need to demonstrate
authority through vengeance hinged on the division of the powers in the
Christian tradition. The general assumptions underlying this tradition were
threefold and stemmed from divine mandate: first, the material and spiritual

---

[71]   Peter of Blois, *Passio Raginaldi Principis Antiochie*, ed. R. B. C. Huygens, CCCM
194 (Turnholt, 2002), p. 35. References to Jeremiah 12:1 and Job 21:7.

[72]   Gerald of Wales, *Itinerarium Kambriae*, ed. J. F. Dimock, RS 21:6 (London, 1868),
p. 126.

[73]   Ibid., p. 113.

[74]   See above pages 19–31.

powers, or swords, were distinct (except with reference to the person of the pope); second, the material and spiritual powers must cooperate; and third, the spiritual power was superior.[75] As Otto of Freising wrote:

> One [person of the Church] ... should take in hand the sacraments of Christ and exercise ecclesiastical justice with the spiritual sword. The other carries the material sword against the enemies of the Church, and by defending the poor churches of God against the incursion of evildoers and by punishing the criminal, [the material sword] should be thrust forward in secular justice.[76]

Furthermore, a distinction was made between the possession of a power, the right to command a power, and the right to exercise a power. Both spiritual and secular powers were coercive, embodying the ability to judge and punish, but the means of punishment differed. Traditionally, the spiritual sword had at its disposal the coercive tools of conviction, admonition, excommunication, and deposition.[77] If these tools failed, the spiritual power could call on the secular power to take physical action.[78]

But in the mid-twelfth century the balance between the two powers was shifting. The Concordat of Worms in 1122 had introduced a new kind of relationship between the Church and western Europe, a relationship accompanied in the mid-twelfth century by new forms of monasticism, new spiritual emphases within the Church, and the impetus to consolidate and codify the vast theological tradition of the past. In 1139, Pope Innocent II summarized the Church's position concerning this new relationship when he reportedly said at the beginning of the Second Lateran Council that "Rome is the head of the world ... promotion to ecclesiastical dignity is requested from the Roman pontiff as if by the custom of feudal law and is not legally held without his permission."[79]

The concept of an "independent power of material coercion" belonging to the Church had been growing since before the First Crusade, and in the mid-twelfth century new theories of papal power developed alongside the established

---

[75] John A. Watt, *The Theory of Papal Monarchy in the Thirteenth Century* (London, 1965), p. 13. The New Testament passage frequently cited was Luke 22:38.

[76] Otto of Freising, *Chronica*, pp. 290 and 292.

[77] Watt, *Theory of Papal Monarchy*, p. 17.

[78] Ibid., p. 31.

[79] *Chronicon Mauriacense* III (cited and translated by Colin Morris, *The Papal Monarchy* (Oxford, 1989), p. 187).

tradition.[80] Gratian argued that, although churchmen had a limited right to exercise the material sword, they possessed the *ius auctoritatis* to command it.[81] Bernard of Clairvaux argued that "both [powers] therefore belong to the Church, the spiritual and material sword; but the one is to be used for the Church, the other by the Church."[82] Gratian and Bernard agreed, at least, that the Church held the authority to command both swords.

That raised at least two further questions. Who specifically within the Church had that authority, and towards whom could physical force be directed? Recognizing the former issue, Gratian set himself the question "whether to bishops or to any clerics this authority to move arms by command should be permitted, or to the pope, or to the emperor?"[83] Gratian confirmed that the authority belonged to the pope and (crucially) extended to the avenging of communal, though not individual or personal, injuries.[84] Further in the same *quaestio*, Gratian, working from the New Testament example of the deaths of Ananias and Saphira and the writings of St. Jerome as well as Deuteronomy 13:6, affirmed that "to punish crimes for God is not cruelty but piety."[85] As Chodorow has noted, this argument asserted that it was right to use force "in the interests of the social body."[86]

Gratian's justification of papal punishment of communal injuries was applied to crusading through the vocabulary of vengeance. The *Gesta Stephani* noted that the Second Crusade was sparked by the desire "to avenge the universal injury."[87] The same verse Gratian used, Deuteronomy 13:6, appeared in the sermon put into the mouth of Peter bishop of Oporto in the *De Expugnatione Lyxbonensi*, in which the need to take vengeance on the Muslims was emphasized.[88] In fact, the ideology of vengeance in that sermon was explicitly compatible with Gratian's *Decretum*. The sermon classified the Muslims as criminals, thereby making it right to take vengeance on them:

---

[80]   Stanley Chodorow, *Christian Political Theory and Church Politics in the Mid-Twelfth Century: The Ecclesiology of Gratian's Decretum* (Los Angeles, 1972), pp. 226–7.

[81]   Watt, *Theory of Papal Monarchy*, p. 57.

[82]   Bernard of Clairvaux, *De Consideratione ad Eugenium Papam*, ed. J. Leclerq and H. M. Rochais, SBO 3 (Rome, 1963), p. 454.

[83]   Gratian, *Corpus Iuris Canonici*, ed. A. E. Richteri (2nd edn, 2 vols, Lipsiae, 1879), vol. 1, col. 889. This question is then dealt with in cols 953–65.

[84]   Watt, *Theory of Papal Monarchy*, p. 233.

[85]   Gratian, *Corpus Iuris Canonici*, vol. 1, col. 956.

[86]   Chodorow, *Christian Political Theory*, p. 234.

[87]   *Gesta Stephani*, p. 127.

[88]   For more on this sermon, see Jonathan Phillips, "Ideas of Crusade and Holy War in *De Expugnatione Lyxbonensi* (*The Conquest of Lisbon*)," in Robert Swanson (ed.), *Holy Land, Holy Lands, and Christian History*, Studies in Church History 36 (2000): 123–41.

But now, with God inspiring you, you bear arms with which murderers and plunderers should be wounded, the devious controlled, the adulterers punished, the impious lost from the earth, the parricides not allowed to live, nor the sons of impiety to go forth. You, therefore, brothers, take up courage along with these arms ... Deeds of this kind are the duty of vengeance which good men carry in good spirit ... *It is not cruelty but piety for God.* With the zeal of justice, do not go forth with anger, [instead] wage just war.[89]

Christians had a duty to promote law and order and punish crime with just vengeance, and the Muslims were described here not simply as unfaithful, but as murderers, adulterers, and parricides, criminals who would have deserved vengeance even if they had been Christian.

Indeed, although the texts for the period gave examples of crusading as vengeance for specific wrongs (such as the Muslim seizures of Edessa and Jerusalem), some of the texts suggested that a more fundamental characteristic of the Muslims was an injury that deserved punishment: their hostile and rebellious lack of Christian faith. The Muslims were in and of themselves "the enemies of the cross of Christ, who ought to be his sons."[90] The *Chanson de Jérusalem* and the *Chanson d'Antioche* both emphasized that the Muslims were "they who did not want to believe."[91] William of Tyre referred to the Muslims as an "impious people," an "unclean people" who adhered to the "impiety of superstition."[92] Even the Muslim individual who betrayed Antioch from the inside on the First Crusade was "pious in deed, yet criminal at the same time."[93]

This imputation of willful disbelief was echoed in the accusations of treachery leveled at the Muslims. The *Chanson de Jérusalem* depicted them as "criminal" (*felon*), "unfaithful" (*desfaé*), "disloyal" (*desloiaus*), and "misbelieving" (*mescreans*).[94] *Les Chétifs* also called the Turks "that disloyal people."[95] This was familiar ground for the *chansons de geste*; the *inimici Dei* in these texts were systematically portrayed as political enemies, unbelievers, traitors, and the people of Satan.[96] This type of characterization, and the vocabulary of faithlessness, continually suggested that the Muslims were treacherous. In the texts, the

89 *De Expugnatione Lyxbonensi*, p. 80.
90 Peter of Blois, *Conquestio*, p. 84.
91 *La Chanson de Jérusalem*, p. 42. *La Chanson d'Antioche*, p. 52.
92 William of Tyre, *Chronicon*, pp. 339, 127 and 285.
93 Ibid., p. 299.
94 *La Chanson de Jérusalem*, pp. 35, 56, 73, and 117.
95 *Les Chétifs*, ed. G. M. Myers, OFCC 5 (Tuscaloosa, 1981), p. 92.
96 Marianna Gildea, *Expressions of Religious Thought and Feeling in the Chansons de Geste* (Washington D.C., 1943), pp. 24–7.

Muslims had betrayed their Father and thus were faithless, both in terms of religious belief and in terms of personal character. Their crime of treachery deserved vengeance, in much the same way as did criminals and traitors within Christian society. Although Christian doctrine made it clear that pagan disbelief in Christ alone did not justify vengeance, the fact that the same language was used to describe both lack of Christian faith (which did not technically deserve vengeance) and treachery and betrayal (which certainly did deserve vengeance) may have contributed to the perception of crusading as an act of vengeance.

This language, as well as efforts as in the *De Expugnatione Lyxbonensi* to paint the Muslims as the worst kind of criminals, enabled a clever—if somewhat unconvincing—manipulation of canon law to justify violence against Muslims and confirms our understanding that some Christian contemporaries viewed Christians and Muslims as subject to the same divine law. It highlights the missing connection between Gratian's argument for papal authority to punish criminals through vengeance, and actions against those outside Christian society; despite the suggestive language of faithlessness used to describe both Muslims and traitors, we have as yet seen no formal connection. But in time one was supplied by other thinkers who took Gratian's argument and expanded it logically, building upon the tradition of using the material sword to deal with heretics.[97]

Some blurred the line between Islam and heresy, since traditionally contemporaries confronted heresy with physical coercion when deemed necessary.[98] For example, Peter the Venerable described Muslims as both heretics and *pagani*: "either call them heretics on account of their heresy, and since they understand some part [of truth] with the Church, or call them pagans because of their exceptional impiety."[99] Peter may well have drawn upon the 1127 *Digest of Aimon*, in which William of Malmesbury asserted that Christians, Jews, and Muslims were sects with different opinions about God the Son, but who agreed in their worship of God the Father.[100] Whether the Muslims were heretics or

---

[97]   Watt, *Theory of Papal Monarchy*, p. 31.

[98]   The idea that Islam was a heresy was forged in the Middle East and Spain much before its arrival in northern Europe (John V. Tolan, *Saracens: Islam in the Medieval European Imagination* (New York, 2002), p. 277).

[99]   Peter the Venerable, *Liber contra Sectam sive Haeresim Saracenorum*, ed. J. Kritzeck, *Peter the Venerable and Islam* (Princeton, 1964), p. 227.

[100]   Benjamin Z. Kedar, *Crusade and Mission: European Approaches Toward the Muslims* (Princeton, 1984), pp. 87–8.

pagans was in truth a crucial question in the context of canon law, a question that affected the legality of physical coercion against Islam.[101]

Others used Islamic aggression in the Holy Land to argue that Muslims, like heretics, were actively resisting the rules of Christian society. Circa 1160 the *Summa Parisiensis* stated: "we ought to persecute [Muslims] because they struggle to invade us and our lands, but not the Jews, because they are prepared to serve … so generally we can say, that whether they are Saracens or Jews, as long as they are rebels, we ought to persecute them."[102] Similarly, Henry of Huntingdon described the Muslims killed in Jerusalem in 1099 as rebels: "therefore assaulting the city and climbing its walls with ladders, the sons of God took the city, and killed many rebels (*rebellantes*) in the temple of the Lord, and cleansed the holy city of the unclean peoples."[103] The evidence suggests that some in the mid-twelfth century were extending the legality of vengeance authorized by the pope against those who had committed injuries to the communal good to the Muslims, because they were seen, like heretics, as actively rebelling against Christian society.

Arguments from another direction used the reality of the crusading movement to promote the use of force against the unfaithful within Christian society. As well as arguing that the use of force against Christian criminals logically led to the use of force against non-Christians, Peter the Venerable noted that the use of force against Muslims could be used to justify the use of force against Christians. In 1150, he stated that those who argued for the application of physical coercion to non-Christians should argue as well for the application of physical coercion to Christians:

> But perhaps you say: we take up arms against pagans, but not against Christians. But whom should you fight more, a pagan who does not know God, or a Christian confessing himself in words and deeds to be opposed to [God]? Who should be most persecuted, one who is ignorant and blaspheming, or refusing to acknowledge and fighting? … It is not true that a Christian suffering injustice

---

[101]　For a thorough analysis of Peter the Venerable's thought and attitudes towards Jews, Muslims, and heretics, see Dominique Iogna-Prat, *Order and Exclusion: Cluny and Christendom Face Heresy, Judaism, and Islam*, trans. G. R. Edwards (Ithaca NY, 2002), especially pp. 265–365.

[102]　Kedar, *Crusade and Mission*, pp. 72–3n. It is worth noting that this passage opens the door to persecution of Jews who are rebelling; it demolishes the idea that all Jews, by virtue of being Jewish, are protected from violence.

[103]　Henry of Huntingdon, *Historia*, p. 229.

from another Christian should be less defended with counsel, and indeed by your swords, than a Christian suffering the same from a pagan.[104]

Apparently, not only did physical coercion of criminals lead some to apply physical coercion to Muslims, but vice versa; the persecution of Muslims led some to advocate internal sanctions. Here was great potential for circular reasoning in the future.[105]

The key point is that this just punishment, this material coercion, was described as vengeance. As has already been pointed out, this was partly due to the contemporary understanding of an intimate connection between vengeance, justice and punishment, and it was also partly due to the Biblical language and metaphors with which ecclesiastical minds sought to express their arguments. To give yet another example, Gratian used Old Testament events and vocabulary to explain why sins should be "avenged":

> God is provoked to anger, when the punishment of sins is delayed. And God is vehemently offended when we hesitate to attack and avenge the [sins] of some people; we provoke divine patience to anger. *Did not Achan son of Zerah break the mandate of God, and did not His anger consume the whole people of Israel?*[106]

So is this part of the family tree of crusading as vengeance exclusively ecclesiastical? I suggest that to draw a distinction between the "secular" and "ecclesiastical" sources for the terminology of vengeance may be anachronistic, or at the very least, premature. After all, Bernard of Clairvaux wrote that, during the First Crusade, "God elevated the spirit of kings and princes to take vengeance on the nations and eradicate the enemies of the Christian name from the land," and vernacular poets wrote "since the son of God summons you to avenge him on the lineage of Pharaoh, you indeed ought to be joyful."[107] The two passages emphasized different aspects of vengeance and used slightly different language, but ultimately both promoted the basic ideology of crusading as an act of vengeance on the wrongdoer.

---

[104]   Peter the Venerable, *The Letters of Peter the Venerable*, vol. 1, p. 409.

[105]   In fact, in 1275 Humbert of Romans wrote to Gregory X that this line of thought (if we kill Muslims, why not others who sin?) had been reincarnated yet again, this time to criticize the crusading movement. (Kedar, *Crusade and Mission*, p. 175)

[106]   Gratian, *Corpus Iuris Canonici*, vol. 1, col. 926. Reference to Joshua 22:20.

[107]   Bernard of Clairvaux, *Epistolae*, vol. 8, p. 432. Marcabru, *Marcabru*, p. 310.

Crucifixion and crusade

I was forced to conclude in the previous chapter that although there was a relationship between anti-Jewish sentiment, vengeance, and the First Crusade, it was impossible to make that relationship explicitly clear. Therefore in this chapter there are two questions already waiting to be answered: was there a continued relationship between anti-Jewish sentiment, vengeance, and the First Crusade, and if so, what accounted for it?

Our knowledge of events suggests a continued ideological relationship. On the eve of the Second Crusade, people stirred by crusade preaching attacked Jews in the Rhineland, leading Bernard of Clairvaux to write explicitly against anti-Jewish violence.[108] Jews were threatened with violence and forced conversion on the eve of the Third Crusade, and these threats were annulled only by the quick intervention of Emperor Frederick I.[109] The crusading movement was still inspiring, albeit without official sanction, anti-Jewish sentiment and violence.

There is evidence to suggest that this violence was understood by its victims as the desire to avenge the crucifixion of Christ, as it had been in the late eleventh and early twelfth centuries. The Hebrew *Sefir Zekhirah*, composed by Rabbi Ephraim of Bonn after the Second Crusade, described how some crusaders attacked a certain Master Rabbi Jacob:

> They ripped up a Torah Scroll before his face and took him out to a field. There they argued with him about his religion and started assaulting him viciously. They inflicted five wounds upon his head, saying "You are the leader of the Jews. So we shall take vengeance upon you for the Crucified One and wound you the way you inflicted five wounds on our God."[110]

Direct violent retaliation, five wounds for five wounds, was inflicted by crusaders in repayment for the suffering of Christ over a thousand years before.

On the other hand, it is fair to claim that by the later twelfth century the persecution of Jews was widespread and habitual, rather than merely tied to specific crusading expeditions, even though the call for the Third Crusade did inspire some to anti-Jewish violence. Anecdotes reporting various atrocities supposedly committed by Jews were circulated more regularly to inflame

---

[108]   Bernard of Clairvaux, *Epistolae*, vol. 8, pp. 311–17.

[109]   Robert Chazan, "Emperor Frederick I, the Third Crusade, and the Jews," *Viator*, 8 (1977), p. 88.

[110]   *Sefir Zekhirah*, p. 130.

Christian anger, and writers in the period took note of these stories.[111] In 1180, near Boppard, Jews were accused of murdering a young girl, urged to be baptized, and eventually drowned; one corpse was dragged from town to town.[112] In 1181 Gervase of Canterbury noted that "a certain boy named Robert was martyred by the Jews" and in 1191 King Philip II of France heard of a terrible episode involving a certain Christian:

> whom [the Jews] falsely charged with secret homicide, and whom the Jews, moved by ancient hatred, with his hands bound at his back, and crowned with thorns, led through the whole town, cudgeling him, and afterwards hung from a gibbet, saying among themselves as at the time of the Lord's passion, "*We are not permitted to kill anyone …*"[113]

In 1186, an apparently insane Jew publicly killed a Christian girl. That Jew was immediately killed along with six others, and a few days later his mother was buried alive and his uncle drawn and quartered.[114] Rigord, explaining Philip's decision to expel the Jews in 1180, offered three reasons, two of which are anecdotal and necessarily vague; only one, "for giving money to the Christians uxoriously," seems likely to have been true in any factual sense.[115] Rigord's other explanations were that "in the chalices, in which the body and blood of our Lord Jesus Christ was collected, [the Jews] devoured [Christian] infants made into little bits covered in wine (*infantes eorum offas in vino factas comedebant*)" and "a certain Jew … having the pledges of the Church … plac[ed] them most vilely in a bag in a deep pit where he was accustomed to empty his bowels."[116] Episodes of anti-Jewish violence promoted further acts of anti-Jewish violence, due to an attitude best described as "there's no smoke without fire."[117] As the Jews'

---

[111]   It will interest comparative historians that in nineteenth- and early twentieth-century Spain similar accusations of well poisoning and so forth were made against the Catholic Church. For further discussion, see Bruce Lincoln, *Discourse and the Construction of Society: Comparative Studies of Myth, Ritual, and Classification* (Oxford, 1989), p. 113.

[112]   Robert Chazan, "Ephraim ben Jacob's Compilation of Twelfth-Century Persecutions," *Jewish Quarterly Review*, 84:4 (1994), p. 401.

[113]   Gervase of Canterbury, *Chronica*, p. 296 and Rigord, *Gesta Philippi Augusti*, p. 310. Reference to John 18:31.

[114]   Chazan, "Ephraim ben Jacob's Compilation," p. 403.

[115]   Rigord, *Gesta Philippi Augusti*, p. 144.

[116]   Ibid., pp. 146 and 148.

[117]   Robert Chazan, "The Anti-Jewish Violence of 1096: Perpetrators and Dynamics," in A. S. Abulafia (ed.), *Religious Violence between Christians and Jews: Medieval Roots, Modern Perspectives* (Basingstoke, 2002), p. 37.

maltreatment increased, so too did the fear that they in turn might retaliate with more abominations and sabotage, thus propelling the cycle further along.[118]

Robert Chazan, using as evidence the growth of murder and well-poisoning accusations, has argued that in the period between the First and Second Crusades the hostility between Christians and Jews shifted from the "cosmic" level to a more everyday, earthly animosity and fear.[119] And, indeed, anti-Jewish violence in this period was predominantly justified case by case as vengeance for specific Jewish "crimes" (if it was justified at all), rather than as vengeance for Jewish disbelief or the crucifixion.

It is thus difficult to say based on events whether a relationship between anti-Jewish sentiment and the idea of crusading as vengeance continued in contemporary society just as it had in the very early twelfth century. However, I will now show that *in the texts*, at least, writers continued to draw a link between anti-Jewish sentiment and the idea of crusading as an act of vengeance. The apparent foundation of this link was writers' frequent blurring of the distinction between Jews and Muslims and their treatment.

One particular mindset of the time encouraged grouping Jews and Muslims together. Many in the mid-twelfth century saw the world in black-and-white terms that grouped non-Christians together, emphasizing primarily the division between the faithful and the unfaithful, rather than the divisions between different types of non-Christians. As we have seen, Peter the Venerable asked whether the Muslims should be deemed pagans or heretics, and ultimately decided that it did not greatly matter, even though it was a critical distinction in terms of canon law.[120] It is well documented that the Cistercians, particularly Bernard of Clairvaux, promoted the growing twelfth-century tendency to enforce a unified Christendom through physical coercion.[121] For Bernard, the love of God fed the hatred of those who did not love God:

> for from this it is certain that if [a man] should not return immediately to the love of God, it is necessary that he know, that not only is he now nothing, but nothing at all, or rather, he will be nothing for eternity. Therefore that man [should be] set aside; not only now should he not be loved, moreover he should be held in hatred,

---

[118]   Robert I. Moore, *The Formation of a Persecuting Society: Power and Deviance in Western Europe, 950–1250* (Oxford, 1987), p. 15.

[119]   Robert Chazan, "From the First Crusade to the Second: Evolving Perceptions of the Christian–Jewish Conflict," in M. A. Signer and J. Van Engen (eds), *Jews and Christians in Twelfth-Century Europe* (Notre Dame IN, 2001), pp. 46–62.

[120]   Peter the Venerable, *Liber Contra Sectam*, p. 227.

[121]   Martha G. Newman, *The Boundaries of Charity: Cistercian Culture and Ecclesiastical Reform, 1098–1180* (Stanford, 1996), p. 238.

according to this: *will I not hate those who hate you, Lord, and will I not languish over your enemies?*[122]

Bernard presented a definition of Christian love that effectively served to divide the world in two. Perhaps for similar reasons the Cistercians (and many others) did not distinguish between various types of heresy, choosing instead to present all heresies as "part of an ongoing diabolical battle against the unity of the Church."[123] As Peter of Blois wrote in his crusading narrative, "it is Christ who says: *he who is not with me, is against me, and he who does not unite with me will be scattered.*"[124] At the least, these kinds of opinions created an environment in which it was easier to blur the distinctions between Jews and Muslims.

Predominantly, however, the blurred distinctions between Jews and Muslims, and the relationship between those blurred distinctions and the idea of crusading as vengeance, centered around the crucifixion in four ways. First, there was an obvious and intrinsic link between Jerusalem, threatened by Muslims in the East, and Jerusalem, location of Christ's death at the hands of the Jews. So the city of Jerusalem itself served as a nexus for attitudes towards Jews and Muslims, reminding Christians of the crucifixion of Christ (blamed on the Jews) whilst encouraging violence against the Muslims to regain the holy city. We see this relationship in a number of texts already cited that suggest the First Crusaders stormed Jerusalem while the crucifixion was literally happening, and we see it also in images that depict this exact scenario: crusaders charging up from below, whilst above the Passion and Crucifixion of Christ is carried out.[125]

Second, the rhetorical emphasis writers placed upon avenging Christ's injuries (rather than injuries to the Church or to Christians in the East) drew attention to the crucifixion, making it a convenient ideological focal point. This was no doubt connected with the devotion to the suffering Christ that grew through the twelfth century, which was itself encouraged by the way in which visual depictions of the cross were increasingly replaced by the crucifix, partly in response to contempt for the cross expressed by heretics and Jews.[126] As Christians became more interested in the literal, physical details of Christ's life and painful

---

[122]   Bernard of Clairvaux, *Sermones super Cantica Canticorum*, ed. J. Leclerq and H. M. Rochais, SBO 1–2 (Rome, 1957–58), vol. 2, p. 82. Reference to Psalms 138:21.

[123]   Newman, *Boundaries of Charity*, p. 220.

[124]   Peter of Blois, *Conquestio*, p. 83. References to Matthew 12:30 and Luke 11:23.

[125]   For the textual references, see pages 51 and 99. For the image, see Norman Housley, *Fighting for the Cross: Crusading to the Holy Land* (New Haven, 2008), Plate 11 (from *Histoire d'Outremer* by Guillaume de Tyr).

[126]   Dominique Iogna-Prat, *Order and Exclusion*, p. 188.

death, they experienced "new and more intense emotional reaction[s]."[127] In fact, that was the exact goal aimed at by members of the Church. As Ralph Ardens wrote in one of his twelfth-century homilies, "also for this reason the image of the crucifix is now depicted in church so that we, seeing that our Redeemer voluntarily endured poverty, infirmity, taunts, spitting, beating [and] death for our salvation, may be more and more inflamed to love Him in our hearts."[128] Rupert of Deutz summarized the emotional effect of the crucifixion more succinctly: "we ourselves are aroused internally to love of Him while imagining externally His death."[129] The cultural immediacy of the crucifixion, and the vivid emotional responses it evoked, are clearly evident in later medieval demands for Christians to avenge injuries purportedly done by the Jews on the Eucharist. In those cases, the wounded body of Christ was believed to be literally right there in the present moment.[130] A rising emotional interest in the spectacle of the suffering Christ may have promoted Christian attention to the crucifixion, which in turn may have promoted Christian attention both to the purported Jewish deicide, leading to anti-Jewish violence, and to Jerusalem as the location of Christ's Passion, leading to aggression in the East.[131]

Third, although Chazan may be right that "cosmic" reasons for anti-Jewish persecution were less influential in society than they had been in the late eleventh and early twelfth centuries, in the crusading sources for the later twelfth century those same "cosmic" reasons for violent persecution remained evident and contributed to the ideology of crusading as vengeance against the Muslims. These "cosmic" reasons were fundamentally rooted in what I will refer to henceforth as Christian "mytho-history," the narrative framework underlying contemporary culture in the Christian West that assigned meaning and order to historical events

---

[127] Gavin I. Langmuir, "At the Frontiers of Faith," in A. S. Abulafia (ed.), *Religious Violence between Christians and Jews: Medieval Roots and Modern Perspectives* (Basingstoke, 2000), p. 149.

[128] Ralph Ardens, *Homiles* 55 (cited and translated by Giles Constable, *Three Studies in Medieval Religious and Social Thought* (Cambridge, 1995), p. 197).

[129] Rupert of Deutz, *De Conversione Sua* 3 (cited and translated by Constable, *Three Studies*, p. 211).

[130] Miri Rubin, *Gentile Tales: The Narrative Assault on Late Medieval Jews* (New Haven, 1999), pp. 54–7.

[131] Indeed, Peter the Venerable explicitly encouraged those who blamed the cross for Christ's death to consider instead the human beings in whom fault truly resided: "instead of taking vengeance upon inanimate, unfeeling objects, it made better sense to seek out the guilty, who was of necessity a human being, and demand justice of him for his fault" (Dominique Iogna-Prat, *Order and Exclusion*, p. 184).

on the basis of religious belief.[132] This narrative took actual historical events and reshaped and interpreted them to fit into a presupposed sacred pattern. To give one example already touched on, in this mytho-history the Roman destruction of Jerusalem in 70 C.E. was not perceived primarily as punishment for political rebellion, but as prophesied vengeance for the crucifixion of Christ. The premise that the destruction of Jerusalem was the fulfillment of Christian prophesy led to assertions about events, like the baptism of Titus and Vespasian, that in contemporary minds "must" have happened. Belief and interpretation largely determined what events were acknowledged, and the priority was maintaining a contiguous Christian worldview that used historical events, religious symbolism, and orthodox doctrine to frame the present-day situation.

There is a good example of the key role played by the Jews in Christian mytho-history in Otto of Freising's *Chronica*, a work devoted to describing the entirety of Christian history from the creation to the forthcoming day of judgment. Otto devoted considerable space to the Roman destruction of Jerusalem in 70 C.E., describing it as divine vengeance:

> Therefore when the Jews, forty years after the Passion of the Lord (which they had received as a time for penitence) did not wish to repent the crime they had committed on the Savior ... it was the time for divine vengeance, which had been predicted to them by the Lord, to consume that impious people. However through divine intervention the citizens of Christ were forewarned, so that they could leave the sacrilegious city and the most impious people, just as Lot left Sodom ... This is believed to have been the just judgment of God, so that those who had sinned against God the Father and Son were punished by men who were father and son.[133]

Not only did Otto of Freising deem the Roman destruction of Jerusalem divine vengeance, he described it in a ritualistic manner, allotting the Jews customary time to repent, forewarning the Christians in Jerusalem just as Lot had been warned in the Old Testament, and drawing a symbolic parallel between the crimes committed against two of the three persons of God and the two persons of Vespasian and Titus. In so doing Otto, like many of his contemporaries, transformed a historical fact into a rich, meaning-laden event that played a key role in Christian mytho-history.

---

[132]   The term "mytho-history" is from Jonathan Riley-Smith, "The Military Orders and the Orient, 1150–1291," unpublished (n.d.), p. 18. The definition here is my own.

[133]   Otto of Freising, *Chronica*, pp. 248–50.

But it was not only texts written by high-status bishops that noted the role of the Jews as mytho-historical enemies of Christianity in the mid-twelfth century. The vernacular poem *Chevalier, mult estes guariz* also did so:

> God gave his body to the Jews,
> in order to set us free from prison;
> they wounded him in five places,
> he who underwent death and suffering.
> Now you are ordered against the [Muslims],
> and the rebellious and bloody people
> have done much with their shameful arms:
> now return to them their recompense![134]

The passage suggests that the crusades, and the role the Muslims played as targets of crusading, were incorporated into the Christian mytho-history—and not just by literate members of the Church. Crucially, that incorporation placed the Muslims side by side with the Jews as villains. A chain of cause and effect was forged: the Jews killed Christ, and now vengeance must be taken on the Muslims. The crime of the Jews and the need to take vengeance on the Muslims were linked, both part of the mytho-history that informed medieval Christian actions. It seems likely that this mytho-history continued to aggravate both anti-Jewish and anti-Islamic sentiment and to motivate violence, whether in Europe or on crusade in the East.

Fourth, the texts suggest that Jews and Muslims had committed the same injury. Not only the Muslims in the East actively threatened Christendom. Some writers in the late twelfth century imagined that Christendom was completely encompassed by its enemies:

> not only in the East were the faithful thus oppressed by the impious, but in the West and in all the lands of the earth, especially among those who were called faithful, belief deserted [us] and fear of the Lord was taken away right in the middle [of things], justice concerning things perished.[135]

Most prominently, as is well known, the Jews alongside the Muslims were called *infideles*, "the unfaithful."[136] It is also well-known that Jews were perceived as the enemies of Christianity alongside the Muslims by some crusaders. Orderic

---

[134]   *Les Chansons de Croisade*, p. 9.

[135]   William of Tyre, *Chronicon*, pp. 117–18.

[136]   Rigord, *Gesta Philippi Augusti*, pp. 152 and 154. For comparisons of Jews and Muslims, see also ibid., p. 158.

Vitalis had hinted at an amalgamated target for Christian vengeance during the First Crusade: "these pilgrims held all Jews, heretics, and Saracens equally detestable, whom they all called enemies of God."[137] As Peter the Venerable remarked to Peter of Poitiers, "the three greatest enemies of holy Christianity [are those whom] I name: the Jews and heretics and Saracens."[138]

Of course, the issue here is not whom the Christians deemed enemies of God, but at whom they directed violent acts of vengeance. I have already quoted the *Summa Parisiensis*, which very carefully distinguished between violence against Muslims and Jews.[139] As long as crusaders respected that moral distinction, hatred of the Jews should *not* have led to physical violence against them which would be deemed vengeance. But the historical record shows that not all crusaders did respect the moral difference between violence against Muslims and Jews. The evidence from the mid-twelfth century suggests that the concept of vengeance was invoked for acts of anti-Jewish violence as well as crusading violence against Muslims:

> Look now, we are going a long way to seek out the profane shrine and to avenge ourselves on the Ishmaelites, when here, in our very midst, are the Jews—they whose forefathers murdered and crucified him for no reason. Let us first avenge ourselves on them and exterminate them from among the nations so that the name of Israel will no longer be remembered, or let them adopt our faith and acknowledge the offspring of promiscuity.[140]

Yet, one could easily object that the quotation above also emphasizes the injury the Jews had committed according to Christian mytho-history. That injury was the singular crime of deicide, which surely could not be repeated literally by any other group, no matter how antagonistic toward Christianity. Why therefore (apart from human frailty and incomprehension) was the moral distinction between crusading vengeance on Muslims and on Jews not universally respected?

The first response must be that the Passion was not necessarily a singular, temporally-bound event for twelfth-century contemporaries. As Dominique Iogna-Prat has convincingly demonstrated, for Peter the Venerable and fellow Cluniac Christians, the Passion was truly timeless, a reality in the present as

---

[137]   Orderic Vitalis, *Historia Aecclesiastica*, ed. M. Chibnall (6 vols, Oxford, 1969–80), vol. 5, p. 44.

[138]   Peter the Venerable, "Epistola Petri Pictavensis," in J. Kritzeck (ed.), *Peter the Venerable and Islam* (Princeton, 1964), p. 216.

[139]   See above page 95.

[140]   *Solomon bar Simson Chronicle*, p. 22.

well as in the past.[141] When considering the Eucharist, another timeless event from Peter's perspective, he applied a philosophical principle to demonstrate the way in which the sacrament "condense[d] past, present, and future into one": "*Semel est verum, semper est verum*" (A thing once true is always true).[142] Certainly the sources repeatedly describe the crucifixion as happening in the present—so perhaps our insistence on the crucifixion as a time-bound event is deeply anachronistic.

In addition, although vengeance for the crucifixion and vengeance for the occupation of the Holy Land were strong motivating factors for the persecution of Jews and Muslims respectively in the sources, other "injuries" that the two groups supposedly perpetrated in common may also have encouraged the crusaders to seek vengeance. It has been well documented by Anna Abulafia and others that the Jews' continued refusal to accept the "truth" of Christian doctrine was perceived to be an injury that brought guilt upon their heads.[143] The Jews were not only those who crucified Christ, they were those "who rebel and disbelieve in him," who "disrespect [the Christian god]."[144] As Otto of Freising wrote in his *Chronica*, "the Jews [living at the time of Christ] were not ignorant ... but, to their greater damnation, through prejudice, the circumcised ones did not wish to believe."[145] The conviction that the Jews were guilty, not only for the specific crime of the crucifixion but moreover for their willful rejection of Christ and Christianity, can be traced as far back as the Venerable Bede, although its popularity seems to have noticeably revived in the twelfth century.[146]

In the mid-twelfth century some accused the Muslims of committing the same crime as Jews: willful rejection of the true Christianity.[147] As the Pseudo-Anselm wrote in his *Dialogus inter Gentilem et Christianum*, "because you cannot see the effect of this [the Passion], whether you want to or not, from now on you are to blame."[148] Henry of Huntingdon called the Muslims "*rebellantes*," those

---

141   Dominique Iogna-Prat, *Order and Exclusion*, p. 183.

142   Ibid., pp. 196–7.

143   See in particular Anna Sapir Abulafia, *Christians and Jews in the Twelfth-Century Renaissance* (London, 1995).

144   *Solomon bar Simson Chronicle*, pp. 25 and 26.

145   Otto of Freising, *Chronica*, p. 232.

146   Jeremy Cohen, "The Jews as Killers of Christ in the Latin Tradition, from Augustine to the Friars," *Traditio*, 39 (1983), p. 11.

147   Noted also by Debra H. Strickland, *Saracens, Demons and Jews* (Princeton, 2003), p. 241, though she discusses "destruction" in general rather than the more specific "vengeance."

148   Cited and translated by Abulafia, *Christians and Jews*, p. 86.

who were rebelling.[149] And during the siege of Lisbon, the Muslims supposedly deliberately blasphemed Christian rites: "Christ was actually blasphemed by the unbelievers, saluted with false bows, wet with the spit of the evil, afflicted with chains, crushed with cudgels, affixed to the cross with hate."[150] In this passage the Muslims repeated two "Jewish" crimes: the crucifixion (albeit symbolically) and the derogation of Christianity.

The idea that the Jews willfully rejected Christianity surely drew a parallel in some minds between Jews and heretics. Heretics had also willfully rejected true Christianity, and it had long been acceptable to take vengeance on them. Moreover, as shown above, for some there was a similar parallel between Muslims and heretics.[151] The comparison of Jews and heretics, and Muslims and heretics, suggested both that Jews and Muslims had committed similar injuries and that those injuries might be justifiably punished with vengeance, as heretics were punished.

Furthermore, the crucifixion was specifically connected with the view of the Jews as belligerent non-believers by some twelfth-century thinkers: "the external evil [the Jews] did [when they crucified Christ] was a sign of the greater evil they conceived within, that is, to snuff out their spiritual understanding."[152] After all, if the Passion was seen as timeless and continual, then so too was the role of the Jews as tormentors of Christ.[153] Rupert of Deutz expressed this by claiming that, through circumcision, Jews negated Christ and his suffering.[154] Rigord, as we have seen, stated that Jews did, indeed, reenact the crucifixion in the present time.[155] The Muslims also were accused of recreating the crucifixion. On some occasions, they were accused of killing crusaders by imitating the crucifixion literally, as in the case of Rainald Porcet:

---

[149]   Henry of Huntingdon, *Historia*, p. 229.

[150]   *De Expugnatione Lyxbonensi*, p. 132. For an earlier example of similar desecration, see Albert of Aachen, *Historia Ierosolimitana*, ed. S. Edgington (Oxford, 2007), p. 414. See also Baldric of Bourgueil, *Historia Jerosolimitana*, in RHCOc. 4 (Paris, 1879), p. 101.

[151]   See above pages 94–5.

[152]   Joachim of Fiore, *Expositio Magni Prophete Abbatis Joachim in Apocalympsum* ... (cited by Anna Sapir Abulafia, "The Intellectual and Spiritual Quest for Christ and Central Medieval Persecution of the Jews," in A. S. Abulafia (ed.), *Religious Violence between Christians and Jews: Medieval Moots and Modern Perspectives* (Basingstoke, 2002), p. 78).

[153]   Miri Rubin, "Mary and the Jews," paper given in Cambridge, 30 March 2004.

[154]   Rupert of Deutz, *Anulus sive Dialogus inter Christianum et Iudaeum* (cited by Abulafia, *Christians and Jews in the Twelfth-Century Renaissance*, p. 102). While Rupert was explicitly referring to Jews, and not to Muslims, we cannot help but recognize that circumcision was a ritual performed by both Jews and Muslims.

[155]   Rigord, *Gesta Philippi Augusti*, p. 310. Quote given above at page 98.

they [the Muslims] extended him freely in a cross on the table,
laying out his arms and putting his feet near each other ...[156]

According to the mid-twelfth-century *De Expugnatione Lyxbonensi*, during the siege of Lisbon the citizens of the city taunted the crusaders: "Christ was actually blasphemed by the unbelievers, saluted with false bows, wet with the spit of the evil, afflicted with chains, crushed with cudgels, affixed to the cross with hate."[157]

The belief that both Jews and Muslims were scornfully imitating the crucifixion may well have been connected with the accusations that both Jews and Muslims willfully rejected Christian faith. Iogna-Prat has shown that, for some twelfth-century Christians, the cross "was the sign of signs subsuming all the possible ways in which the mystery of salvation could be signified."[158] I would suggest that, in a parallel manner, the crucifixion may also have served as a "sign of signs"; in this case signifying the ultimate rejection of Christ. Put another way, the crucifixion of Christ may have served as a template, a standard by which to assess the malevolence of non-Christians.[159] If in some sense the crucifixion was the physical embodiment of the crime of disbelief, and thus the crucifixion symbolized the threat the unfaithful posed to Christian society, it is not so surprising that, for some at least, Jews were *infideles* to be attacked alongside the Muslims, and Muslims were guilty of the crucifixion alongside the Jews.

Moreover, the influence of this sense of a crime committed by both Jews and Muslims may well have been bolstered by the trend in canon law to claim papal authority to dispense vengeance on Muslims.[160] When at least some of the canon lawyers had justified crusading as vengeance in terms of direct papal punishment of Muslims, the blurring of distinctions between non-believers, alongside the Christian mytho-history and an emphasis on both Jews and Muslims as the culpable unfaithful, may have encouraged the relationship between anti-Jewish sentiment, vengeance, and the crusading movement in the sources, despite the undisputed fact that, in strict theological terms, violence against the Jews simply because they were Jews remained unjustifiable.

---

[156]   *La Chanson d'Antioche*, p. 196.

[157]   *De Expugnatione Lyxbonensi*, p. 132.

[158]   Dominique Iogna-Prat, *Order and Exclusion*, p. 187.

[159]   One could almost argue that, in the case of the crucifixion, human history itself was seen as ritual, or, more specifically, as the ritualistic re-enactment of the founding myth of blood sacrifice according to the model of religious violence proposed by René Girard.

[160]   Tolan has also noted that, as Jews and Muslims were polemically linked, there was also "an increasing judicial association" (Tolan, *Saracens*, p. 278).

Identity and hierarchy

Vengeance was also tied to crusading in this period, as in the early twelfth century, through the demand for vengeance as *auxilium* and *caritas*, a form of social obligation rooted in the conscious identity of the crusaders. To briefly recapitulate the argument of the previous chapter: in the period from 1095 to 1137 vengeance was perceived as a part of the duty to provide *auxilium* and to express *caritas* to friends. In this case the "friends" were fellow crusaders, fellow Christians, and God, as signaled by the terminology of family and lordship relationships. It was imperative that the crusaders perceived (and remembered) themselves as united, and the language used to convey that social unity carried with it certain expected behavior.[161]

It is still evident that in this period the crusaders saw themselves as part of a group characterized with the language of family and kin, and that membership in that group bound the crusaders to avenge what they perceived as the injuries of those within the group upon those who stood outside it. Much of the imagery in late twelfth-century accounts was identical to that used in the immediate aftermath of the First Crusade, and terms for close family relationships again figured prominently.

Jerusalem was "our mother," Christians were "her sons" and "brothers." As Peter of Blois exclaimed:

> If [Jerusalem] is your mother, where are her sons? Truly, whoever allows their mother to be deceived, despised, and prostituted are not sons, but stepsons, and what is more, they will become known for their shameful treachery, if they do not defend the patrimony of their mother, the inheritance of their Lord ... The blood of Naboth cried out, the blood of Abel cried out from the ground for vengeance, and found vengeance. The blood of Christ clamors for aid, and does not find anyone to help.[162]

In the *De Expugnatione Lyxbonensi*, Peter, Bishop of Oporto, was said to have quoted Ambrose in his stirring sermon:

> The mother church cries to you as though with limbs chopped off and face deformed, she seeks the blood and vengeance of her sons through your hands. She cries out, indeed she cries out! ... *He who does not drive back injury from his*

---

161   Norman Daniel, "Crusade Propaganda," in H. W. Hazard and N. P. Zacour (eds), *A History of the Crusades 6: The Impact of the Crusades on Europe* (Madison WI, 1989), p. 77.
162   Peter of Blois, *Conquestio*, p. 83.

brothers and associates, although he is able to, is as much to blame as the man who
strikes the blow. Therefore you, good sons of the mother church, drive back the
hostile force and [thrust back] the injury.[163]

The Church was represented as a wounded and bereaved mother clamoring
for revenge; any "sons" who resisted her pleas would be as culpable as those
who had injured her in the first place. In this context, to take vengeance would
be a sign of righteous innocence, and to deny vengeance a sign of guilt and
complicity. Inaction would signify collusion: there were only two sides from
which to choose. I speculated that, in the earlier period, to take vengeance was
sometimes interpreted as an act of love. It is clear now that to *not* take vengeance
was sometimes seen as a malicious act of rejection and a repudiation of the all-
important group identity of the crusaders.

God was seen as a father, and in the texts those taking the cross sometimes
remarked upon their duty to "avenge the injury of the highest Father."[164] Henry
of Huntingdon described the First Crusaders as "sons of God" fighting against
"the sons of the devil."[165] The perception of God as a father was complemented
by the idea of the East as God's hereditary estate to be reclaimed. William of
Tyre reported Pope Urban II at Clermont informing the crowd that the holy
land "was worthy to be called [God's] inheritance ... he says through Isaiah *my
inheritance is Israel* and again *the vineyard of the Lord of the Sabbath is the house
of Israel*."[166] Furthermore, as before, the crusaders went to avenge the injuries of
their "brothers" in the East.[167]

Although the language of family relationships and the need to provide
vengeance were stressed in the emotional appeals for crusade in these texts, it
was not always the case in the narrative accounts of the battlefield. In the early
twelfth century, the crusaders were frequently described *en masse* remembering
their group identity and avenging their injuries on the battlefield, but in the later
twelfth century, William of Tyre alone described the crusaders as moved to seek
vengeance as aid to their "brothers" on the battle field, and he did so only twice.[168]
Writers in the late twelfth century did not paint exactly the same pictures of
battlefield emotion and vengeance as *auxilium* in the midst of battle.

Furthermore, the sources hint at the importance of lordship, in addition to
and comparison with family relations. Earlier in the twelfth century, Baldric of

163   *De Expugnatione Lyxbonensi*, p. 78. Reference to Ambrose, *De Officiis* i.36.
164   Gerald of Wales, *Itinerarium Kambriae*, pp. 14–15.
165   Henry of Huntingdon, *Historia*, p. 225.
166   William of Tyre, *Chronicon*, p. 131. References to Isaiah 19:25 and 5:7.
167   Ibid., pp. 739–40.
168   Ibid., pp. 276 and 800.

Bourgueil, Albert of Aachen, and Orderic Vitalis had written that, when First Crusaders were ambushed at Port St. Symeon, others longed to avenge their "brothers."[169] Regarding the same attack, William of Tyre described Godfrey of Bouillon exhorting that "enemies of the name and faith of Christian have triumphed over our lords and brothers ... let us either die with them or avenge the injury done to the Lord Jesus Christ."[170] When compared with the earlier accounts, William had inserted the term "lords" alongside "brothers" to describe those who deserved to be avenged. This is a subtle change, but significant when other episodes are also examined. In another late twelfth-century source, although Eustace of Bouillon did avenge the death of his fellow crusader Rainald of Beauvais on the plains of Ramla, the language of brotherhood was not used to explain his actions. The same went for the crusaders' reaction to the torture and death of Rainald Porcet at the hands of the Muslims, and the death of Eudo of Beauvais avenged by Hugh the Great.[171] Crusaders still sought vengeance on the battlefield, but these quests for vengeance were sometimes described with the language of family, and sometimes with that of lordship or simple "friendship". As the Old French crusading song *Pour lou peuple rescon forteir* stated about the desecration of the Holy Land:

> Do you know why God endures it?
> He wants to prove his friends,
> who have offered their service to him
> to take vengeance on his enemies.[172]

I have discussed how the ability to take vengeance became more and more the responsibility and the privilege of those in power.[173] It is therefore not surprising that in the late twelfth-century sources the individuals who were portrayed seeking vengeance for personal injuries were almost exclusively high-ranking men: Tancred, Baldwin, Conrad, Fulk.[174] These were the kind of men expected and allowed to take personal or familial vengeance as they wished. The one "average" crusader who took vengeance on the battlefield and was singled out for exemplary narrative treatment was a "certain Fulbert of Cannes," who bravely avenged not a family member, but his lord. In the anecdote William of Tyre attributed Fulbert's good deed solely to the political aspect of the relationship:

---

169   See above page 59.
170   William of Tyre, *Chronicon*, p. 276.
171   *La Chanson de Jérusalem*, p. 224. *La Chanson d'Antioche*, pp. 197 and 337.
172   *Les Chansons de Croisade*, p. 79.
173   See above pages 19–31.
174   William of Tyre, *Chronicon*, pp. 228, 461, 463–4, 636, 770 and 825–6.

"learning the injury that his lord had suffered, suffering equally with his whole heart he was concerned in his mind how such an injury could be avenged."[175] In another narrative from the period, when Hugh of St. Pol mourned for the death of his son Engelrand in the First Crusade he was advised by Hugh the Great to simply accept what had happened:

> "Hey, Hugh of St. Pol, I wish to pray to God for you
> that you might set aside your grief: you ought to be well pleased—
> if your son is dead, it was in order to avenge God.
> He is lodged there in the sky with the angels."[176]

The message would seem to be clear: among the Christian crusaders, those in power could and should avenge personal or familial injuries, whilst those in the ranks avenged their lords, and their desire for family vengeance was to be set aside when necessary.

Furthermore, narratives like *Les Chétifs* emphasized that subordinates should seek their superior's permission to pursue familial vengeance, and if they did not, dire consequences would ensue. For example, when Baldwin of Beauvais wished to avenge the death of his brother Ernoul on the dragon Sathanas, he begged his lord for permission to do so:

> "... if [you and] God will allow me I will willingly kill it,
> for my brother whose death has dismayed my heart."[177]

Only after his lord took counsel with his other men and approved the request did Baldwin set off in pursuit of the dragon. Ambroise similarly described the Muslim troops' request to be allowed to take vengeance when they learned that Salah al-Din had made peace with King Richard I of England after the Third Crusade:

> And they called out to him: "Ha! Worthy Saladin
> now it would be well right and timely
> to avenge ourselves for the massacre
> that happened to us before Acre.
> Sire, allow us to avenge our fathers,
> our parents, our sons and our brothers,

---

[175]   Ibid., pp. 351–2.

[176]   *La Chanson de Jérusalem*, p. 253.

[177]   *Les Chétifs*, p. 48.

> for there they are dead and buried;
> now each one can be avenged."[178]

Soudans, a powerful Muslim leader, sought vengeance for the death of his son Brohadas in *Les Chétifs*, albeit through the relatively impersonal form of public judicial combat.[179] But when the families of the two Muslim combatants who died in the judicial combat subsequently sought their own family vengeance contrary to the wishes of their lord, they were markedly unsuccessful, and all were killed.[180] These humble requests to be allowed to pursue vengeance for dead kin, and the striking morality tale of the downfall of those who did not seek approval, contrast somewhat with the earlier sources, in which one who failed to immediately avenge his loved ones and peers was held in contempt even by the writers of the texts themselves.

Of course, there is a risk in reading the sources in this way. Do they reflect "real life" attitudes and behavior, or do they merely represent an idealized society? And, if we conservatively claim that they represent a cultural ideal, then whose cultural ideal is it—that of society at large, or that of the particular author of the particular source? Following on this, do the changes in the sources—the contrast between earlier and later texts—represent a change in society, a change in crusading, and/or a change in genre or authorship?

Ultimately these questions cannot be answered with complete certainty, at least not now. Future research comparing family and lordship relations over time, and the social values associated with those relationships, will support or undermine this portion of my argument. In the meantime, it seems that, although the rhetoric of vengeance for the Christian "family" was still used to promote the crusades, and although the concept of aid was still a crucial link between crusading and vengeance, nevertheless the authority for vengeance resided more clearly with the powerful—*at least within the texts.*

This was surely due in large part to the environment in which the texts were written. The twelfth century was a time of political construction, when both Church and secular governments were forming in response to the "implantation of customary coercive lordships."[181] The idea of crusading as vengeance in the later twelfth century echoes this time of change and its complex ideals. The language

---

[178]   Ambroise, *The History of the Holy War*, vol. 1, p. 193. A similar passage can be found in the later *Itinerarium Peregrinorum et Gesta Regis Ricardi*, ed. W. Stubbs, RS 38:1 (London, 1864), p. 434.

[179]   *Les Chétifs*, pp. 6–9.

[180]   Ibid., pp. 30–31.

[181]   Thomas N. Bisson, *The Crisis of the Twelfth Century: Power, Lordship, and the Origins of European Government* (Princeton, 2009), p. 574.

of family was still used heavily in rhetorical appeals to crusading in this period, and the importance of family history was a key element in chivalric crusading ideals as well. Time and again reference was made to the First Crusaders, the crusaders' predecessors and sometimes also their ancestors, as a link between past and present.[182] Crusaders were exhorted to remember their ancestors and maintain the family honor:

> Remember France, full of such countryside,
> may God make us powerful enough to return healthy and whole,
> and see our lineage, that is our desire.[183]

But, at the same time, crusaders and knights in general were expected to set family relationships and family honor aside for the sake of political relationships, as we have already seen. This complicated set of ideals was epitomized in the argument between Oliver and Roland in the *Chanson de Roland*. Roland refused to blow the horn to summon aid because it would reflect badly on his family's honor; at the same time, he explained that:

> for his lord a man ought to suffer great evils
> and endure great heat and fierce cold,
> for him a man ought to lose his blood and his body.[184]

The texts recognized that men longed, and were expected, to avenge the death of their kin, but they were also supposed to respect and submit to the hierarchy of power around them.

For some modern thinkers, including the philosopher Franz Borkenau, this ideological conflict in the *Chanson de Roland* foreshadowed "an essential characteristic of Western civilization ... the compulsion to choose between mutually exclusive principles of conduct."[185] However, the evidence suggests that the principles of vengeance for family on the one hand, and vengeance in accord with the wishes of the powerful on the other, were not mutually exclusive. An individual need not choose one or the other set of values to determine all future actions, but rather was free to lean one way or the other as circumstance dictated. There was room between the two sets of principles for a man to maneuver, and the texts show individuals doing that by accommodating the desire and

---

[182]   For example, see *La Chanson de Jérusalem*, p. 58.

[183]   *Les Chétifs*, p. 16.

[184]   *La Chanson de Roland*, ed. C. Segre, TLF 968 (Geneva, 2003), p. 144.

[185]   Franz Borkenau, *End and Beginning: On the Generation of Cultures and the Origins of the West* (New York, 1981), p. 430.

expectation of family vengeance to the values of the political power structure that surrounded them.[186]

Another, related explanation for the greater emphasis on the idea that crusading vengeance should conform to the wishes of the powerful is the changing nature of crusading itself. The First Crusade was led by a number of powerful lords, not by kings; none of the First Crusade leaders completely outranked all of the others, and no one individual had the power to say yea or nay. In addition, because of the incredible hardships undergone by the First Crusaders, many of the nobility wound up walking on foot, as desperate for food and drink as those who would have been more clearly subordinate back home. And the First Crusaders were not facing a united, hierarchical Muslim force—they were engaging with a variety of local rulers who were often engaged in local conflicts, as well as a Muslim world divided between the Sunni Seljuks and the Shi'ite Fatimids. The Second and Third Crusades, on the other hand, were led by European monarchs, who were, in turn, fighting against a powerful Islamic army that was clearly united under Zengi, Nur al-Din and Salah al-Din. Therefore the Third Crusade, in particular, may have required participants on both sides to acknowledge vertical hierarchies—lordship relations—more than the First Crusade. This, in turn, may also be partly responsible for the shift we see in the sources.

Given the tendency to suggest that the idea of crusading as vengeance was linked solely to what we might call secular values, it is worth repeating here that the connection between social relationships and crusading as vengeance was not simply a case of socio-political values "outweighing" or "infiltrating" Christianity. The authority quoted by the Bishop of Oporto was Ambrose; the values he was espousing had long been part of the Christian tradition, and were very close if not identical to the passage by Bernard of Clairvaux in which love for God begets hatred for the ungodly.[187] As Suger of St. Denis wrote to King Louis VII of France in 1149, "will I not hate those who hate you, and languish over your enemies?"[188] Even the tendency to use family relationships to characterize the two group identities was not exclusively "secular"; one has only to glance through the Bible to see similar language employed to distinguish between the righteous and the unrepentant.[189]

---

[186]   Dominique Barthélemy, "Knightly Feud in Tenth-Century France," in S. Throop and P. Hyams (eds), *Vengeance in the Middle Ages: Emotion, Religion and Feud* (Ashgate, 2010), pp. 110 and 113.

[187]   See above page 100.

[188]   Suger of St. Denis, *Epistolae*, in RHGF 15 (Paris, 1878), p. 509.

[189]   A few examples from the New Testament are Matthew 12:50 (*quicumque enim fecerit voluntatem patris mei qui in caelis est ipse meus et frater et soror et mater est*); Romans

*   *   *

The idea of crusading as vengeance manifested in most, but not all, of the crusading texts from the later twelfth century. Despite the fact that some texts referred to vengeance while others did not, the vast majority of the sources emphasized similar themes and reasons for crusading. Because of the thematic similarities, I have continued to investigate the three patterns of thought identified in the previous chapter as contributing to the idea of crusading as vengeance. This has led me to three general conclusions.

The concept of an independent material power aimed at injuries done to the communal good and authorized by the pope strongly influenced the continually evolving ideology of crusading, just as the crusading movement itself championed the power of the papacy.[190] Some applied this legal theory to actions against the "criminal" Muslims, or, by classifying the Muslims as heretics, incorporated anti-Islamic violence into the already established tradition of violence against heretics. This violence was described with the terminology of vengeance, thanks to both the application of Biblical terminology and also contemporary secular understandings of justice, vengeance, and punishment. Although surely the secular aspects of culture impacted on and promoted the ideology of crusading as vengeance, so too did canon law and Biblical tradition.

The sources demonstrated a continued textual link between anti-Jewish sentiment and the idea of crusading as vengeance. A number of factors in the texts contributed to the blurring of distinctions between Jews and Muslims, and thus suggested vengeance was owed on both groups. A basic belief that the world was divided into those who loved God and those who did not encouraged blurred distinctions. A strong triangular relationship between Jews, Muslims, and the crucifixion further encouraged this trend. Muslims wrongly threatened Jerusalem, the city in which the Jews had purportedly killed Christ. A rhetorical emphasis on injuries to Christ and devotional trends of the twelfth century further promoted attention to the crucifixion, an event that linked the Jews and Muslims through the nexus of Jerusalem. In the sources, Muslims were incorporated into the Christian mytho-history alongside the Jews, thus tied also to the crime of the crucifixion. Both groups were accused of denigrating

---

8:14 (*quicumque enim spiritu Dei aguntur hii filii sunt Dei*), Hebrews 12:8 (*quod si extra disciplinam estis cuius participes facti sunt omnes ergo adulteri et non filii estis*); and 1 John 3:10 (*in hoc manifesti sunt filii Dei et filii diaboli omnis qui non est iustus non est de Deo et qui non diligit fratrem suum*). There are many more such passages.

[190]   Yael Katzir, "The Second Crusade and the Redefinition of *Ecclesia, Christianitas* and Papal Coercive Power," in M. Gervers (ed.), *The Second Crusade and the Cistercians* (New York, 1992), pp. 6 and 8.

and desecrating the crucifixion, at the same time as both groups were accused (by some at least) of the common injury of rebellious disbelief, suggesting that the crucifixion represented, or served as a template for, the crime of willful infidelity.

Terms for family members continued to be used to characterize the relationships between crusaders, and between crusaders and God. Alongside the terms of family, however, there was also a noticeable emphasis on language associated with lordship and simple friendship, and the texts went to some length to show the importance of respecting the wishes of the powerful when desiring vengeance for kith and kin. This evidence illustrates changing twelfth-century society, its different, but not necessarily mutually exclusive, principles of conduct, and the way in which those principles affected the pursuit of vengeance. It also points towards the changing nature of crusading itself.

Chapter Four

Popular—or Papal? Crusading as Vengeance, 1198–1216

In 1198, an ambitious young man named Lothario dei Conti di Segni became Pope Innocent III at the remarkable age of 37. Innocent's enthusiasm for crusading is well-known, and during his tenure, crusading expanded and changed significantly—sometimes due to papal direction, sometimes despite strenuous objections from Rome. He wasted no time, launching his first crusade appeal, *Post miserabile*, in August 1198. He planned for a large and impressive expedition, and outlined the clerical taxation and employment of mercenaries that would, in his mind, facilitate such an army. Because there was a truce until 1203 between the Kingdom of Jerusalem and al-'Adil, Salah al-Din's surviving heir, Innocent's initial target was to be the Egyptian city of Alexandria, a wealthy port with a large Christian population that could potentially serve as a staging ground for a reconquest of Jerusalem.

Things did not go as Innocent had planned. Unable to pay the Venetians all they owed for ships and sea transport, the crusaders assisted the Venetians to sack the Christian city of Zadar, a city under the lordship of King Emeric of Hungary, who had himself taken the cross. The crusaders and Venetians then restored the Byzantine prince in exile, Alexius IV Angelus, to the throne in Constantinople. Alexius not only failed to fulfill his promises to the crusaders and the Venetians, but also to solidify support in Constantinople, and in January 1204 his rule was overthrown by Alexius V Dukas Mourtzouphlos, a man distinctly hostile to the Western forces, who still expected payment. In April 1204, the frustrated crusaders and Venetians sacked the city of Constantinople, establishing a short-lived Latin Empire. The pope had expressed his disapproval most forcefully at virtually every stage of these proceedings, from the initial attack on Zadar to the final assault on Constantinople, but with little result.

Remarkably, this series of events did not persuade Innocent III to pursue crusading any less enthusiastically. Among other expeditions, he authorized crusades in the Baltics and crusades against his political opponent, Markward of Antweiler, as well as crusades in southern France against the Cathar heretics (commonly known as the Albigensian Crusades). And by 1208 he was already thinking about launching another crusade to the East—this would, in time, become the disastrous Fifth Crusade (1218–21).

Largely thanks to Innocent's endeavors, the early thirteenth century is rich in crusading sources. And, even while new crusades occurred in the late twelfth and early thirteenth centuries and were documented, writers continued to look at the First Crusade anew, retelling its story in the context of the century that followed it. As a result, crusading texts from the short period from 1198–1216 describe and document quite a variety of crusades, from the First Crusade up through the Fourth, expeditions against the Cathars in southern France, and the first calls for what would become the Fifth Crusade. A correspondingly varied group of sources has been examined for the period: letters to and from Pope Innocent III and the eminent crusade preacher James of Vitry, general chronicles, crusading narratives in Latin and the vernaculars, sermons, *exempla* and crusading songs.

In the previous chapter, I concluded that the idea of crusading as vengeance was more prevalent in the later twelfth century than it had been in the aftermath of the First Crusade. This suggested momentum, and it is tempting to assume an upward swing that continued through the early thirteenth century—but only the evidence can tell if the trend continued, and if the same supporting themes promoted the idea of crusading as vengeance.

What, then, does the evidence say? The idea of crusading as an act of vengeance certainly did appear in many of the early thirteenth-century sources: two letters to and almost all letters from the pope, four chronicles, six narrative crusading accounts, two related epic poems and the poetry of Conon of Béthune. However, at the same time, it was absent from other sources: three narrative accounts of the Fourth Crusade, a Provençal narrative of the events in Languedoc, the poems of Raimbaut of Vaqueiras, and the writings of James of Vitry in the period (with the exception of one brief passage from a sermon). Faced with this suggestive, yet equivocal, body of evidence, it is clear that we can make no assumptions. Instead, we must ask whether the apparent popularity of the idea of crusading as vengeance (such as it was) was the result of the appeal of the idea itself, or merely the effect of pervasive use of the idea in papal correspondence.

Vengeance—or not

There was only one passage referring to the First Crusade as vengeance from the early thirteenth century. The Provençal *Canso d'Antioca* briefly proclaimed the intention to wreak vengeance upon non-Christians during the First Crusade:

To the end of the world loss and suffering will be great,
and the Saracens and pagan peoples should know
that still vengeance will be taken![1]

Regrettably, the *Canso d'Antioca* did not make it clear why vengeance was sought. The one example of crusading as vengeance from the writings of James of Vitry in the period was similarly vague as to why vengeance was needed and simply made it clear that those who sought vengeance for God through crusading were worthy Christians: "those who are not signed [with the cross] come from the devil and are against those who, worthy of their Lord, wish to take vengeance."[2]

On the other hand, early thirteenth-century texts dealing with the Third, Fourth and Albigensian Crusades continued to call upon the reasons for crusading as vengeance earlier identified (loss of land, Christian deaths, and injuries to the cross and Christ). Sometimes the Christian loss of Jerusalem in 1187 was attributed through hindsight to a reluctance to take vengeance: "*therefore their sons became orphans, and their wives became widows in a foreign land*, they who did not wish to avenge the heredity of the Crucified One and their own [land]."[3] Certainly Salah al-Din's success drove many to call for vengeance to retrieve the lost territory. According to Arnold of Lübeck:

[Pope Clement II] mourning the destruction of the church in Jerusalem sent letters to the whole Roman world, writing to all churches about the impious surrender and slaughter of the servants of God and about certain abominations perpetrated by the Saracens in the Holy Land, inciting all to zeal against the impious and to vengeance for the holy blood."[4]

A participant in several crusades, Conon of Béthune wrote similarly in the poem *Ahi! Amors, con dure departie*:

Now it appears that those who would be known as honorable
will go to avenge the grievous shame
for which each man ought to be angry and ashamed;

---

[1]   *Canso d'Antioca*, ed. C. Sweetenham and L. M. Paterson, in *The Canso d'Antioca: An Occitan Epic Chronicle of the First Crusade* (Aldershot, 2003), p. 228.

[2]   James of Vitry, *Sermones*, ed. C. T. Maier, in *Crusade Propaganda and Ideology* (Cambridge, 2000), p. 92 (Sermo 1).

[3]   *De Expugnatione Terrae Sanctae per Saladinum*, ed. J. Stevenson, RS 66 (London, 1875), p. 248. Reference to Lamentations 5:3.

[4]   Arnold of Lübeck, *Chronica*, in MGHSS 21 (Hanover, 1869), p. 169.

for lost to us is the holy place
where God suffered for us a painful death.[5]

The death of Christians also deserved vengeance alongside the seizure of land in the East. Arnold of Lübeck thus described the response to papal appeals: "therefore the husband went forth from his bed to take vengeance for the house of a zealous God and to avenge the just blood."[6] Emperor Frederick I had promised "to take vengeance for a zealous God and to avenge the holy land and the effusion of blood of the servants of God."[7]

Writers sometimes chose to focus on the need to avenge injuries to the cross, though these too were linked with the 1187 loss of the Holy Land. The *Itinerarium Peregrinorum* remarked that Joscius, Archbishop of Tyre was partly responsible for getting news from the Latin East to the West: "announcing to all the faithful that Christ's inheritance was occupied by the gentiles, he reduced some to tears and fired others to vengeance."[8] The *Itinerarium Peregrinorum* also described the crusaders as "avengers of the injury of the cross" and noted that Richard, Count of Poitou, took the cross "on account of the injuries of the cross."[9] The *De Expugnatione Terrae Sanctae per Saladinum* noted that the Archbishop of Tyre "bore forth the news ... to the Christian world, bringing innumerable numbers to tears, and inciting many to vengeance. First among all the magnanimous Count Richard of Poitou was signed with a cross to avenge the injury of the Cross."[10] According to another account, Pope Clement III had sent messengers to Christians throughout western Europe, seeking that:

> they would aid the strength of their suffering mother, remembering her breasts, with whose milk the primitive church of Jerusalem was nourished ... and that with the cross put on in remission of sins, proud of themselves as servants of the cross, they would avenge the shame of the cross, which was held by pagans, for the praise and glory of the Crucified One.[11]

---

[5] Conon of Béthune, *Les Chansons de Conon de Béthune*, ed. A Wallensköld, CFM 24 (Paris, 1921), p. 7.

[6] Arnold of Lübeck, *Chronica*, p. 170.

[7] Ibid., pp. 172–3.

[8] *Itinerarium Peregrinorum et Gesta Regis Ricardi*, ed. W. Stubbs, RS 38:1 (London, 1864), p. 32.

[9] Ibid., pp. 32 and 59.

[10] *De Expugnatione Terrae Sanctae per Saladinum*, p. 251.

[11] Otto of St. Blasien, *Chronici ab Ottone Frisingensi episcopo conscripti continuatio auctore ... Ottone Sancti Blasii monacho*, in MGHSS 20 (Hanover, 1868), p. 319.

Otto of St. Blasien confirmed Emperor Frederick I's commitment to vengeance, but suggested that it was vengeance for "the shame of the cross" rather than specifically the loss of Jerusalem and Christian deaths: "he announced in public that he would avenge the shame of the cross."[12] Conon of Béthune suggested that continued failure to take vengeance for the cross would result in God's retribution in turn upon the Christians:

> and when the cross cannot be protected,
> with his crusaders God will be much aggrieved
> if he is not avenged a little in the end.[13]

Arnold of Lübeck noted about the Third Crusaders in the year 1197: "now, however, the heirs of Christ and sons of God in hymns and confessions praised the Lord, speaking and praying that their devotion would be accepted and that worthy vengeance would fall upon the enemies of the cross."[14] Injury to Christ himself deserved vengeance as well. According to Robert of Auxerre, Kings Philip II of France and Richard I of England went on the Third Crusade "to avenge the abuse of Christ."[15] Ralph of Coggeshall described Richard I at Jaffa encouraging his men:

> he set forth to them that death should not at all be feared, [death] which was inflicted by the pagans for defending Christianity and avenging the injury of Christ; for it would be more magnificent to fall in honor for the laws of Christ, and to be prostrate before the enemies of Christ in death, than to give oneself like a coward to the enemies.[16]

The Fourth Crusade was also described in the early thirteenth century as an act of vengeance for the loss of the Holy Land and injuries done to the cross and Christ. Geoffrey of Villehardouin noted that, from the beginning, the aim of the Fourth Crusade was to exact vengeance and retake Jerusalem. According to Geoffrey of Villehardouin, the Frankish crusaders in 1201 took the sign of the cross in order "to avenge the shame of Jesus Christ and conquer Jerusalem."[17]

---

[12]   Ibid., p. 319.

[13]   Conon of Béthune, *Les Chansons*, p. 9.

[14]   Arnold of Lübeck, *Chronica*, p. 205.

[15]   Robert of Auxerre, *Chronicon*, in MGHSS 26 (Hanover, 1882), p. 253.

[16]   Ralph of Coggeshall, *Chronicon Anglicanum*, ed. J. Stevenson, RS 66 (London, 1875), pp. 44–5.

[17]   Geoffrey of Villehardouin, *La Conquête de Constantinople*, ed. E. Faral (2 vols, Paris, 1938), vol. 1, p. 20.

In the same year, according to the same text, Geoffrey of Joinville spoke thus to the Venetians:

> "Lords, the highest and most powerful lords of France have sent us to you, and they ask you mercy, that they might pray you to take pity on Jerusalem which is in service of the Turks, in order that for God you would wish ... to avenge the shame of Jesus Christ."[18]

In 1205, Innocent urged the Venetians to be faithful to their crusading vows. Since they had taken vengeance on Zadar with God's help, Christ should be helped to take vengeance in turn: "[something derogatory could be said about you] if now that you have avenged your injury, you did not avenge the insult [done to] Jesus Christ"[19]

Even once the Fourth Crusade had diverted to Constantinople, some still perceived the Western objective in Byzantium as vengeance on a large scale. Once the crusaders were considering an assault on Constantinople, according to Robert of Clari, Doge Henry Dandolo asked the bishops if it would be a sin to fight eastern Christians; "the bishops responded and said that it would not be at all a sin, moreover it would be a great mercy, for they ... could aid [the true ruler] to conquer his right and take vengeance on his enemies."[20] Some suggested that to take Constantinople was vengeance for Christ. According to Arnold of Lübeck, Baldwin IV of Flanders (then emperor of Constantinople) wrote to Pope Innocent III from Constantinople, reporting the sins of the eastern Christians and concluding that when "these and similar monstrosities, which a small letter cannot lay forth ... provoked Lord Christ to disgust, divine justice through our ministration struck with worthy vengeance and, when the people who hated God were expelled, he gave to us, those who love him, the land and all good things."[21] Gunther of Pairis viewed the taking of Constantinople as just vengeance:

---

[18]   Ibid., vol. 1, p. 28.

[19]   Innocent III, *Die Register Innocenz' III*, ed. O. Hageneder and A. Haidacher (Vols 1–8, Graz, 1964–2001), vol. 7, p. 365 (*Venientes ad apostolicam sedem*).

[20]   Robert of Clari, *La Conquête de Constantinople*, ed. P. Lauer, CFM 40 (Paris, 1924), p. 40.

[21]   Arnold of Lübeck, *Chronica*, p. 230.

Now run forth, run forward, revered knight of Christ,

run forward, to the city which Christ has given to the victor!

... you have fought the wars of Christ, vengeance for the just Christ

you have sought ...[22]

Otto of St. Blasien concluded:

and thus God, the severe omnipotent judge, avenged the injuries of his pilgrims

... God the lord of vengeance, returning retribution to the proud, nevertheless did

not forget mercy in his anger, for he inflicted this lash on the sons of pestilence

through the Christians, not through the pagans ...[23]

Some in the early thirteenth century depicted the crusades against the Cathars in Languedoc as vengeance for injuries done to God. One of the most articulate of these writers was Peter of Les Vaux-de-Cernay. According to Peter, the region of Toulouse was where "from fathers to sons the successive and superstitious venom of unfaithfulness is diffused ... for which reason the avenging hand is said to have justly sustained such a killing of the population in vengeance for such a crime."[24] When the Franks marched against the Cathars in 1209, they were "all of the faithful marked to avenge the injury of our God."[25] When Béziers was destroyed, he considered that the city had "received worthy vengeance for its crime."[26] At Carcassonne, a cleric attempted to reason with the inhabitants and warned them of God's vengeance:

You do not want to listen to me? Believe me ... even you should know most

certainly that, even if the walls of this city were of iron and were most high, you

could not defend yourselves, because for your disbelief and malice you will receive

worthy vengeance from the Most Just Judge![27]

Arnold Amaury, a papal legate, wrote to Rome to announce the victories at Béziers and Carcassonne as divine vengeance:

---

[22]   Gunther of Pairis, *Hystoria Constantinopolitana*, ed. P. Orth, Spolia Berolinensia: Berliner Beiträge zur Mediävistik 5 (Zurich, 1994), p. 155.

[23]   Otto of St. Blasien, *Chronici*, p. 332.

[24]   Peter of Les Vaux-de-Cernay, *Hystoria Albigensis*, ed. P Guébin and E. Lyon (3 vols, Paris, 1926–39), vol. 1, p. 7.

[25]   Ibid., vol. 1, p. 80.

[26]   Ibid., vol. 1, p. 93.

[27]   Ibid., vol. 1, p. 100.

the city of Béziers is captured, and our men not sparing any order, sex, or age, killed nearly twenty thousand people in the jaws of the sword; and when the greatest slaughter of the enemies was finished, the city was completely looted and burned, with divine vengeance raging miraculously throughout.[28]

Peter reported the Pope expressing the same idea:

the highest Pope had sent general letters to all his prelates, counts, barons, and all people living in the kingdom of Francia, in order that he might move the faithful people to most promptly extirpate the pest of heresy, warning and exhorting them that they should hasten to avenge the injury of the Crucified One in the province of Narbonne.[29]

Pope Innocent III's surviving letters support Peter's vision of a papal appeal for vengeance for an injury done to Christ, not only on the Cathars but also in the period preceding the Fourth Crusade. Innocent made a connection between vengeance and traditional themes of pilgrimage when he expanded on Matthew 16:24 in his letter *Quanta sit circa*: "*he who wishes to come after me, must deny himself, and take up his cross, and follow me*, putting on the sign of the cross you ought to seek to avenge the injury of Jesus Christ."[30] In his 1198 letter *Si ad actus*, Innocent III promised the Count of Forcalcquier indulgence for his sins "if he would personally take up the journey to avenge the injury of the Crucified One, as is proper for such a prince, [if] he would be honorably persistent in the defense of the eastern land."[31] Innocent III's 1198 letter *Post miserabile* stated:

But ... may our tongue adhere in our mouths if we do not remember [Jerusalem], for this reason the apostolic seat clamors and raises its voice as though it were a trumpet, desiring to excite the Christian people to the battle of Christ and to avenge the injury of the Crucified one ... but now our princes ... are absent in adulterous embraces, consumed with pleasures and crimes; and while they pursue each other with inexorable hatred, while one strives to avenge his injuries on another, there is not one who is so moved [to take vengeance] by the injuries of Christ.[32]

---

[28]   Innocent III, *Epistolae*, ed. J.-P. Migne, PL 214–16 (Paris, 1890–91), vol. 216, col. 139 (*Sanctissimo patri et*).

[29]   Peter of Les Vaux-de-Cernay, *Hystoria Albigensis*, vol. 1, p. 74.

[30]   Innocent III, *Die Register*, vol. 1, p. 22 (*Quanta sit circa*).

[31]   Ibid., vol. 1, p. 611 (*Si ad actus*).

[32]   Ibid., vol. 1, pp. 499–500 (*Post miserabile*).

In *Plorans ploravit Ecclesia*, also written in 1198, Innocent III remarked: "we have sent letters ... so that sons may avenge the injuries of the Father, and brothers may arm to avenge their slain brothers."[33]

Again and again Innocent III called for vengeance for injuries done to Christ and the Church. *Justus et misericors*, written in 1201, noted that "we, however, rejoice in the Lord, because he, who gave cause for penitence, has bestowed the state of penitence within many, and mercifully has inspired them, that, taking up the sign of the cross, they wish to avenge the injury of Jesus Christ."[34] This example strikingly described vengeance for Christ as an act of penance, usually a component of the ideology of crusading as pilgrimage and penitential war. In 1203, Innocent further wrote, "we beget these [letters] with tears ... advocating the word of the Lord, and exhorting friends of the Christian name to avenge the injury of Jesus Christ."[35]

In 1204, Innocent wrote about the Cathars to King Philip II of France: "may ... the secular sword of power, which is carried by the king and princes to avenge the evildoers ... be unsheathed to avenge the injury of the Savior."[36] In 1207, he told Raymond VI of Toulouse that he should stop "persecuting the Church of God": "listen, wretch, and tremble because for the double offense of two-faced prevarication vengeance will be taken on you, even while you treacherously prepare warlike destruction and the pest of heresy injures the flocks of God."[37] Writing again to Philip II in 1207, Innocent asked his "most loved son ... to avenge the injury of Jesus Christ and capture the little foxes which will not stop destroying the vineyard of the Lord of the Sabbath."[38] In 1208 he wrote to archbishops throughout France and Languedoc:

> to those however who are inflamed with zeal for the orthodox faith to avenge just blood, which does not stop crying out from earth to the heavens, until the Lord of vengeance may descend to earth from heaven to confound the subverters and those subverted, [to those who] manfully join together against this pestilence, against those who fight against unity, peace, and truth, we promise the remission of their sins by God.[39]

The Pope then exhorted Philip II specifically:

---

[33]   Ibid., vol. 1, p. 431 (*Plorans ploravit Ecclesia*).

[34]   Ibid., vol. 4, p. 304 (*Justus ad misericors*).

[35]   Ibid., vol. 6, pp. 163–4 (*Cum in manu*).

[36]   Ibid., vol. 7. p. 373–4 (*Ne populus Israel*).

[37]   Innocent III, *Epistolae*, vol. 215 col. 1166 (*Si parietem cordis*).

[38]   Ibid., vol. 215 col. 1247 (*Inveterata pravitatis haereticae*).

[39]   Ibid., vol. 215 col. 1356 (*Ne nos ejus*).

> Go forth therefore, knight of Christ, go forth most Christian prince, may the
> moans of the universal holy Church move your most religious heart, may pious
> zeal inflame you to avenge such an injury done to your God ... The time has come
> for doing justice, and do not turn your ears from the cries of the Church saying to
> you: *go forth, and judge my cause* ... most beloved son, take up the sword which is
> for vengeance on the evildoers, but for the praise of the good; gird on our sword,
> so that we may both be avenged on these criminal and inhuman evildoers.[40]

In the same year, 1208, Innocent directed the same rhetoric at the French
nobility, with almost word-for-word repetition, suggesting that the papal curia
was not averse to reusing particularly good material.[41] And when the pope turned
his attention back to the East, he wrote members of the Church: "we seek and
pray the Lord ... that you, fired with zeal for the Christian faith, will lead ... the
faithful to take vengeance for the injury of the Crucified One."[42]

Turning from papal correspondence to vernacular literature, the late twelfth-
century *chanson de geste* known as *La Venjance de Nostre Seigneur* also contained
some elements of the ideology of vengeance for the crucifixion, although the
historical expedition that formed the basis for the narrative had occurred almost
a thousand years before the First Crusade, the avengers were not Christian until
baptized at the end of the poem, and the targets were Jews, not Muslims. In the
text, the Romans were surprisingly depicted as virtuous (and eventually baptized)
Muslims, prone to exclaiming in conversation "by Mohammed!" in a manner
familiar to readers of the *chansons de geste*.[43] But imprecations to Mohammed
did not cure Vespasian of leprosy, and eventually he was healed by Veronica and
consequently heard of the death of Jesus. Outraged by the story of the Passion,
he and his son Titus embarked on a military expedition to take "vengeance for
the royal Father whom the Jews tortured, those lying gluttons."[44] They destroyed
Jerusalem, and took vengeance for the betrayal of Jesus by selling thirty Jews for
one denarius. Almost all of the Jews were killed, once the Romans realized they
had swallowed their gold and silver and subsequently disemboweled them to
get at the loot. The few Jews left alive were sold into slavery, Pontius Pilate was
punished, and the Romans were baptized.

La Venjance de Nostre Seigneur emphasized the need for vengeance for the
crucifixion of Christ. So too did one version of the exploits of Charlemagne

---

[40]   Ibid., vol. 215 col. 1358 (*Si tua regalis*). Reference to Psalms 73.
[41]   Ibid., vol. 215 col. 1359–60 (*Rem crudelem audivimus*).
[42]   Ibid., vol. 216 col. 822 (*Pium et sanctum*).
[43]   *La Venjance de Nostre Seigneur*, ed. L. A. T. Gryting, in *The Oldest Version of the Twelfth-Century Poem La Venjance Nostre Seigneur* (Ann Arbor, 1952), p. 34.
[44]   Ibid., p. 33.

and Roland in Spain, the *Historia Karoli Magni et Rotholandi*, which asserted that the entire expedition against the Muslims had been driven by the desire to take vengeance and convert Muslims. The best evidence for this overall theme comes from the speeches attributed to Roland and Charlemagne. The *Historia Karoli Magni et Rotholandi* devoted considerable narrative time to the "passion of Roland," describing Roland soliloquizing to his sword:

> O how greatly have I avenged the blood of our Lord Jesus Christ, how many enemies of Christ have I killed, how many Saracens have I killed through you [the sword], how many Jews and traitors have I destroyed for the exaltation of the Christian faith, through you the justice of God is increased ... As many treacherous Jews and Muslims as I have killed, to such a degree, I think, I have avenged the blood of Christ.[45]

When Roland finally died many pages later, his prayers to God assumed a similar tone: "Lord, may the bowels of your mercy be moved for your faithful who have died today in war; from far away regions into these barbarous times they came to fight the treacherous people, exalt your holy name, avenge your precious blood, and declare your faith."[46] Like so many other sources from the period, the *Historia Karoli Magni et Rotholandi* emphasized the need to take vengeance for Christ's blood, and notably did not greatly differentiate between killing Muslims and Jews.

So quite a few early thirteenth-century texts portrayed crusading (or wars that resembled crusading) as an act of vengeance. That said, three accounts of the Fourth Crusade did not characterize the sacking of Constantinople, or indeed the Fourth Crusaders' original intentions in the East, as vengeance: the *De Terra Iherosolimitana* by the Anonymous of Soissons, the *Devastatio Constantinopolitana*, and the *Gesta* by the Anonymous of Halberstadt. In addition, Robert of Auxerre, who did not hesitate to describe the Third Crusade as vengeance, did not use the vocabulary of vengeance in reference to the Fourth Crusade. The writer of the early portion of *La Chanson de la Croisade Albigeoise* did not refer to the crusades against the Cathars as vengeance, even though he clearly supported the expeditions. In addition, James of Vitry, who played a key role in preaching the crusades against the Cathars and the Fifth Crusade, did not refer directly to the idea of crusading as vengeance in either his letters of the period or his *exempla*, and only mentioned it once in one of his sermons.

---

[45]   *Historia Karoli Magni et Rotholandi*, ed. P. G. Schmidt, in *Karollelus atque Pseudo-Turpini Historia Karoli Magni et Rotholandi* (Stuttgart, 1996), p. 136.

[46]   Ibid., p. 148.

The divide in the evidence does not correspond to membership in the ecclesiastical hierarchy, nor does it correspond to participation in the events described or language of composition. So what does account for it? First, it is possible that there was uncertainty about the application of vengeful rhetoric to Christian adversaries, particularly in the case of the Fourth Crusade. Perhaps some western Christians were uncomfortable characterizing the Byzantines alongside Muslims, Jews, and heretics. Certainly, early thirteenth-century western Christians had differing views about the ethics of fighting a crusade against eastern Christians, and the Fourth Crusade put these views to the test.

The crusading texts reflect the fact that there was no unanimous sentiment towards the Greeks. Some Fourth Crusaders spoke against attacking Constantinople in favor of moving on to Jerusalem, saying "Ba! What would we do in Constantinople? We have our pilgrimage to make."[47] In response to these arguments, Conon of Béthune reportedly replied that "[the Greeks] have held [Constantinople] wrongly and have sinned against God and against reason."[48] Similarly, in the same text, when Alexius IV was displayed to the Greeks before restoration to the imperial throne, the Franks announced "see your natural lord … for the one whom you have obeyed as lord you held wrongly, and as a sin against God and against reason; and you well know how he disloyally acted against his lord and his brother."[49] The lack of vocabulary of vengeance in some accounts of the Fourth Crusade may correspond to the fact that not all writers at the time were entirely confident that they knew who was a proper target of crusading violence and who was not, what was just vengeance and what was a wrongful war of self-interest.

However, the evidence for the crusades against the Cathars weakens the argument that the silence of the sources stems from uncertainty about the justice of the crusades in question. The Cathars were most definitely perceived as heretics by the Church. Their violent persecution was compatible with canon law and the Christian tradition of just vengeance, but yet, not all who discussed the crusades against the Cathars in the early thirteenth century used the terminology of vengeance. One possible explanation for this discrepancy is that perhaps the claims of heresy were not believed by all to be the real cause of the crusade. Yet, the writers I examined definitely supported the crusade against the Cathars, and did not hesitate to refer to them as heretics—they just did not link their persecution with the idea of vengeance.

---

47 Robert of Clari, *La Conquête*, p. 32.
48 Geoffrey of Villehardouin, *La Conquête*, vol. 1, p. 144.
49 Ibid., vol. 1, pp. 146 and 148.

In searching for explanations for the divided nature of evidence from the early thirteenth century, we cannot overlook the potential impact of Pope Innocent III on crusading ideology, and on our perceptions of crusading ideology. Colin Morris has summarized Innocent's papacy as one devoted to "crusade, reform, and the correction of heresy," and Innocent's pursuit of political power for the Church is well known.[50] It is striking that Innocent's letters were one of the richest sources of the idea of crusading as vengeance around 1200. Perhaps the emphasis on the ideology within the period in general is due in large part to papal enthusiasm. It is conceivable that recipients of papal correspondence, or those who aligned themselves with papal discourse, may have reused the idea of vengeance precisely because it was so vigorously employed by the pope. On the other hand, those who received such correspondence infrequently or indirectly, or who were not consciously concerned with mimicking papal language, may not have had the same impetus to talk about vengeance.

It also must be acknowledged that the nature of the historical record suggests a distortion of evidence. Innocent III clearly rather liked the idea of crusading as vengeance, and used it unceasingly. Because he was a pope, rather than an anonymous monk, his views and words were transmitted widely and show up in many other sources, like the writing Peter of Les Vaux-de-Cernay. Moreover, his views and words (at least, the official ones) have survived the centuries largely intact, providing evidence for historians investigating the idea of crusading as vengeance. It is easy to accord Innocent's words with great weight, and he was powerful, articulate, and ambitious for crusading success. Yet, how far can we take the words of one man, even if he was a pope? Did Innocent's fondness for the vocabulary of vengeance accurately reflect his times, or merely his personality? And what would have happened to the idea of crusading as vengeance in this period, if it had not been championed by such a dominant figure?

These are important questions, and expose the inherently problematic nature of the sources—a familiar experience for any medievalist. Ultimately, only continued work on the idea of crusading as vengeance throughout the thirteenth century and beyond will clarify affairs during Innocent's papacy. However, it is nevertheless possible, and necessary, to continue to investigate the underlying patterns of thought contributing to the concept of crusading as vengeance. What links were drawn between crusading and vengeance in this period, did they mirror those of earlier crusading texts, or was the idea of crusading as vengeance moving in a different direction?

---

[50]   Colin Morris, *The Papal Monarchy* (Oxford, 1989), p. 450. See also Christopher Tyerman, *God's War: A New History of the Crusades* (Cambridge MA, 2006), pp. 479–88.

Christian unity

As in the twelfth century, vengeful crusading was associated with divine justice in early thirteenth-century texts, and this justice was to be enacted through human agents. Geoffrey of Villehardouin noted that King Philip II of France told the Venetians "you go for the sake of God and for right and for justice."[51] The taking of Constantinople by the Fourth Crusaders was described as when "divine justice through our ministration struck with worthy vengeance."[52] Pope Innocent III urged Philip II concerning the Cathars to "take this opportunity to do justice, and do not turn your ears from the cries of the Church saying to you: *go forth, and judge my cause.*"[53]

Other passages suggested that just vengeance proceeded from God directly. The battle of Hattin called for the "judgment of God, which certainly no one can evade, which He like a father of mercies exercises more through defense than through hostility. Nevertheless ... certainly he exercises just vengeance."[54] The expeditions against the Cathars were attributed to God's own need "to avenge just blood," and at Carcassonne a cleric supposedly told the citizens: "you will receive for your disbelief and malice worthy vengeance from the Most Just Judge."[55] Otto of St. Blasien concluded about the Fourth Crusade that "thus the stern judge, omnipotent God, avenged the injuries of his pilgrims."[56]

Clearly, early thirteenth-century crusading texts upheld the idea of crusading as God's vengeance, God's justice. This was so even when God's vengeance was directed at Christians. Arnold of Lübeck not only called for Christians to take vengeance on Salah al-Din, but described Salah al-Din's conquest of Jerusalem itself as divine vengeance upon the Christians: "because of these [sins] the justice of God was imposed, which truly no one can evade, which [God], although like a father of mercies, exercises now more as a warning than a punishment ... certainly he exercises just vengeance."[57] Moreover, those who would not take vengeance for God risked receiving divine vengeance themselves.[58] That, after all,

---

51   Geoffrey of Villehardouin, *La Conquête de Constantinople*, vol. 1, p. 92.

52   Arnold of Lübeck, *Chronica*, p. 230.

53   Innocent III, *Epistolae*, vol. 215, col. 1358 (*Si tua regalis*). Reference to Psalms 73.

54   Arnold of Lübeck, *Chronica*, p. 163.

55   Peter of Les Vaux-de-Cernay, *Hystoria Albigensis*, vol.1, pp. 60 and 100.

56   Otto of St. Blasien, *Chronici*, p. 332.

57   Arnold of Lübeck, *Chronica*, p. 163.

58   *De Expugnatione Terrae Sanctae per Saladinum*, p. 248. Conon of Béthune, *Les Chansons*, p. 9.

was seen by some as the reason God allowed the Fourth Crusaders to conquer Constantinople.[59]

To a certain degree, early thirteenth-century texts emphasized the more down-to-earth reasons why the Muslims deserved retribution. The Muslims had taken back large areas of land in the East. Jerusalem itself had fallen to Salah al-Din in 1187, and many Christians in the Latin East had died trying to keep the Muslims at bay. These were very concrete injuries that justly deserved vengeance in contemporary minds, and many writers at the time of the Third and Fourth Crusades dwelt upon them. For some (and not only the laity), the conquests of Zadar and Constantinople by the Fourth Crusade armies were also just endeavors precisely because they were acts of vengeance for those who had been wrongly injured; as acts of vengeance, they corresponded with the medieval concept of just war.[60] Following the Augustinian tradition, the canonist and Fourth Crusade participant Sicard, Bishop of Cremona, wrote that a just war was determined by two factors, one of which was cause: "just wars [are] for vengeance, for defense of the body, and [for defense] of the fatherland, the faith, and peace."[61]

Another more tangible injury that required vengeance was the death of the papal legate, Abbot Peter of Castelnau, in southern France. Peter of Les Vaux-de-Cernay wrote about the matter to the Pope in 1208: "he [the abbot] who, a pious man of Christ having a care for his impious attacker, following the example of his master and Saint Stephen, said to [the attacker]: God forgive you, since I forgive you ... [yet] he does not stop crying out from the earth to heaven for vengeance for his just blood."[62] Peter of Les Vaux-de-Cernay heavily played upon the need to avenge injuries to Christ and the Church, but alongside these claims lay the reality of one man's death. For the Third, Fourth, and Albigensian Crusades, the reality of human death, injured honor, and lost territory were also used to mobilize people to a vengeful crusade, and were acceptable within a Christian framework due to Gratian's judgment, again following Augustine, that it was a duty to avenge the wrongful injuries of others and that a war of vengeance was one type of just war.[63]

---

59   Otto of St. Blasien, *Chronici*, p. 332.

60   Raymond H. Schmandt, "The Fourth Crusade and the Just-War Theory," *Catholic Historical Review*, 61 (1975), pp. 207 and 210; for example, Robert of Clari, *La Conquête*, p. 40.

61   Sicard of Cremona, *Summa decretorum*, Causa 23 Quaestio 2 (cited by Schmandt, "The Fourth Crusade," p. 200n).

62   Peter of Les Vaux-de-Cernay, *Hystoria Albigensis*, vol. 1, pp. 56 and 60.

63   Stanley Chodorow, *Christian Political Theory and Church Politics in the Mid-Twelfth Century: The Ecclesiology of Gratian's Decretum* (Los Angeles, 1972), p. 233.

This is not to say that the usual epithets applied to Muslims were missing from these texts. Muslims were "that nefarious people," "the enemies of Christ."[64] They were "misbelieving traitors" or, more simply, "the unfaithful."[65] The Cathar heretics were even more thoroughly painted with the rhetoric of vengeance for unfaithfulness. In early thirteenth-century texts they were those who particularly deserved vengeance because their "disbelief and malice" had injured Christ and Christendom.[66] Pope Innocent III called for the French nobility to "take vengeance for the injury to your God," "avenge just blood ... manfully join together against these pestilent [people], against those who fight against unity, peace, and truth."[67]

What is clearest from the early thirteenth-century evidence, taken together, is that Christian unity was of the utmost importance and was threatened not only by Muslims (and Jews), but also by some who claimed to possess Christian truth—that is, heretics. James of Vitry for one was concerned about "impious Christians ... men of Belial..profane Christians."[68] He noted that in the Holy Land there were as many "heretics" to be "converted" as there were Muslims.[69] James explained in one of his *exempla* that "Christians who blaspheme are worse than gentiles and Jews."[70] As Innocent III described the situation, "[the world] is overflowing with heretics, schismatics, traitors, tyrants, simoniacs, hypocrites, the ambitious, the greedy, thieves, robbers, the violent, blackmailers, usurers, liars, the impious, the sacrilegious ..."[71] St. Francis of Assisi, also, linked preaching to Christians and preaching to Muslims, illustrating the importance of building

---

[64]   Ralph of Coggeshall, Chronicon, pp. 37 and 48–9.

[65]   *Canso d'Antioca*, p. 218; and James of Vitry, *Lettres de Jacques de Vitry*, ed. R. B. C. Huygens (Leiden, 1960), p. 130.

[66]   Peter of Les Vaux-de-Cernay, *Hystoria Albigensis*, vol. 1, p. 100. Full quote above at page 130.

[67]   Innocent III, *Epistolae*, vol. 215, col. 1358 (*Si tua regalis*); Innocent III, *Epistolae*, vol. 215, col. 1354 (*Ne nos ejus*).

[68]   James of Vitry, *Lettres*, p. 136. Reference to Deuteronomy 13:13 and Judges 19:22.

[69]   James of Vitry, *Lettres*, pp. 96–7. The leaders of the First Crusade expressed similar concerns to Urban II in a letter written 11 September 1098: "for we have fought Turks and pagans, but heretics, Greeks and Armenians, Syrians and Jacobites we have not fought, therefore we ask and demand that you, our dearest father, as our father and head should come to the place of your fatherhood ... and that you may eradicate and destroy with your authority and our strength all heresies" (*Epistulae et Chartae ad Historiam Primi Belli Sacri Spectantes*, ed. H. Hagenmeyer (New York, 1973), p. 164).

[70]   James of Vitry, *The Exempla*, ed. T. F. Crane (London, 1890), p. 124.

[71]   Innocent III, *De Miseria Condicionis Humane*, ed. R. E. Lewis (London, 1980), p. 203.

a united Christendom through both internal reform and external expansion.[72] And both reform and expansion through crusading involved exercising just vengeance on those who erred.

In effect, as seen in sources dating from the twelfth century, for some the world was divided into black and white, the faithful and the unfaithful. As James of Vitry noted, "nevertheless the Lord says: *he who is not with me, is against me*."[73] This translated easily to the crusading context and amounted to a condemnation not only of those who deserved vengeance, but also those who did not want to seek vengeance for God, who were deemed to come "from the devil."[74]

The sources emphasized the need for preaching and conversion alongside vengeance for Muslims and heretics alike. James of Vitry preached both crusade and conversion; crusading, the Christian conquest of land, was seen as the means for furthering conversion.[75] As James of Vitry wrote, there was "one group who defend the faith with words, like *doctores* against heretics, and another who defend the faith with the sword, like knights of Christ, and a third group who [use] neither word nor sword, and these are of the devil."[76] In this sort of rhetoric a Christian had only the choice of which type of defensive weapon to use, words or the sword, not the choice to abstain altogether.

Crusade and conversion both aimed to redress the balance in favor of Christianity, and for some they were not antithetical but rather different tools for largely the same end. James of Vitry wrote to Pope Honorius III from the Holy Land in early 1220:

> there appears to us a great host for the subjugation of the unfaithful and to
> increase the power (*imperium*) of Christ, so that..where the cursed name of the
> treacherous Mohammed is invoked by all ... now the blessed name of Jesus Christ
> is invoked ... so that the lords of Egypt understand and convert to him [Christ]
> and from the West to the East the light of truth returns."[77]

Although "the abominable law of the impious people would be exterminated with many cut down by the sword, others would convert to the faith of Christ."[78] Ralph of Coggeshall, writing about the early Fifth Crusade, warned that

---

[72]   Benjamin Z. Kedar, *Crusade and Mission: European Approaches toward the Muslims* (Princeton, 1984), p. 134.

[73]   James of Vitry, *Lettres*, p. 96. Reference to Matthew 12:30.

[74]   James of Vitry, *Sermones*, p. 92 (Sermo 1). Full quote in next paragraph.

[75]   Kedar, *Crusade and Mission*, pp. 117–18 and 128.

[76]   James of Vitry, *Sermones*, p. 90.

[77]   James of Vitry, *Lettres*, p. 123–24.

[78]   Ibid., p. 152.

Prester John (a legendary Christian king in the Far East) was rumored to be coming with a large army to convert the Muslims: "and all paganism would be destroyed, unless they converted themselves to the faith of Christ."[79] For some, the Christian desire to convert the Muslims—that is, to eliminate their religious identity through baptism—was mirrored by their perception of the Muslim desire to do the same to Christianity: "[Salah al-Din] ... hopes to seize a great opportunity for his error, if the name of the Crucified One can be eliminated with the inhabitants of the land."[80]

The Cathars were also apparently given the choice to die or recant. In 1210 at one city:

> the abbot therefore ordered that the lord of the castle and all who were in the castle, even those believing in heresy, if they wished to be reconciled and to stand by the mandate of the Church, would escape to live, with the castle remaining to the count; and even the Perfects among the heretics would escape ... if they wished to convert to the Catholic faith.[81]

Those who refused were burned. At Cassés in 1211 a similar event occurred: "the bishops who were in the army entered the castle and seized the heretics, willing them to turn back from error; but, since they could not convert even one, they left the castle; the pilgrims however, seizing the heretics ... burned them with great joy."[82] In *La Chanson de la Croisade Albigeoise*, the armed attacks against the Cathars had in fact been preceded by attempts to persuade them to "convert": Arnold Amaury, "that most holy man ... preached to the heretics that he wished [them] to convert."[83]

The verb used by the medieval writers for heretical recantation was the same as that used for Muslims and Jews, *convertere*. Writers did not make a semantic distinction between the recantation of heresy and religious conversion. The means allowed to convert the groups were different (force could not be used to convert *infideles*, in theory at least), but the outcome was the same and the vocabulary indicates this.

Indeed, it seems that underneath the need to avenge lost land and Christian deaths, another purpose of the vengeance to be unleashed on the unfaithful through the crusading movement was to further promote conversion, baptism, and the general elimination of religious identities other than orthodox

---

79   Ralph of Coggeshall, *Chronicon*, p. 190.
80   *De Expugnatione Terrae Sanctae per Saladinum*, pp. 235–6.
81   Peter of Les Vaux-de-Cernay, *Hystoria Albigensis*, vol. 1, p. 159.
82   Ibid., vol. 1, pp. 232–3.
83   *La Chanson de la Croisade Albigeoise*, ed. M. Zink (Paris, 1989), p. 42.

Catholicism. This desire caused, among other things, some confusion about how the Byzantine Church should be treated. Despite attempts by Innocent III to emphasize that the Christians stood united in opposition to the Muslims and Jews, one of the justifications for the conquest of Constantinople in medieval minds was that the Christian Church, divided by schism, would truly be united again through Rome.[84] The monk Gunther of Pairis condemned the Byzantines as "an impious people ... a people untaught to rule, subdued by no law ... sacrilegious citizens, impious people."[85] It would be tempting to ascribe this confusion about the Byzantines to the laity, but Gunther of Pairis obviously was not a layman.

It does not seem that the goal of creating a uniform Catholic identity through vengeance was a conscious ideology, but, rather, that the common theme of creating a world united by "true" Christian faith through the means of just war and subsequent conversion lay behind one strand of the ideology of crusading as vengeance, and was particularly evident in the early thirteenth-century sources.[86] At the same time, the concept of just vengeance for specific, concrete injuries—the events of 1187, the later failure of the Third Crusade, and the death of Peter, Abbot of Castelnau—also contributed to the ideology of crusading as vengeance.

Jews, Muslims, heretics—and the crucifixion

Heretics, Jews, and Muslims were supposed to be treated in fundamentally different ways by Christians. Heretics, rebels who had rejected Christ and injured the Church, were legitimate targets of Christian vengeance, and it is not surprising therefore that early thirteenth-century crusading texts used extreme language to describe the Cathars in Languedoc. Heretics were "members of Antichrist, firstborn of Satan, wicked seed, criminal sons," "criminal and inhuman wrongdoers," "depraved in every way with heretical impiety," "deserters of the faith," "enemies of Christ."[87]

---

[84]   Innocent III, *Die Register*, vol. 7, p. 356 (*Evangelica docente scriptura*). Geoffrey of Villehardouin, *La Conquête*, vol. 2, p. 24.

[85]   Gunther of Pairis, *Hystoria*, p. 136.

[86]   Tolan has suggested a similar argument, linking European "denigration of the other" with Christian universalism (John V. Tolan, *Saracens: Islam in the Medieval European Imagination* (New York, 2002), p. 283).

[87]   Peter of Les Vaux-de-Cernay, *Hystoria Albigensis*, vol. 1, p. 12 ; Innocent III, *Epistolae*, vol. 215, col. 1358 (*Si tua regalis*); Robert of Auxerre, *Chronicon*, pp. 276 and 272; Peter of Les Vaux-de-Cernay, *Hystoria Albigensis*, vol. 1, pp. 158.

However, the early thirteenth-century sources continued to reveal connections between vengeance against heretics and the need to seek vengeance on Jews and Muslims as well. The heretics of Béziers were not only heretics, but also "plunderers, the unjust, adulterers and the worst criminals, full of all kinds of sins," just as the Muslims in the sermon of the bishop of Oporto in the *De Expugnatione Lyxbonensi* had been described as adulterers and parricides.[88] The conceptual overlap between Jews, Muslims, and heresy was conveniently demonstrated by Ralph of Coggeshall, who called both Jews and Muslims "that nefarious people" and "enemies of Christ," and referred to the Muslims as "all those infected by the most impious sect of the heretic Mohammed."[89] According to Ralph of Coggeshall, the Jews "blasphemed our Lord Jesus Christ with their sacrilegious mouths not only in their secret meetings, but even with an impious public voice, and offended by railing openly [against] our faith and the sacraments of the Church."[90] They did not simply lack Christian faith, they willfully refused to believe and expressed animosity towards God. In 1205, Pope Innocent III noted in a letter to the bishop of Paris that the Jews were treacherous, using the crucifixion as ultimate proof of their infidelity: "although the Jews, whose crime submitted them to perpetual servitude, crucified the Lord ... Christian piety receives and sustains their cohabitation, whom even the Saracens, who persecute the Catholic faith, do not tolerate, on account of their treachery."[91]

Furthermore, Jews, Muslims, and heretics were all portrayed as enemies seeking to injure Christianity through active animosity. This animosity for all three groups was illustrated through acts of aggression against the crucifixion, a highly useful focal point due to the reasons already discussed above: namely, current devotional trends and the crusading target of Jerusalem, and the role of the city as the place of Christ's life and death. The dualist denial of the Eucharist also surely concentrated attention on the crucifixion of Christ in the crusading context.

For some, the Jews were literally reenacting the crucifixion in their times. Arnold of Lübeck reported that a "certain Jew" miraculously converted to Christianity after he watched some fellow Jews crucifying a "waxen image [of Christ]," which Arnold made clear the Jew understood as Christ himself, lest anyone lessen the crime by suggesting ignorance.[92] (Furthermore, Arnold's insistence that the Jew understood his actions reinforced the belief that the Jews

---

88   Peter of Les Vaux-de-Cernay, *Hystoria Albigensis*, vol. 1, pp. 86–7. For the passage from the *De Expugnatione Lyxbonensi*, see above page 93.

89   Ralph of Coggeshall, *Chronicon*, pp. 27, 28, 37, 48, 49 and 69.

90   Ibid., pp. 27 and 28.

91   Innocent III, *Die Register*, vol. 8, p. 221 (*Etsi Judeos quos*).

92   Arnold of Lübeck, *Chronica*, p. 190.

knew what they had done when they had killed Christ.) Arnold commented that "those [Jews] were satisfying the standards of their fathers, calling down [condemnation] on themselves and their own as they said: *his blood be on us and on our sons.* Crucifying the image struck with wounds, truly they did crucify [Christ] ... through hatred, through curses, touching [Christ] with hands of malice."[93] For Arnold, the Jews were maliciously recrucifying Christ in the present as they had done in the past.

Peter of Les Vaux-de-Cernay attributed to Cathars the kinds of host desecration and crucifix defamation usually blamed on the Jews, and on Muslims in the East. This related to the understanding that the Cathars denied the real presence of Christ in the Eucharist. According to Peter, the citizens at Béziers attacked a priest and "urinated in [the chalice] in contempt for the body and blood of Jesus Christ."[94] Roger of Foix was accused of "striking with arms and legs the image of the Crucified One ... in contempt for the Lord's Passion."[95] At Lavaur in 1211, when the crusaders set up a cross outside the city, the people of the city attacked the cross fiercely, "but the Dedicator of the cross avenged that destruction miraculously and manifestly ... the enemies of the cross, who exulted in the destruction of the cross ... were captured on the feast of the Cross."[96] These injuries centered on the crucifixion, all rooted in supposed contempt for "the body and blood of Jesus Christ," "the Lord's Passion," and "the cross." These injuries deserved vengeance, as the crucifixion had done in the legendary past.

Like the late twelfth-century sources, some early thirteenth-century crusading texts connected the Jews, the crucifixion of Christ, and crusading against the Muslims through the narrative structure of Christian mytho-history. For example, Raimbaut of Vaqueiras wrote:

> God allowed himself to be sold to save us,
> and he suffered death and accepted the passion,
> and for us the criminal Jews outraged him,
> and he was beaten and bound to a pillar,
> and was lifted onto the beam which stood in the mire
> and was scourged with scourges of knots
> and crowned with thorns on the cross:
> for which a man is hard of heart who does not grieve
> that the Turks who wish to retain

---

[93] Ibid., p. 190. Reference to Matthew 27:25.
[94] Peter of Les Vaux-de-Cernay, *Hystoria Albigensis*, vol. 1, p. 87.
[95] Ibid., vol. 1, p. 205.
[96] Ibid., vol. 1, p. 223.

the land where God wished to exist, alive and dead,
so a great war and a great combat falls to us.[97]

In this passage, the crucifixion, blamed on the Jews, was tied to contemporary crusading against the Muslims: one necessitated the other, both bound by the role of Jerusalem as the site of Christ's death. The *Canso d'Antioca* implied a similar association between the crucifixion and the crusades:

> Lords, Frankish knights, citizens and sergeants!
> We have the belief and know it true
> that God was born on earth for our salvation;
> and the Jews then killed him through treachery;
> and he rose on the third day from the true holy sepulchre;
> and he arose into the sky ...
> And he will return to hold his judgment ...
> these proud Turks, misbelieving traitors,
> think to contradict us ...
> you must prove the truth to them through a judicial process
> so that they are defeated and vanquished in battle.[98]

The Jews killed Christ willfully "through treachery," and then the Muslims, also "misbelieving traitors," obstinately did not believe the truth of the matter, making it necessary for the Christians to defeat them in battle in order to prove the Christians right, almost as though the Christians faced the Jews and Muslims in a judicial duel. The Roman destruction of Jerusalem was interpreted as vengeance on the Jews for the crucifixion; directly linking the Roman destruction with the crusades against the Muslims may well have encouraged the perception of the crusades as vengeance for the crucifixion.[99]

But influence no doubt was circular: the crusading movement in turn promoted attention to the legends and traditions associated with Jerusalem. Brian Stock has pointed out that social change viewed as unprecedented often provoked "a series of imaginative attempts to fit contemporary experience into models from the distant past."[100] It seems likely that *La Venjance de Nostre*

---

[97]   Raimbaut of Vaqueiras, *The Poems of the Troubadour Raimbaut de Vaqueiras*, ed. J. Linskill (The Hague, 1964), p. 218.

[98]   *Canso d'Antioca*, pp. 216–18.

[99]   For example, as in *La Chanson d'Antioche*, ed. J. Nelson, OFCC 4 (Tuscaloosa 2003).

[100]   Brian Stock, *The Implications of Literacy: Written Language and Models of Interpretation in the Eleventh and Twelfth Centuries* (Princeton, 1983), p. 527.

Seigneur, a narrative of almost unparalleled popularity in the Middle Ages, served just such a function, providing a historical parallel to the crusades that placed the Jews side by side with the Muslims. Moreover, as Miri Rubin has noted, commonly held beliefs about the present generate in turn commonly held beliefs about the past.[101] This connection between past and present may well also have fed into the formulation of a united Christendom, since emotional attachment to a communal memory often leads to belief in a communal identity (and vice-versa).[102]

Once again, the crucifixion served as a focal point, a litmus test of willful infidelity and deliberate injustice. Desecration of the cross and Christian ritual by Muslims, Jews, and heretics symbolized the threat all three groups posed to Christian society. The desecrations reminded Christians of the crucifixion, an event long associated with the concept of religious vengeance on non-Christians in the tradition of the Roman destruction of Jerusalem, and also emphasized the difference between a united Christendom and those who threatened that unity. Moreover, the desecrations called for vengeance: on Muslims, on Jews, and on heretics.

Friendship, aid, and vengeance

The need to avenge family members was still used alongside the language of lordship in crusading appeals in the early thirteenth century. Christians were brothers, sons of the Mother Church and Jerusalem, and sons of God. When the Christians in the East were attacked by Muslims in May 1187, the Master of the Templars reportedly addressed his men: "most beloved brothers and my comrades in arms ... you require vengeance on those whom you have always defeated. Therefore get ready, stand fast in the battle of the Lord, and be mindful of your fathers the Maccabees."[103] Otto of St. Blasien described Pope Clement III's response to 1187 with the vocabulary of family:

> [Clement sent messengers] to the sons of the mother Church, conquering confusion with paternal affection, [seeking] that they would aid the strength of their suffering mother, remembering her breasts, with whose milk the primitive church of Jerusalem was nourished ... and that with the cross put on in remission

---

[101]   Miri Rubin, *Gentile Tales: The Narrative Assault on Late Medieval Jews* (New Haven, 1999), p. 2.

[102]   Bruce Lincoln, *Discourse and the Construction of Society: Comparative Studies of Myth, Ritual, and Classification* (Oxford, 1989), p. 23.

[103]   *De Expugnatione Terrae Sanctae per Saladinum*, pp. 211–12.

of sins, proud of themselves as servants of the cross, they would avenge the shame of the cross.[104]

As the *Itinerarium Peregrinorum* succinctly stated, "here equally and completely a common cause of the Christians and the common vengeance for fraternal injuries moved [the crusaders]."[105] In *Plorans ploravit Ecclesia*, Pope Innocent III remarked: "we have sent letters..so that sons may avenge the injuries of the father, and brothers may arm to avenge their murdered brothers."[106] Following the same metaphor, Innocent wrote in 1204 that heretics were "sons against their mother."[107] Even when crusade efforts failed, the failure itself was described in terms of injuries to family; when Jerusalem finally surrendered to Salah al-Din in 1187, one text stated about the Christians that *"their sons became orphans, and their wives are widows in an alien land*, they who did not want ... to avenge the inheritance of the Crucified One"[108] Clearly, family relationships still demanded vengeance; crusading was still described with the language of family, and thereby writers contributed to the ideology of crusading as vengeance.

The political relationships of lordship also required vengeance, and thus the language of lordship continued to be applied to the crusades and to the ideology of crusading as vengeance. The crusaders were "those who took the cross and did service for God," who "did service for God and Christianity."[109] Conon of Béthune noted that "[my] body goes to serve Our Lord."[110] This "service" was specifically related to the political relationships between men and their lords in contemporary society, a relationship applied to crusading. As James of Vitry explained on one occasion (and then subsequently downplayed), "the Lord through the cross ... invested his vassals in the heavenly kingdom."[111] Lordship required, specifically, service as vengeance, and this too was incorporated into the need to take vengeance for God. In one *exemplum*, a Parisian knight assaulted a burgher for swearing and was brought before the king for punishment. The knight spoke in his own defense:

> Lord, you are my earthly king and liege lord, if I were to hear anyone saying anything to slander you or to say wrongly about you, I could not endure it but

---

104   Otto of St. Blasien, *Chronici*, p. 319.
105   *Itinerarium Peregrinorum*, p. 60.
106   Innocent III, *Die Register*, vol. 1, p. 431 (*Plorans ploravit Ecclesia*).
107   Innocent III, *Epistolae*, vol. 215, col. 527 (*Ne populus Israel*).
108   *De Expugnatione Terrae Sanctae per Saladinum*, p. 248.
109   Geoffrey of Villehardouin, *La Conquête*, vol. 1, pp. 4 and 24.
110   Conon of Béthune, *Les Chansons*, p. 6.
111   James of Vitry, *The Exempla*, p. 57.

I would rightly wish to avenge your wrong. This man said such things about my heavenly king before I struck him, and he injured him by blaspheming so much, that just as I could not endure it said of you, I could not tolerate [it] about the highest Lord.[112]

Moreover, the crusaders were avenging not only their Lord, but also the other servants of their Lord. Arnold of Lübeck stated that Pope Clement III hastened to spread the news of "the impious betrayal and slaughter of the servants of God."[113] In the same text, Emperor Frederick I was moved to take vengeance for "the effusion of blood of the just servants of God."[114]

It is tempting to view vengeance for family relations, and vengeance for lordship relations, as markedly separate lines of thought. Yet, the distinction between the two was not as defined as one might think. Both ideas shared in common a clear sense of hierarchy and obligation. The classical "family" was defined by authority and hierarchy just as was the "state," and some of this seems to have survived into the Middle Ages. Knowledge of where one fit into the socio-political hierarchy, both within the family and in relation to one's lord and peers, informed one of where lay the obligation to defend (and to take vengeance if defense proved futile).[115]

Furthermore, as we have already seen, alongside authority and hierarchy a tool used to reinforce social bonds in medieval thought was *caritas*. This concept has been already demonstrably linked to the need to take vengeance for injuries done to those within one's group.[116] Whereas authority and hierarchy stipulated vengeance for vertical relationships, lords and vassals, fathers and sons, *caritas* may well have emphasized the need to avenge those horizontally related to oneself through Christian love. This is not to say that *caritas* did not motivate vengeance for father and lords—rather, in situations where a hierarchical relationship was not clearly evident (for example, the relations between crusaders from disparate parts of western Europe), that the obligation to love may have bolstered the sense that these people, too, deserved help and vengeance.

As before, crusading was linked with the concept of aid. Early thirteenth-century sources confirmed that crusading continued to be described by writers as an act of aid; *auxilium* in Latin, *secorre* or *aie* in Old French. Otto of St. Blasien

---

[112] Ibid., p. 91.

[113] Arnold of Lübeck, *Chronica*, p. 169.

[114] Arnold of Lübeck, *Chronica*, p. 173.

[115] See, for example, Thomas of Chobham: "*ita meritorium est socio socium defendere, et servo dominum, et patrifamilias hospitem et familiam ...*" (*Summa Confessorum*, ed. F. Broomfield (Paris, 1968), p. 444).

[116] David Herlihy, "Family," *American Historical Review*, 96 (1991), pp. 5–9.

referred to the expedition of 1197 as a Christian attempt to help in the East: "they journeyed to aid the Church overseas."[117] Geoffrey of Villehardouin stated that the purpose of the Fourth Crusade was to "aid the land overseas."[118] Robert of Clari likewise noted that Boniface I of Montferrat "took the cross, for love of God and to aid the land overseas."[119] Conon of Béthune stated that God "had need of aid" and that the crusaders "now prepared how they could aid him."[120] This aid, or military obligation, was tied to vengeance: Pope Innocent III, asking King Philip II of France to rout the heretics in southern France in 1207, wrote "we invoke your aid, dearest son, to avenge the injury of Jesus Christ."[121] Aid, again, was a concept related to political relationships between lords and vassals, but also to family relationships and networks of social obligation in general.

Who most deserved vengeance on his or her behalf? Father, mother, lord, vassal, brother or friend? James of Vitry argued persuasively that the relationship with God trumped all others.[122] In one of his *exempla*, he described the actions of a man condemned to death who visits three friends. The first offers him a shroud, the second offers to attend his execution, but the third, an old friend recently neglected, offers to die in his place: "the third and old friend is Christ."[123] In one of his sermons, James argued that true friends help each other in difficult circumstances: the Lord had lost his patrimony, so his faithful vassals should offer him aid.[124] Family hierarchy, political authority, and Christian love all dictated that vengeance for God was paramount.

*   *   *

The early thirteenth-century crusading texts present clear evidence for a Christian desire to create a uniform Catholic society through both internal reform and external expansion. This was demonstrated by blurred distinctions between the treatment of Christian heretics and those of other religions altogether, with both being urged to either convert or suffer the just vengeance of God. Furthermore, heretics, Jews, and Muslims were all accused of crimes of malicious desecration

---

[117]   Otto of St. Blasien, *Chronici*, p. 327.

[118]   Geoffrey of Villehardouin, *La Conquête*, vol. 1, p. 74.

[119]   Robert of Clari, *La Conquête*, p. 6.

[120]   Conon of Béthune, *Les Chansons*, p. 6.

[121]   Innocent III, *Epistolae*, vol. 215, col. 1247 (*Inveterata pravitatis haereticae*).

[122]   In doing so he followed a tradition dating back to Origen, who depicted an *ordo caritatis* that placed, in order of importance, God, parents, children, domestics, and neighbors (Herlihy, "Family," p. 7).

[123]   James of Vitry, *The Exempla*, p. 55.

[124]   James of Vitry, *Sermones*, p. 98 (Sermo 1).

centered on the crucifixion of Christ. The crucifixion, seen in the Christian mytho-history as a timeless event repeated by the unfaithful, continued to demand vengeance.

Crusading continued to be described with terms for family relationships, lordship relationships, and *caritas*. By using these terms, writers informed individuals of the obligation to pursue crusading as an act of vengeance. Whether as servants of their Lord, sons of their Father God and Mother Church, or friends of their best and truest friend Christ, Christians were duty bound to aid and avenge injuries committed against their God. Furthermore, early thirteenth-century texts revealed even more references to figures from history and contemporary literature. These examples and characters from other texts often echoed the ideology of crusading as vengeance, confirming interplay between crusading ideology and contemporary literature.

Finally, the assortment of evidence from the early thirteenth century suggests that the idea of crusading as vengeance continued to be popular—to a degree, and in large part due to the enthusiastic promotion of the idea by Pope Innocent III. It is striking that between 1137 and 1197 no popes used the idea of crusading as vengeance in their correspondence, while, at the same time, the idea was used more frequently in other sources—chronicles, epic narratives, poetry, and so on. Then, between 1198 and 1216, the idea of crusading as vengeance was milked dry by Innocent III, and used in some other sources, but, in general, appeared with less frequency than in the late twelfth-century texts. Future research on later thirteenth-century sources is needed to clarify two points: First, did the idea of crusading as vengeance wax, wane, or remain the same in terms of cultural presence in the later Middle Ages? And second, what relationship, if any, existed between papal patronage of the idea and its expression in overall culture?

Chapter Five

Zelus: An Emotional Component of Crusading as Vengeance[1]

Thus far we have examined the intellectual and social components of the idea of crusading as an act of vengeance. Inherent in this examination has been the premise that, on some level, the idea of crusading as vengeance was appealing because it was emotionally attractive to medieval minds. Indeed, it was traditionally assumed that the notion of crusading as vengeance was entirely due to overemotional reactions, and the concept of "vengeance" in our own times is steeped with emotional overtones, resonant with the "irrational" passions that we assume drive people to seek vengeance. In essence, then, we face two assumptions about crusading as vengeance: first, and morally neutral, that there was an emotional element to the ideology; second, and morally judgmental, that to some degree, that emotional element was opposed to rational thought and conscious control.

The second of these assumptions, about the irrationality of vengeful emotion, is, I would argue, a reflection of our own cultural context and does not necessarily tell us anything about the medieval emotion/s associated with crusading as vengeance. Extensive research in the social and natural sciences has led to the theory that emotional change within any given culture is the product of humanity's emotional capacities and a specific historical context.[2] No scholar who accepts in this way that emotion is subject to the influence of culture could simply assume that the emotional component of crusading as vengeance is self-explanatory and universal. Just as *vindicta* and *ultio*, the two primary medieval Latin terms I have investigated, did not signify precisely the same concept in the twelfth century as the modern English term *vengeance* does today, so the emotions associated with *vindicta* and *ultio* must have been in some way understood differently than the emotions the modern individual ascribes to

---

[1]   This material has also appeared in "Zeal, Anger and Vengeance: The Emotional Rhetoric of Crusading," in S. Throop and P. R. Hyams (eds), *Vengeance in the Middle Ages: Emotion, Religion and Feud* (Ashgate, 2010), pp. 177–202. I am grateful to Ashgate for allowing me to include it again here.

[2]   William Reddy, *The Navigation of Feeling: A Framework for the History of Emotions* (Cambridge, 2001), p. 45.

vengeance. The question that needs to be asked is: what emotions did twelfth-century contemporaries relate to crusading as vengeance, and how did those emotions further connect to the ideology as a whole?

The evidence for the importance of *zelus*

When reading the primary source evidence for crusading in twelfth- and early thirteenth-century Latin texts, it quickly becomes apparent that one word was time and again used to describe, expand, or otherwise modify the idea of crusading as vengeance: *zelus*. Not merely the proximity of the different words in the texts is suggestive—the frequency with which the terms appear is related. As the twelfth century progressed, the idea of crusading as vengeance appeared more frequently in the texts and, at the same time, the term *zelus* appeared more frequently alongside those references to vengeance.

I believe it is well worth outlining the evidence in detail, so that the reader can gain a sense of scope of the passages in question, and so that other scholars can build from this work.[3] For convenience I have translated *zelus* and its derivatives as "zeal," but the deeper, more exact meaning of *zelus* will be discussed at much greater length later in the chapter.

Early twelfth-century sources

In crusading texts from the early twelfth century, *zelus* was associated with crusading by only two writers. Orderic Vitalis wrote of Raymond of St. Gilles that on the way to Jerusalem from Antioch, "in no way giving way to laziness or indolence, rather he was continuously hostile to the gentiles owing to zeal."[4] Describing the violent persecution of the Jews by First Crusaders on their way to the East, Ekkehard of Aura wrote that "they had enough to do, either to eliminate the execrable Jewish people they discovered, or even to compel them into the lap of the church, serving with the zeal of Christianity even in this thing."[5] Later in the same work he noted that those who persecuted the Jews "[had] the zeal of God, but not according to the knowledge of God." In other words, the crusaders were motivated by the right sentiment, but nevertheless acted against God's

---

[3]   That said, because some of the following material has already been introduced to support other elements of my argument, some readers may wish to advance to the next major section, "Christian love and righteous anger," which begins on page 152 below.

[4]   Orderic Vitalis, *Historia Aecclesiastica*, ed. M. Chibnall (6 vols, Oxford, 1975), vol. 5, p. 134.

[5]   Ekkehard of Aura, *Hierosolymita*, RHCOc. 5 (Paris, 1895), p. 20.

plan.[6] Their moral failing lay in their action, not in the emotion that moved them.

Mid twelfth-century sources

Crusading texts in the mid-twelfth century revealed more frequent connections between zeal, crusading and vengeance. King Louis VII of France supposedly went on crusade because "zeal for the faith burned in the king."[7] Bernard of Clairvaux wrote similarly to those preparing for the Second Crusade.[8] After the Second Crusade, Peter the Venerable asked King Roger II of Sicily to attack the Greeks for their alleged role in the expedition's failure: "therefore rise up, good prince ... rise up to aid the people of God, just as the Maccabees were zealous for the law of God; avenge such shames, such injuries, so many deaths, such great and impious shedding of blood of the army of God."[9] Peter, Bishop of Oporto, was depicted exhorting the second crusaders before the siege of Lisbon with the vocabulary of vengeance, justice and zeal: "good men with good minds, implement legitimate deeds of vengeance here and now. *Cruelty for God is not cruelty but piety.* With the zeal of justice, not the bile of anger, wage just war."[10]

Late twelfth-century sources

In late twelfth-century crusading texts, references to zeal and vengeance with regard to crusading substantially increased in number. At Damascus the army of King Baldwin II of Jerusalem was described as "having zeal for the faith, immediately they all strove to avenge their injuries."[11] King Baldwin III was described in similar terms at the siege of Edessa.[12] William of Tyre also depicted Pope Urban II speaking at Clermont: "therefore, let us be armed with the zeal of

---

6   Ibid., p. 21.

7   Odo of Deuil, *De Profectione Ludovici VII in Orientem*, ed. V. G. Berry (New York, 1965), p. 6.

8   "... the zeal of God burns in you ..." Bernard of Clairvaux, *Epistolae*, ed. J. Leclerq and H. M. Rochais, SBO 7–8 (Rome, 1974–77), vol. 8, p. 314.

9   Peter the Venerable, *The Letters of Peter the Venerable*, ed. G. Constable (2 vols, Cambridge MA, 1967), vol. 1, p. 395.

10   *De Expugnatione Lyxbonensi*, ed. C. W. David (New York, 1936), p. 80.

11   William of Tyre, *Chronicon*, ed. R. B. C. Huygens, CCCM 63 (Turnholt, 1986), p. 609.

12   "... zeal seized arms to take vengeance on the iniquitous ..." William of Tyre, *Chronicon*, p. 719.

God, let us as one gird on our powerful sword, let us go forth and be powerful sons ... anyone who has zeal for the law of God, he will help us."[13]

People in western Europe purportedly responded with enthusiasm to calls for the Third Crusade:

> zeal incited [the men] to greater fervor to embrace the journey without delay ... [the pope] ran forward to the cross held by the priests with speedy zeal and pious passion, so that now it is not a question of who will be signed with the cross, but rather who will not take on such pious work.[14]

Kings Philip II of France and Henry II of England took the cross "incensed with zeal for God."[15] When King Richard I's men captured a Muslim vessel in June 1191, the Muslims killed a few Christians in the fighting. In response, according to the *Itinerarium Peregrinorum*, the crusaders were "pregnant with fervent anger and zeal for vengeance ... [they] raged courageously at the bitter insult."[16] In 1199, Pope Innocent III wrote to the Armenians "may the house of the Lord employ your zeal so that [you may] take vengeance for the injury done to the Crucified One and to his Temple and his inheritance."[17]

Zeal was invoked to describe actions against Jews and heretics as well as Muslims. When preachers spoke convincingly against heretics in southern France, purportedly the crowd were "moved with vehement admiration and inflamed with zeal for the Christian faith."[18] Kings Henry II of England and Louis VII of France had supposedly taken action against the heretics "filled with zeal for the Christian faith ... they decided that they would eliminate the aforesaid heretics from their borders."[19] Rigord reported that King Philip II of France felt likewise about the Jews in France: "inflamed with zeal for God he commanded that ... the Jews should be captured ... despoiled ... and sent forth,

---

[13]   Ibid., p. 134. William also described the first crusaders before Jerusalem was taken: "there was in that group not one man who was old or sick or from a small estate whom zeal did not move and whom the fervor of devotion did not incite to the battle" (ibid., p. 970.)

[14]   *Itinerarium Peregrinorum et Gesta Regis Ricardi*, ed. W. Stubbs, RS 38:1 (London, 1864), p. 139.

[15]   Rigord, *Gesta Philippi Augusti*, in *Rigord: Histoire de Philippe Auguste*, ed. E. Carpentier, G. Pon and Y. Chauvin, Sources D'Histoire Médiévale 33 (Paris, 2006), p. 246.

[16]   *Itinerarium Peregrinorum*, p. 208.

[17]   Innocent III, *Die Register Innocenz' III*, ed. O. Hageneder and A. Haidacher (Vols 1–8, Graz, 1964–2001), vol. 2, p. 468 (*Etsi modernis temporibus*).

[18]   *Gesta Regis Henrici Secundi*, ed. W. Stubbs, RS 49:1 (London, 1867), p. 201.

[19]   Roger of Howden, *Chronica*, ed. W. Stubbs, RS 51:2 (London, 1868–71), p. 150.

just as the Jews themselves despoiled the Egyptians."[20] Some of Philip's actions against Christian enemies were also attributed to zeal for the Christian faith.[21] When he moved against Hugh of Burgundy in 1185, Philip, "inflamed with zeal for the Christian faith ... told [Hugh] that ... he must restore things stolen to the aforesaid churches and must not do such things again, and, if he did not want to restore that money to the churches, [Philip] would take serious vengeance upon him."[22]

Some writers in the late twelfth century connected zeal with crusading through self-sacrifice rather than aggression.[23] In 1181, Pope Alexander III described the crusaders in 1096 as "zealous for the law of God, they were able to tolerate the slaughter of the faithful with patient mind."[24] In 1187, Pope Gregory VIII wrote in his crusading bull *Audita tremendi* that the Christians should "pay attention to how the Maccabees were zealous for divine law, experiencing great dangers to free their brothers, and they learned to relinquish not only their belongings, but even their persons for their brothers."[25] Zeal was associated with self-sacrifice on the field of battle as well. When Reynald of Châtillon died, the *Itinerarium Peregrinorum* lauded his martyrdom: "O zeal of faith! O fervor of the soul!"[26] Similarly, when a woman died of exhaustion after carrying stones at Jerusalem, the *Itinerarium Peregrinorum* noted that "without a break the tireless woman went back and forth, exhorting others more diligently, driven by zeal to find the end of her life along with the end of her labors ... O admirable faith of the weak sex! O inimitable zeal of the woman!"[27]

---

[20]   Rigord, *Gesta Philippi Augusti*, p. 132.

[21]   Ibid., pp. 134 and 166.

[22]   Ibid., p. 184.

[23]   Intriguingly, this seems to relate to the parallel behavior for priests and warriors discussed by Philippe Buc: that priests seek martyrdom, and warriors seek vengeance ("La Vengeance de Dieu: De l'Exégèse Patristique à la Réforme Ecclésiastique et à la Première Croisade," in D. Barthélemy, F. Bougard, and R. Le Jan (eds), *La Vengeance 400–1200* (Rome, 2006), p 458). As Buc notes, to a degree the Maccabees were, thus, both priests and warriors, as they were at the same time "mártyrs et vengeurs" (ibid., p. 468). And, as we have seen, crusaders were frequently compared to the Maccabees, who were also depicted as "zealous."

[24]   Alexander III, *Epistolae*, ed. J.-P. Migne, PL 200 (Paris, 1855), col. 1294 (*Cor nostrum*).

[25]   Gregory VIII, *Epistolae*, ed. J.-P. Migne, PL 202 (Paris, 1855), col. 1542 (*Audita tremendi*).

[26]   *Itinerarium Peregrinorum*, p. 16.

[27]   Ibid., pp. 101–2.

Early thirteenth-century sources

Early thirteenth-century crusading texts also revealed numerous textual connections between zeal, vengeance, and crusading. According to Arnold of Lübeck, in 1187 Pope Clement III "incit[ed] all to zeal against the impious and to vengeance for the holy blood."[28] Arnold of Lübeck also noted that Emperor Frederick I was moved "to the vengeance of the zeal of God and the vengeance of the holy land."[29] This was confirmed by Robert of Auxerre, who wrote that "Frederick Augustus was happy when he heard the news ... a discreet man and one zealous for justice."[30] The Third Crusade was described as undertaken "by many, inflamed with zeal ... with fervent zeal."[31] Each man who took the cross, "zealous to take vengeance for the house of God went forth to avenge the just blood."[32] Ralph of Coggeshall also described the Third Crusaders as "inflamed with zeal for God."[33] According to a German chronicler, even the Byzantines in 1189 reportedly "marveled that ... [the Third Crusaders] did this with one agreement or promise, by which they swore, to take vengeance for a zealous God and the holy land and the effusion of just blood of the servants of God."[34]

Peter of Les Vaux-de-Cernay described crusaders in southern France in 1209 as "on fire with zeal for the orthodox faith."[35] Robert of Auxerre noted that those who fought the Cathars were "armed with zeal for the faith against the deserters of the faith."[36] According to Robert, in 1210, "the pilgrimage [to Languedoc] was celebrated ... because of the zeal for the faith inflamed in the minds of the faithful against those who corrupt the faith."[37]

James of Vitry made it clear that he admired zealous Christians, or, at least, that he chose to depict individuals worthy of praise as zealous. Robert of Courçon, a papal legate, was "a man literate and devout, affable, generous and benign, having zeal for God and ardently desiring the liberation of the holy

---

28   Arnold of Lübeck, *Chronica*, MGHSS 23 (Hanover, 1869), p. 169.

29   Ibid., p. 172.

30   Robert of Auxerre, *Chronicon*, MGHSS 26 (Hanover, 1882), p. 252.

31   Arnold of Lübeck, *Chronica*, p. 203.

32   Ibid., p. 170.

33   Ralph of Coggeshall, *Chronicon Anglicanum*, ed. J. Stevenson, RS 66 (London, 1875), p. 24.

34   Arnold of Lübeck, *Chronica*, p. 172–3.

35   Peter of Les Vaux-de-Cernay, *Hystoria Albigensis*, ed. P. Guébin et E. Lyon (3 vols, Paris, 1926), vol. 1, p. 74.

36   Robert of Auxerre, *Chronicon*, p. 272.

37   Ibid., p. 275.

land."[38] Reiner, the prior of Saint Michael, "inflamed with zeal of the faith he did not fear to go to the enemies' army [and preach]."[39]

Pope Innocent III continued to use the word *zelus* often in the thirteenth century. In 1206 he wrote to Peter II of Aragon that good men, who "are zealous about divine law," should take as their own what formerly belonged to heretics in southern France: "while you endeavor to exterminate them with zeal for the orthodox faith, you may retain [their goods] freely for your own use."[40] In 1208, he wrote "the Lord of vengeance descends to earth with those who are on fire with zeal for the orthodox faith, to avenge the just blood ... .may pious zeal inflame you to so avenge the injury of your God."[41] He also wrote to King Philip II of France and, later, the Frankish nobility, using practically identical words.[42] In that year Innocent also wrote to all clerics that "on fire with zeal for the orthodox faith, you have decided to fight heretical depravity."[43] Those crusaders who fought the Cathars were "on fire with zeal for the orthodox faith to avenge just blood," and "the zeal of the Lord had armed [them] in a holy army against the subverters of the faith."[44] And as Innocent began preparations for the Fifth Crusade, he wrote that he hoped that "those inflamed with zeal for the Christian faith ... [would] avenge the injury of the Crucified One."[45]

As in the late twelfth-century crusading texts, there was one example of zeal inspiring self-sacrifice in the early thirteenth-century sources. In one of James of Vitry's *exempla*, a pilgrim was captured by the Muslims in the holy land. He faced death because the Muslims believed him to be a Templar and they (so the story went) killed all Templars. At first the pilgrim truthfully denied he was a Templar, but finally, "inflamed with zeal for the faith he said, with his neck stretched forth, 'in the name of the Lord I am a Templar.'" He was killed immediately and "went to the Lord, happily crowned in martyrdom."[46]

---

[38]   James of Vitry, *Lettres de Jacques de Vitry*, ed. R. B. C. Huygens (Leiden, 1960), p. 100.

[39]   Ibid., pp. 132–3.

[40]   Innocent III, *Epistolae*, ed. J.-P. Migne, PL 214–16 (Paris, 1890–91), vol. 215, cols 915–16 (*Cum secundum evangelicam*).

[41]   Peter of Les Vaux-de-Cernay, *Hystoria Albigensis*, vol. 1, pp. 60 and 63 (see also p. 74).

[42]   Innocent III, *Epistolae*, vol. 215, col. 1358 and 1359 (*Si tua regalis* and *Rem crudelem audivimus*).

[43]   Ibid., vol. 215, col. 1469. (*Cum orthodoxae fidei*)

[44]   Ibid., vol. 216, col. 152 (*Nuntios et apices*); vol. 215, col. 1356 (*Ne nos ejus*); and vol. 216, col. 151 (*Habuisse bajulos Dominici*).

[45]   Ibid., vol. 216, col. 822 (*Pium et sanctum*).

[46]   James of Vitry, *The Exempla*, ed. T. F. Crane (London, 1890), p. 39.

Clearly the term *zelus* was increasingly used in crusading texts in the twelfth and early thirteenth centuries, often alongside the vocabulary of vengeance. But what did the medieval Latin word actually mean? What concepts underpinned its usage? What can it tell us about medieval emotions, crusading, and vengeance?

Christian love and righteous anger

On closer examination, the context of the evidence itself, in particular the evidence related to specific passages from the Bible, provides crucial information about the meaning of the term. The Biblical verse Ekkehard of Aura cited when referring to those who had killed Jews on their way to the East in 1096 was Romans 10:2–3. In this passage Paul expressed his doubt that the Jews could or would come to know Christ: *testimonium enim perhibeo illis quod aemulationem Dei habent sed non secundum scientiam ignorantes enim Dei iustitiam et suam quarentes statuere iustitiae Dei non sunt subiecti.*[47]

Romans 10:2–3 was frequently cited to signify right intention but incorrect action. For example, Bernard of Clairvaux wrote to a young monk that he should desist from his desire to live an eremitical life: "acquiesce to the counsel of your seniors, since although by chance you may have the zeal of God, [it is] nevertheless not according to the knowledge [of God]."[48] The idea that zeal was good, and blameless, even if the action it motivated was not, was also evident in a letter from Bernard of Clairvaux to another professed religious: "for you may have the zeal of God in this matter, and thus your intention should be excused; but I do not see that in any way your will has been enacted according to the knowledge [of God]."[49] Zeal for God and intention were distinguished from knowledge of God and action. Similarly, in one of James of Vitry's *exempla*, a group of Dominicans heard the confession of a community of nuns. Shocked by the sins some of the nuns had committed, the Dominicans concluded that all were "evil" and publicly proclaimed this, causing great scandal. James disapproved of the public disclosure, and commented "I have known some of those preachers who are called truly religious and are seen to have zeal, but not according to the knowledge [of God]."[50]

---

[47]   Romans 10:2–3. As you will see, twelfth-century writers frequently substituted *zelus* for *aemulatio* when citing this verse; I discuss the significant relationship between *zelus* and *aemulatio* at length below.

[48]   Bernard of Clairvaux, *Epistolae*, vol. 8, p. 508.

[49]   Ibid., vol. 7, p. 294.

[50]   James of Vitry, *The Exempla*, p. 36.

In addition, there was already a historical precedent for using the verse to evaluate the guilt or innocence of those who committed violence for religious reasons. Departing from the Augustinian tradition, Bede had used the verse to question the Jews' ignorance of their crime in killing Christ in reference to Christ's request on the cross that God forgive his murderers.[51] Bede held that those possessing zeal but doing the wrong thing should be forgiven, since they acted out of ignorance and right intention. Some of the Jews, on the other hand, acted with wrong intention, and should not be forgiven. It should be noted that Bede's judgment that some of the Jews had wrongly intended to kill Christ did not resurface in textual sources until the twelfth-century *Glossa Ordinaria*.[52]

It seems reasonable to conclude that, at least within a religious context, zeal was used to signal the partial mitigation of guilt—it was the right sentiment, even when it motivated the wrong action. This is very different from our modern notion of zeal as simply a "passion," a strong emotion that derives its moral value from context. In the medieval sources I have examined, there appears to be no such thing as "bad" zeal—zeal was always "good," even when the actions it inspired were not; and thus the possession of zeal partially mitigated responsibility for those "bad" actions.[53]

Some texts even suggested that, because zeal was the right sentiment, the possession of zeal would in general lead to success. For example, Joachim of Fiore wrote of the Second Crusade:

> [all were] zealous for the injury of their King and desiring to take vengeance on the unfaithful people ... There were many such zealous ones and they were moved, not only in spirit but in body. Wherefore then did they fail? I think that [it was because] in being zealous they did not maintain the proper order (*rectum ordinem*).[54]

Joachim was clearly very surprised that the zeal of the Christians had not guaranteed their victory, and concluded that, although they rightly possessed zeal, their actions were not governed by the proper discipline. Many things could compromise the actions of the zealous—lack of discipline, as with Joachim

---

[51]   Jeremy Cohen, "The Jews as Killers of Christ in the Latin Tradition, from Augustine to the Friars," *Traditio*, 39 (1983), p. 11. Cohen cites Bede, *Lucae Evangelium Expositio*.

[52]   Ibid., p. 11.

[53]   Of course, I cannot claim to have exhaustively looked at every medieval text in existence. Only time will tell if this argument will hold up.

[54]   Joachim of Fiore, *Expositio in Apocalypsim* 6.1 (cited by Benjamin Z. Kedar, *Crusade and Mission: European Approaches Toward the Muslims* (Princeton, 1984), p. 222).

above, or ignorance of "God's will," as with Bernard and Ekkehard—but it was not because their zeal was itself problematic.

Looking beyond the Biblical passages, zeal was intimately connected to the concepts and terminology of justice and love.[55] In 1133, Peter the Venerable wrote to Pope Innocent II about the sentence handed down on the murderer of Thomas, Prior of St. Victor:

> since therefore the king's sword was withheld in this [matter], we seek, and all who are zealous for the law of God pray you with us, that the episcopal, that is, the spiritual sword [in this case excommunication], which is the word of God, according to the Apostle, should not be hidden ... so that the impious may be punished with deserved vengeance and others may be deterred.[56]

Those who were "zealous for the law of God" prayed that the "impious may be punished with deserved vengeance." Arnold of Lübeck was fond of the appellation "a man zealous for justice," and used it to praise Bertold, Achbishop of Bremen, Pope Urban II, and Henry of Glinden.[57] Likewise, Bernard of Clairvaux urged Pope Eugenius III to be more zealous and actively avenge injuries to the papacy and God: "your zeal, your clemency, and the discretion [which serves] to moderate between these virtues should be known; as often as you pardon injuries, you should avenge them, having prudently observed the means, the place, and the time for each."[58] Bernard also urged Eugenius to love justice, according to Proverbs 1:1: "it is of little account to possess justice, unless you love it. Those who possess it, possess it; those who love [it], are zealous. One who loves justice seeks justice and prosecutes it."[59]

The moral argument connecting vengeance and justice was not that *all* acts of vengeance were just, but that vengeance could be, and sometimes necessarily was, just. Thomas of Chobham summarized the complicated position taken by the Church on vengeance, noting that "it is permitted for the laity to seek to regain their belongings from criminals through judgment and to demand the death

---

55   Sometimes *caritas*, but also *amor* and others.

56   Peter the Venerable, *The Letters of Peter the Venerable*, vol. 1, p. 25.

57   Arnold of Lübeck, *Chronica*, pp. 131, 158 and 231.

58   Bernard of Clairvaux, *De Consideratione ad Eugenium Papam*, ed. J. Leclerq and H. M. Rochais, SBO 3 (Rome, 1963), p. 428. The translation of *donandis* is debatable. The more usual sense of the word would lead to the following translation: "as often as you give injuries, you should avenge them." But the verb can also mean to forgive, pardon, or remit, and I chose—conservatively, I think, given the rest of the passage—to use this sense when translating.

59   Ibid., p. 437.

penalty if they are evildoers and murderers, as long as they do this with a zeal for justice and not a vengeful desire [*libido*]."[60] Here, Thomas did not distinguish between actions per se, but rather between the emotional motivations behind those acts—approving of a "zeal for justice" and condemning "vengeful desire." But a few pages on, he qualified this statement, implying that in some cases even "vengeful desire" was appropriate: "for it is one thing to avenge one's own injury, and another to avenge a common injury."[61] For Thomas of Chobham, there was licit and illicit vengeance by the laity, although the ways in which the moral value of retributive action was to be judged was complicated and hinged upon internal motivations and whether the injury was considered to be personal or communal. The connection between justice, vengeance, love and zeal dates back at least as far as Anselm of Lucca, who wrote:

> just as Moses the lawgiver by divine inspiration allowed to the people of God an
> eye for an eye, a tooth for a tooth, and so forth to repress the ungodliness of the
> peoples, so we will and applaud that princes should exercise vengeance against the
> enemies of the truth according to zeal, to a purpose of divine love and to the duty
> of godliness.[62]

Zeal was a sentiment that drove the actor to pursue just vengeance on wrongdoers—because it was compatible with the "purpose of divine love."

The relationship between zeal and love was emphasized by other writers as well. The Anonymous of Halberstadt noted that when Arnulf was made Bishop of Halberstadt he was "aroused by the zeal of love and devotion."[63] Suger of St. Denis also made it clear that one who has "zeal according to the knowledge [of God]" would act "out of love for the Church."[64] Moreover, at least sometimes zeal was an emotion tied to the desire to force non-conforming members of society to convert to orthodox Christianity. Bernard of Clairvaux wrote of the use of force to convert heretics:

> we approve the zeal, but we do not recommend the deed, since faith should be
> suggested not enforced. Although it is beyond doubt better that they be coerced

---

[60]   Thomas of Chobham, *Summa Confessorum*, ed. F. Broomfield (Paris, 1968), p. 436.

[61]   Ibid., p. 440.

[62]   Anselm of Lucca, *De Caritate* (cited and translated by H. E. J. Cowdrey, "Christianity and the Morality of Warfare during the First Century of Crusading," in Marcus Bull and Norman Housley (eds), *The Experience of Crusading 1: Western Approaches* (Cambridge, 2003), p. 179).

[63]   Anonymous of Halberstadt, *Gesta*, MGHSS 23 (Hanover, 1874), p. 92.

[64]   Suger of St. Denis, *Epistolae*, RHGF 15 (Paris, 1878), p. 529.

by the sword, namely [the sword] of those who do not carry the sword without cause, than that they be allowed to drag others into their error. For that man is *the minister of God, he takes vengeance in anger on he who does wrong.*[65]

In this sense, zeal was again completely compatible with the notion of Christian love as correction that motivated crusaders. And, again, as with Ekkehard, there was partial approval for the zeal of those who converted others by force. The action was wrong, but the driving emotion was right.

It would seem from the evidence that because those who were zealous acted out of a love for God and justice, their zeal could limit their culpability, even when their actual deeds were less than ideal. But what was the specific sentiment of zeal behind the terminology that was understood in this way?

Charles Du Cange gave an in-depth analysis of the vocabulary associated with *zelus* and the great variety of meanings the terms could signify, and the primary sources I have looked at bear out his conclusions. I have already shown that "zeal" was linked with love, and Du Cange also linked *zelus* with passionate love. *Zelus* could signify passion or love (*studium* and *amor*) and, similarly, the verb *zelare* could mean to favor (*favere*), to be passionate (*studere*), to desire (*expetere*), and to very much wish (*peroptare*).[66]

Appropriately then, *zelare* was to burn or be fervent (*fervere*). Indeed, images of fire surrounded *zelus* in the primary source passages. Crusaders were *zelo accensi, zelo succensi, zelo inflammati*, and *zelo incensi*. Zeal was often burning, *zelo fervente*, and it was eager, *alacri zelo*. As Bernard of Clairvaux urged Pope Eugenius III, "if you are a disciple of Christ, ignite your zeal."[67] The connection between fiery images, *zelus* and love for God may have been related to the way in which the Holy Spirit manifested as Pentecostal flame upon the heads of the disciples in the Acts of the Apostles.[68]

Also appropriately for such committed love, *zelare* could mean to protect unthinkingly (*impense protegere*).[69] A *zelator* was both desirous (*cupidus*) and a guardian (*fautor*).[70] The loving, protective aspect of zeal goes some way towards explaining the connection between zeal and vengeance, since I have already

---

[65] Bernard of Clairvaux, *Sermones super Cantica Canticorum*, ed. J. Leclerq and H. M. Rochais, SBO 2 (Rome, 1958), pp. 186–7. Reference to Romans 13.4.

[66] Charles Du Cange, *Glossarium Mediae et Infimae Latinitatis* (6 vols, Paris, 1840–50), vol. 6, p. 933.

[67] Bernard of Clairvaux, *De Consideratione*, p. 409.

[68] Acts 2:1–4. I am very grateful to Gary Dickson for bringing this point to my attention.

[69] Du Cange, *Glossarium*, vol. 6, p. 932.

[70] Ibid., vol. 6, p. 932.

discussed how Christian love was used by some to encourage vengeance for God and other Christians.[71]

But there was another aspect of *zelus*. The verb *zelare* could mean to love jealously, and the adjective *zelosus* meant one "burning ... full with love, to us *Jaloux*," while *zelotes* signified a rival (*aemulator*).[72] A *zelator* was a rival and enemy (*aemulator, inimicus*).[73] William of Tyre noted that, when Hugh II of Jaffa was suspected of dallying with his cousin's wife, King Fulk I of Jerusalem "inflamed with the zeal of a spouse was said to conceive inexorable hatred against him."[74] Pope Innocent III elsewhere discussed the example of the spouse faced with a rival: "who can endure a rival with equanimity? Suspicion alone fiercely afflicts the zealous, for it is written, *they will be two in one flesh*, but a zealous man cannot suffer two men in one flesh."[75] It would seem that jealousy and rivalry were also emotional components of zeal.[76]

As well as signifying passion and longing, *zelare* could mean to mock (*irridere*), and *zelus* sometimes meant anger (*iracundia*) and hatred (*odium*).[77] Niermeyer also defined *zelus* as "hatred, envy, [and] jealousy."[78] Of course, the images of flames and burning emotion associated with zeal in the sources are as potentially appropriate for depicting anger and hatred as love and devotion.

The textual evidence given above has in part elucidated what the term *zelus* meant. As a general term, it was an emotional composite of the modern concepts of love, passion, jealousy, protectiveness and angry rivalry/hostility. In a Christian context, because it was directly associated with the desire to pursue God's purpose, on the one hand it was a virtuous loving passion and on the other one apparently centered on hatred, anger, and jealousy. It is worth repeating that, when this sentiment led a Christian to incorrect action, it nevertheless served to mitigate the offence.

---

[71]   See above pages 57–64 and 108–14.

[72]   Du Cange, *Glossarium*, vol. 6, pp. 932 and 933 (Du Cange here called attention to Exodus 20.5, a verse with significance for this chapter and discussed below accordingly. The term *aemulatio* will also be further analyzed below).

[73]   Ibid., vol. 6, p. 932.

[74]   William of Tyre, *Chronicon*, p. 652.

[75]   Innocent III, *De Miseria Condicionis Humane*, ed. R. E. Lewis (London, 1980), p. 123. Reference to Genesis 2:24.

[76]   Noted independently by Nira Pancer, who writes about Gregory of Tours that "le terme *zelus* peut être employé dans le context amoureux aussi bien que dans le context religieux" ("La Vengeance Féminine Revisitée: Le Cas de Grégoire de Tours," in D. Barthélemy, F. Bougard, and R. Le Jan (eds), *La Vengeance, 400–1200* (Rome, 2006), p. 321). As an aside, it would seem that this dual aspect of *zelus* goes back to the Greek root, *zelos*.

[77]   Du Cange, *Glossarium*, vol. 6, pp. 932 and 933.

[78]   Jan F. Niermeyer, *Mediae Latinitatis Lexicon Minus* (Leiden, 1997), p. 1138.

Emotion and action

As the twelfth century progressed, and the popularity of the idea of crusading as vengeance increased, the term *zelus* appeared more frequently in crusading texts. The actions zeal inspired crusaders to take were both acts of violent persecution (often labeled acts of vengeance) and acts of self-sacrifice. Why was *zelus* especially associated with crusading, both as vengeance and as self-sacrifice?

The concept of zeal as Christian love desirous of doing God's purpose was linked to crusading in now-obvious ways, as Jonathan Riley-Smith's previous work on the matter has shown, and also to the ideology of crusading as vengeance.[79] But the concept of zeal as a sentiment involving hatred, anger, and jealousy has been less analyzed in relation to crusading ideology.

The very existence of a connection between zeal and anger/hatred hints at why zeal was associated with the terminology of vengeance. Paul Hyams has noted the ways in which the terminology of anger and vengeance were associated and used together to justify acts of violence. For example, in 1281 Archbishop Pecham stated at the Council of Lambeth that *ira* was "a passion for vengeance."[80] Fortunately, it is possible to take the analysis beyond this hint. Anger is one emotion that other medieval historians have examined, and these studies, together with medieval Christian perceptions of anger, are extremely helpful in defining the aspect of zeal as anger/hatred and its relationship with crusading.

In the ninth century, Hincmar of Rheims differentiated between virtuous anger, directed inwards against the sinful self, and vicious anger, directed outwards at others. According to Hincmar, only anger against the sinful self was acceptable in a Christian.[81] But by the time Thomas of Chobham wrote his *Summa Confessorum* in the late eleventh or early twelfth century, anger against the self was no longer the only acceptable anger: Thomas of Chobham also condoned anger against "wrongdoers." He called this anger against the wrongdoer *ira per zelum*.[82]

---

[79]   Jonathan Riley-Smith, "Crusading as an Act of Love," *History*, 65 (1980): 177–92.

[80]   Paul Hyams, *Rancor and Reconciliation in Medieval England* (Ithaca NY, 2003), p. 50.

[81]   Hincmar of Rheims, *De Cavendis Vitiis et Virtutibus Exercendis* (cited by Richard Barton, "'Zealous Anger' and the Renegotiation of Aristocratic Relationships in Eleventh- and Twelfth-Century France," in B. H. Rosenwein (ed.), *Anger's Past: The Social Uses of an Emotion in the Middle Ages* (Ithaca NY, 1998), p. 157).

[82]   Barton, "Zealous anger," p. 157. Intriguingly, *ira per zelum* seems remarkably like "moral anger" as described by Aristotle in the Nicomachean Ethics, an emotion that

For Thomas, *ira per vitium*, anger stemming from vice, was shown when "someone moves to kill or injure another, and if reason does not immediately proceed to refrain that motion to injure."[83] It was least sinful when the anger led only to hatred, moderately sinful when anger "burst forth in general disorder," and most sinful when "from anger proceeds assault and homicide."[84]

Ira per zelum was a different matter:

> Anger through zeal is when we are angry against vice and against the vicious, and we can hope that this anger increases, because it is a virtue. Nevertheless we ought to resist it as much as we can lest it become fastened [to us], that is lest the outward agitation increase ... However that which is called anger through zeal is a virtue, especially when someone moves through hatred of the vicious, and is impassioned to eliminate them ... The Lord was moved by such anger when he threw out the sinners and merchants from the temple.[85]

Anger through zeal (as opposed to vicious anger) was characterized by how rational (that is, morally justifiable) the sentiment of anger was in the circumstances. Of course, anger against sin was always eminently justifiable.[86] So, in part, zeal was a component of the emotion of righteous, or justified, anger against the wrongdoer. This association with righteous anger corresponds to the way in which zeal was portrayed as a virtue that mitigated guilt.[87] Zealous righteous anger also complements the idea of zeal as love, since from Augustine onwards Christians were urged to undertake chastisement and punishment of sin in a spirit of love.

If *ira* signified the emotional arousal of anger, and *ira per zelum* signified "righteous anger" as apart from other forms of anger, then it would seem that *zelus* could be defined in part as righteousness, the desire to eliminate what was wrong, just as when Christ threw people out of the temple in Jerusalem. This

---

positively required action on its behalf (Peter A. French, *The Virtues of Vengeance* (Lawrence KS, 2001), pp. 94–5).

[83]   Thomas of Chobham, *Summa Confessorum*, pp. 414–15.

[84]   Ibid., pp. 415 and 420.

[85]   Ibid., p. 414. Reference to Matthew 21:12–13.

[86]   Daniel L. Smail, "Hatred as a Social Institution in Late-Medieval Society," *Speculum*, 76 (2001), p. 115.

[87]   Edward Muir and Natalie Zemon-Davis have noted that anger was sometimes used to mitigate guilt in courts of law in the later Middle Ages, though not (apparently) in ecclesiastical courts (Smail, "Hatred as a Social Institution," p. 101). Perhaps *ira per zelum* was one form of anger that could be used in ecclesiastical courts in that way, since many clearly felt it mitigated guilt because it indicated right intention.

is confirmed by Pope Innocent III's description of the three natural powers of man: "the potential for reason, so that he may discern between good and evil, the potential for anger, that he may reject evil, and the potential for desire, that he may long for good."[88] Zeal was in some ways both the anger that led one to reject evil and the love that led one to desire good, both according to the purposes of God.

The role of zeal as loving anger that rejected what was evil and promoted what was good (according to divine will) is confirmed by an examination of the Hebrew tradition of zealotry. This tradition stemmed from the exemplary Old Testament story of Phineas who took violent action to stop the Israelites from mixing with other races and thus ended a plague and restored God's favor.[89] Jewish zeal involved both non-physical and violent coercion, and was, at least for some modern scholars, concentrated "on the internal affairs of the Jewish community ... obsessed with sin and sinners."[90] For Paul, writing in Galatians, Judaism was the old way of "zeal for the Law," whereby religious faith equaled action.[91] To possess zeal was to act on God's behalf in the Jewish tradition, and intriguingly this tradition (and not Paul's New Testament reinterpretation) seems to have continued to be true of the term *zelus* in the twelfth century.

The working definition of zeal as a desire to eliminate actively what was wrong and promote what was good on God's behalf is perfectly compatible with the demonstrated connections between zeal, anger, and Christian love. It may seem incongruous to connect anger and Christian love, but the link was evident both in contextual evidence and also in direct statements by those who promoted crusading. For Bernard of Clairvaux, the love of God fed the hatred of those who did not love God:

> it is certain that if [a man] should not return immediately to the love of God, it
> is necessary that he know, that not only is he now nothing, but nothing at all, or
> rather, he will be nothing for eternity. Therefore that man [should be] set aside;

---

[88]   Innocent III, *De Miseria*, p. 99.

[89]   Numbers 25:11. To see how Phineas still serves today as a symbol of the justifiable use of violent force to enact divine will, one need look no further than the so-called "Phineas Priesthood," purportedly a paramilitary faction of the modern "Christian Identity" movement. See Timothy K. Beal, "The White Supremacist Bible and the Phineas Priesthood," in Jonneke Bekkenkamp and Yvonne Sherwood (eds), *Sanctified Aggression: Legacies of Biblical and Post-Biblical Vocabularies of Violence* (New York, 2004), pp. 120–31.

[90]   David Rhoads, *Israel in Revolution, 6–74 c.e.* (cited by Robert Hamerton-Kelly, *Sacred Violence: Paul's Hermeneutic of the* Cross (Minneapolis, 1992), p. 73n). Richard Horsley, *Jesus and the Spiral of Violence* (cited by Hamerton-Kelly, *Sacred Violence*, p. 73n).

[91]   Hamerton-Kelly, *Sacred Violence*, p. 74.

not only now should he not be loved, moreover he should be held in hatred, according to this: *'will I not hate those who hate you, Lord, and will I not languish over your enemies?'*[92]

Fervent love for God and the godly necessitated fervent hatred for the ungodly, and *zelus* seems to have reflected the need to act that was required by both love and hatred. The zealous individual loved God and fellow believers, was angry at those who did not, and took action.

One such action was vengeance, for at least two possible reasons. Stephen White has connected anger and vengeance in medieval social relationships. In his outline of how anger functioned as a political tool in medieval France, White outlined a basic pattern of emotional transformations, a "script" for the quasi-ritual enactment of lordly anger. If a lord was injured, he would feel shame. That shame would lead to zealous anger, and the anger to acts of vengeance. Richard Barton demonstrated that this anger was specifically known as "zealous anger." In a sense, a display of anger could also serve to indicate to others that a prior action was indeed an injury in cases where there was uncertainty about the action.[93] Eventually, vengeance led to reconciliation and the restoration of peace.[94] Daniel Smail has further shown that, if vengeance was not taken, the anger did not fade but rather was deemed hatred, a long-standing and publicly recognized hostile relationship between those involved.[95]

The reason why White called the pattern he identified a "script," and why Smail followed his lead, is because the patterns seem to have been almost universally recognized, understood and manipulated within Western medieval discourse. To make reference to part of the "script" was to bring to mind the rest of the pattern; hence, to display lordly anger was to firmly state that an injury had been committed and that due vengeance would follow. Like any metaphor, "script" is imperfect, in that it may seem to suggest a strictly controlled series of events without room for individual decision-making.

The "scripts" of White and Smail correspond almost perfectly to the evidence found in crusading texts in the twelfth and early thirteenth centuries. Christ, or the Church, or Christianity, was "injured" in some way, either by the taking of territory or the killing of Christians. Upon hearing of this shameful injury,

---

[92]   Bernard of Clairvaux, *Sermones super Cantica Canticorum*, p. 82. Reference to Psalms 138:21.

[93]   Stephen D. White, "The Politics of Anger," in B. H. Rosenwein (ed.), *Anger's Past: The Social Uses of an Emotion in the Middle Ages* (Ithaca NY, 1998), p. 140. Barton, "'Zealous Anger,'" p. 157.

[94]   White, "The Politics of Anger," pp. 142–4.

[95]   Smail, "Hatred as a Social Institution," pp. 90–92.

Christians were moved by anger to avenge the injury. Both Latin and vernacular texts marked the importance of shame and anger as emotions that motivated crusaders. A vernacular example is found in one of the interpolations of the *Chanson d'Antioche*, where Peter the Hermit recounted his experiences in the Holy Land:

> I am Peter the Hermit who made this voyage
> to avenge God for this grievous shame
> that they have done against him ...
> I went to Rome, full of grief and rage,
> the pope heard my grief and my pain;
> he sends letters to you and your barons.[96]

However, the correspondence between the ideology of crusading as vengeance and the "script" is at first glance imperfect because it would seem that, in the context of crusading, Christian anger and desire for vengeance did not fade once vengeance had been taken. The understanding that Jerusalem had already been destroyed as vengeance for the crucifixion in 70 C.E. did not stop some in the twelfth century calling for further vengeance for the crucifixion, and the success of the First Crusade did not stop the movement of Christians to the East to fight Muslims from the early twelfth century onward. But the extraordinary twelfth-century failures of the Christians in the East, especially the fall of Edessa and loss of Jerusalem, in a sense created new injuries to be avenged, and of course the Latin Christians in the East were under military pressure from their Muslim neighbors constantly, pressure that may have been interpreted as injury.

Nevertheless, one would imagine that when a specific injury had been avenged, at the least the angry desire for vengeance would be attributed to a different injury. Instead, the same themes, the rhetoric of crusading as vengeance for the same injuries, only escalated, if anything, as time went on. So the correlation between the "script" outlined by White and Smail and crusading depends greatly on what was deemed to have been the primary injury deserving vengeance, whether it was thought that vengeance had successfully been achieved, and (perhaps) whether a particular injury was judged likely to motivate sufficient numbers of Christians. In any event, Smail's conclusion that unfulfilled vengeance led to hatred, a formalized antagonistic relationship, would seem compatible with Christian attitudes towards Islam as the crusading movement continued.

The virtuous *ira per zelum* also led humans to take vengeance because, to medieval minds, divine anger at sin led God himself to take divine vengeance.

---

[96] *La Chanson d'Antioche*, ed. J. Nelson, OFCC 4 (Tuscaloosa, 2003), p. 352.

God's vengeance was to come in this life and the next; in the words of Pope Innocent III, "if a just man is barely saved, how can the impious man and the sinner be spared?"[97] For "God is eternally angry at the reprobate, because it is just that since the impious delayed in [the time available to him], God should take vengeance in his [eternity]."[98] Or, as Bernard of Clairvaux wrote in 1138, when confronted with sin "God sees and grieves, he is wretched and he girds on his sword to take vengeance on the malefactors, but also to praise the good."[99] In essence, according to medieval interpretations, zeal as righteous anger rooted in love for what was good and the desire to eliminate what was evil was a "script" established by God himself.

God enacted this emotional pattern in part through crusading. Baldric of Bourgueil made that clear when he wrote at the beginning of his account of the First Crusade "*[God] changes kings and times*: he corrects the pious, that he might advance them; he punishes the impious, that he might set them straight."[100] That God was following a traditional sequence of divine zeal and vengeance through crusading was also communicated by one of Innocent III's letters. In 1206, he wrote "[God] *said I the Lord am zealous, avenging the sins of the father, even to the third and fourth generations, on those who hate me*, that is, on those who imitate their fathers' hatred against me."[101] In this passage Innocent quoted Exodus 20:5–6, but with significant changes. The text of Exodus 20:5–6 in the Latin Vulgate reads: *ego sum Dominus Deus tuus fortis zelotes visitans iniquitatem patrum in filiis in tertiam et quartam generationem eorum qui oderunt me et faciens misericordiam in milia his qui diligunt me et custodiunt pracepta mea.* Innocent accurately remembered that the Old Testament text described God as *zelotes*. However, he turned *visitans iniquitatem* into *vindicans peccata*, linking the punishment of sin with divine vengeance.

To a certain degree, then, at least in the mind of Innocent III, Exodus 20:5–6 was a pattern of thought establishing divine zeal leading to divine vengeance, and purportedly spoken in God's own words. James of Vitry confirmed that pattern in a letter written in 1221 from Egypt, relating that Damietta was in Christian hands, but that

> many of our men, unmindful and ungrateful of such blessings, *provoked the Lord to anger* with various crimes ... for which the Lord, angry, permitted them to

---

97 Innocent III, *De Miseria*, p. 227. Reference to 1 Peter 4:18.
98 Ibid., p. 217.
99 Bernard of Clairvaux, *Epistolae*, vol. 7, p. 381.
100 Baldric of Bourgueil, *Historia Jerosolimitana*, RHCOc. 4 (Paris, 1879), p. 9.
101 Innocent III, *Epistolae*, vol. 215, col. 805 (*Nisi cum pridem*).

perish in the sea and on the land in manifest vengeance, with some held captive by
the Saracens, some drowned in the sea, and others [killed] by their own.[102]

This vision of a zealous God who sought angry retribution on the wrongdoer
and lovingly praised the good was directly related to the idea of crusading as
vengeance, not only because the Muslims had committed the singular crimes
of killing Christians and taking land in the East, but also because the targets of
crusader violence were all repeatedly described as those who maliciously turned
away from God by rejecting Christianity again and again, *qui oderunt [Deum]
in tertiam et quartam generationem*, so to speak. The Jews were certainly often
described as willfully perpetuating the sins of their fathers. For example, Arnold
of Lübeck wrote, "those [Jews] were satisfying the standards of their fathers,
calling down on themselves and their own as they said: *his blood be on us and
on our sons*."[103] The heretics in Toulouse supposedly passed their unfaithfulness
from generation to generation: "from father to sons with successive poison the
superstition of infidelity was spread."[104] The Muslims surely also were "those who
imitate their fathers' hatred": to Christian eyes, Muslims were "the enemies of
the cross of Christ, who ought to be his sons."[105] More specifically, Muslims were
"illegitimate sons," the sons of Ishmael—truly their sins were in the family.[106]

If one of the main reasons why vengeance was sought through the crusades
was the "injury" of willful disbelief, it is no surprise that Pope Innocent III
applied Exodus 20:5–6 to the crusades, directly suggesting that *zelus* was the
angry desire for vengeance on the malicious unfaithful who had injured God
by continuing to disbelieve. God, as a zealous God, grew angry at sin and took
vengeance, and the crusaders in effect enacted this divine characteristic by also
taking vengeance on Muslims, heretics, and sometimes Jews. Or rather, more
precisely, the pope, who authorized the crusades, enacted that divine characteristic
as God's representative. As Bernard of Clairvaux advised Pope Eugenius III, "let
him fear the spirit of your anger, who does not fear men or the sword. Let him
fear your words, who is contemptuous of admonitions. He at whom you are

---

[102]   James of Vitry, *Lettres*, pp. 134–5. Reference to Deuteronomy 4:25 and 9:18.

[103]   Arnold of Lübeck, *Chronica*, p. 190.

[104]   Peter of Les Vaux-de-Cernay, *Hystoria Albigensis*, vol. 1, pp. 7–8 (see also p. 2).

[105]   Peter the Venerable, *Summa Totius Haeresis Saracenorum*, ed. J. Kritzeck, *Peter the
Venerable and Islam* (Princeton, 1964), p. 206. Peter of Blois, *Conquestio de Dilatione Vie
Ierosolimitane*, ed. R. B. C. Huygens, CCCM 194 (Turnholt, 2002), p. 84.

[106]   Albert of Aachen, *Historia Ierosolimitana*, ed. S. Edgington (Oxford, 2007),
p. 411.

angry will think that God is angry, not a man."[107] It is debatable to what degree the crusading armies also perceived themselves as God's agents directly.

There was another factor in the increasing depiction of zeal as a crusading virtue, particularly in the context of Romans 10:2, the verse that was used to indicate correct intention but incorrect action. Ekkehard of Aura, Bernard of Clairvaux, and Bede all used the term *zelus* to indicate that correct intention. Yet, the word in the Latin Vulgate is not *zelus*, but *aemulatio*: *enim perhibeo illis quod aemulationem Dei habent sed non secundum scientiam*. The authors just mentioned substituted *zelus* for *aemulatio*, but Guibert of Nogent did not. He did, however, use *aemulatio* in a way that suggests its close relationship to *zelus*. He wrote of the First Crusaders that "they seemed to have the *aemulatio* of God, but not according to his knowledge, nevertheless God who bends many deeds begun in vain to a pious end ... brought success out of their good intention."[108] For some, at least, it would seem that *zelus* and *aemulatio* were roughly interchangeable terms, and were used in the same way to signify good intention.[109]

This is surprising: *aemulatio* is not a term one would normally expect to be used in a positive way within a Christian context. The classical term signified "rivalry, emulation, competition," and the verb *aemulor* "to rival, vie with, emulate, envy, be jealous of."[110] Du Cange rather unhelpfully noted that *aemulamen* often meant *aemulatio*, and also simply an example (*exemplum*), without signaling what kind of example he meant (positive or negative).[111] He (or his editor) further stated that the verb *aemulare* meant "to excite jealousy, *donner de la jalousie*, or rather to act like a spouse."[112] Niermeyer, meanwhile, defined *aemulatio* as "ardent zeal, indignation, hostility," and the verb *aemulari* as "to be zealous, to be angry."[113]

The context of Romans 10:2 confirms that the term connoted some sort of mimicry, a desire to imitate: *for I allow that they* [the Jews] *have the* aemulatio *of God but not according to knowledge of Him*. The verse also upholds the negative connotations of jealousy and rivalry, since the term was applied to the Jews' unsuccessful and ultimately wrong religious beliefs and practices; they were

---

107   Bernard of Clairvaux, *De Consideratione*, p. 466.

108   Guibert of Nogent, *Dei Gesta per Francos*, ed. R. B. C. Huygens, CCCM 127A (Turnholt, 1996), p. 120.

109   Again, also noted by Pancer, who further draws a link between *aemulatio*, jealousy and envy ("La Vengeance Feminine Revisitée," pp. 311–12).

110   Charles Lewis, *An Elementary Latin Dictionary* (Oxford, 1977), p. 34.

111   Du Cange, *Glossarium*, vol. 1, p. 117.

112   Ibid., vol. 1, p. 117.

113   Niermeyer, *Lexicon Minus*, p. 374.

trying to be godly, but because they ignored true knowledge of God through Christ, Paul felt they would always fail to see the truth.

Aemulatio therefore did not mean precisely the same as *imitatio*, though certainly the two terms are closely related. Giles Constable has argued that the term *imitare* implies conforming to and identifying with an ideal.[114] On the other hand, *aemulatio* seems to have contained a sense of aroused emotion and hostile, obstinate perseverance, not merely passive conformity. In a sense it may be closer to the notions of *imitatio* as passionate longing highlighted by Christina Heckman.[115] What is striking then, at first glance, is that this term and its frequent substitute, *zelus*, both associated in part with a negative connotation of hostility and rivalry, were used to depict a Christian crusading virtue that was linked with a virtuous love for God.[116]

A clue may lie in the fact noted above that, in the sources, crusading zeal led to two actions—the first vengeance and the second self-sacrifice. Crusading texts in the later twelfth and early thirteenth centuries more than once portrayed individuals actively giving up their lives because they were moved by zeal. I propose two potential reasons for this association: zealous self-sacrifice through crusading as an act of love, and zealous self-sacrifice through crusading as emulation of God.

First, part of the classic understanding of crusading as an act of love hinged upon the willingness of the crusaders to sacrifice themselves for their Christian brothers in the East.[117] With the term *zelus* so closely tied to the notion of love, particularly Christian love, it is not surprising therefore that some texts described those who possessed zeal as willing to sacrifice their lives through crusading. This basic explanation accounts for most of the passages expressing zeal as self-sacrifice noted in this chapter.

However, it does not account for the striking *exemplum* of James of Vitry in which a Christian who was not a Templar was captured by Muslims. He faced death only if he was a Templar, and he was not; yet "inflamed with zeal for the

---

[114]   Giles Constable, *Three Studies in Medieval Religious and Social Thought* (Cambridge, 1995), p. 146.

[115]   Christina Heckman, "*Imitatio* in Early Medieval Spirituality: *The Dream of the Rood*, Anselm, and Militant Christianity," *Essays in Medieval Studies*, 22 (2005): 141–53.

[116]   This usage, along with the apparent medieval continuation of a Jewish sense of true faith as zealous action on behalf of God, deserves further independent research. It should be noted that Christina Heckman's work at least partially supports the complex relationship between *aemulatio*, *imitatio*, *zelus*, and vengeance that I outline here. For example, she, too, marks the potential danger of strongly affective religious belief: namely, that it "could lead to despair or violence just as easily as it could aspire to sublime identification with the divine" ("*Imitatio* in Early Medieval Spirituality," p. 150).

[117]   Riley-Smith, "Crusading as an Act of Love," p. 182.

faith" he falsely claimed to be a Templar, thus choosing to die for an untrue statement.[118] He was not a crusader, killed in battle; he was a Christian pilgrim, captured alone, who chose to lie and thereby to seal his fate rather than speak the truth and be spared, because he was "inflamed with zeal."[119] What was this "zeal" that so drove him to dishonesty and self-sacrifice?

I proposed above that crusaders saw zeal as a characteristic of God the Father, a divine attribute the pope imitated and they enacted through love for God and their fellow Christians. Christians, especially Christian leaders, were to act as God's ministers, possessing zeal and taking vengeance, as evidenced by the popular Biblical verse applied to crusading, *minister enim Dei est, vindex in iram ei qui malum agit.*[120] Crusaders were also encouraged to be like the second person of God; the *imitatio Christi* was another, albeit limited, strain of crusading rhetoric.[121] In the early Church, martyrs were the most perfect imitators of Christ, and the imitation of Christ was seen as a "process of divinization or deification."[122] Crusaders who imitated Christ bore their sufferings in silence and relinquished their lives when necessary, thereby coming closer to the divine.

In comparison with *imitatio*, the *aemulatio Christi*, zeal as emulation, based on what we know of the term *aemulatio*, surely involved attempting to accord to an ideal, but in an envious, perhaps competitive way. The Jews aimed at the emulation of God but failed; *aemulatio* was negative imitation in the way that Satan had tried to be like God and fallen from divine grace.

Nevertheless, some in the Church attempted to harness *aemulatio* for good ends. Bernard of Clairvaux wrote to Pope Eugenius III that he must act as a good example for the people around him and below him in the Church hierarchy. The rebellious people of Rome were "impious in God, rash in holy things, always seditious, rivals (*aemuli*) with their neighbors, inhuman to outsiders."[123] Eugenius should counter that by encouraging them to attempt to rival each other in virtue, as Bernard himself did with the pope: "I rival you with good rivalry [*aemulatione bona*]"[124] This corresponds with what Miller has

---

[118] James of Vitry, *The Exempla*, p. 39.

[119] It is interesting that the description of this pilgrim rather resembles the description of Christ found in *The Dream of the Rood*—see Heckman, "*Imitatio* in Early Medieval Spirituality," p. 143.

[120] Romans 13:4.

[121] William Purkis, "Elite and Popular Perceptions of *Imitatio Christi* in Twelfth-Century Crusade Spirituality," in K. Cooper and J. Gregory (eds), *Elite and Popular Religion*, Studies in Church History 42 (Woodbridge, 2006), pp. 54–64.

[122] Constable, *Three Studies*, pp. 149 and 150.

[123] Bernard of Clairvaux, *De Consideratione*, p. 452.

[124] Ibid., p. 453.

already noted, using very similar vocabulary, about the contrast between envy as admiration and negative envy.[125] The almost competitive desire to emulate another could be channeled towards virtuous behavior, suggesting that, just as crusaders were described imitating Christ through martyrdom in battle, some, like James of Vitry's knight, were described emulating Christ through zeal: not passively accepting unavoidable death in battle through humility and submission to God's will, but actively seeking it out of defiant, almost angry love for God and, perhaps, a competitive desire for virtue. Crusading texts therefore presented both the imitation and emulation of the second person of the Trinity as goals to be aimed at, culminating in the action of self-sacrifice; although imitation and emulation seem to have differed distinctly with regard to the emotional state of mind leading to that self-sacrifice.[126]

One of the main components of the medieval concept of zeal was to take action on God's behalf based on an angry desire to eliminate evil and on love for the good. Given this, it is not surprising that individuals described as possessing zeal might try to take action in two ways compatible with two related, but distinct, emotional states. Predominantly those who were zealous were depicted seeking to enact the vengeance of God through righteous anger, but at times the desire to emulate God led some to express zeal through active self-sacrifice.

The role of *zelus* as an emotional catalyst

I have demonstrated that zeal was linked to the ideology of crusading through a number of emotional "scripts" or patterns. There was the "script" proposed by White, Barton, and Smail, in which injury led to lordly anger, which in turn led to vengeance.[127] If the desire for vengeance was unfulfilled, anger grew to hatred, another emotion that was used as a narrative strategy to justify actions and mitigate guilt in medieval society.[128] Moreover, there was a longstanding Biblical "script" of God's anger at sin and his love for the good leading him to seek divine vengeance upon wrongdoers.

It must be noted that the emotional patterns that I and others have described are broad and simplistic. Human psychology is never as simple, nor as clearly

---

[125]   William Miller, *Humiliation* (Ithaca NY, 1993), p. 129.

[126]   It is possible, of course, that this difference is so distinct only to the over-scrupulous (and hind-sighted) eyes of modern historians. The necessary caveat, then, is that my careful dissection of meaning is meant to enhance our own understanding of a distant time, rather than to describe a literal play-by-play of conscious thought in the Middle Ages.

[127]   White, "The Politics of Anger," pp. 142–4. Barton, "'Zealous Anger,'" p. 157.

[128]   Smail, "Hatred as a Social Institution," pp. 95, 101 and 109.

delineated, as these models may suggest—as Benjamin Kedar has rightly noted, individual preconceptions always "dictated the extent to which the data [of rhetoric] were absorbed."[129] In fact, the "scripts" were effective *because* they were simple and broad and flexible. They were templates that could be loosely applied to a variety of circumstances with great effect, they contained various options and choices for action, and thus they were compatible with whatever other factors influenced individuals within their own minds as they considered and wrote about crusading.

The fact that the idea of crusading as vengeance grew during the period in question and became more and more associated with the emotional terminology of zeal may have been due to the fact that these patterns of thought were already established, tying together love of God, anger at sin, a passion for justice, and the vocabulary of vengeance. It is crucial that there was more than one such pattern, since the rhetoric was aimed at specific audiences. Multiple patterns ensured more people—in more "emotional communities"—were likely to find a reason in their own minds to link zeal, crusading and vengeance.[130] And even minimal, partial reference may have evoked the entire, commonly understood patterns in individual minds. Thus these pre-existing patterns of thought linking emotion, religion and violence were powerful motivating tools at the disposal of those who encouraged the crusading movement and sought a united Christendom, internally reformed and externally expanding.[131]

There may have been a further dimension to the way in which these patterns worked. In his work on reports of religious visions collected during the much later Spanish Inquisition, William Christian has come to some startling conclusions about the way emotion was interpreted in the later Middle Ages. Apparently, the emotional reaction of the subject of the vision was an important criterion in deciding whether it was a vision from God or from the Devil. The reasoning for this went back to Thomas Aquinas, who in turn relied on the *Life* of St. Anthony by Athanasius: "if fear is followed by joy, we know that the help of God has come to us ... If, on the contrary, the fear remains, then the enemy is present."[132] After extensive research, Christian concluded that "certain emotions seem to

---

[129]   Kedar, *Crusade and Mission*, p. 87.

[130]   Ibid., p. 101. Barbara H. Rosenwein, *Emotional Communities in the Early Middle Ages* (Ithaca and London, 2006).

[131]   Those who sought both internal reform and conversion of the Muslims were usually described as zealous. For example, St. Dominic (*Acta canonizationis S. Dominici*, cited by Kedar, *Crusade and Mission*, p. 121); Ramon of Penyaforte (cited by Kedar, *Crusade and Mission*, p. 138); and St. Francis (James of Vitry, *Lettres*, pp. 132–3).

[132]   William Christian, *Apparitions in Late Medieval and Renaissance Spain* (Princeton, 1981), p. 193.

have been moral indicators, or signifiers ... a form of obscure communication from God. Like dreams, they were messages to be deciphered."[133] I know of no work done to test or verify this conclusion outside the Spanish Inquisition, but if it were true that, in the medieval period as a whole, the right emotion could serve as an indicator of moral rectitude, then "scripts" would be recognized and triggered not only intellectually, but also emotionally: *feeling* the emotion of zeal may have confirmed for the individual that her actions were godly, apart from any intellectual understanding of the situation. Thus the ideology of crusading as vengeance may have functioned both intellectually and emotionally.

John Cowdrey has noted that at the time of the First Crusade martyrdom was not a crucial component of crusading ideology, but rather a "catalyst," a concept that enabled the crusaders to understand "how they could at one and the same time" kill and be martyred.[134] I suggest that the emotional rhetoric of zeal functioned in a similar way as a catalytic discourse that suited both anger and love, imitation and emulation, vengeance and self-sacrifice, and that, because it was such a flexible tool, the emotional rhetoric of zeal was utilized more and more through the twelfth century and into the thirteenth to promote and explain the actions that resulted from crusading ideology.

*   *   *

Throughout the twelfth and early thirteenth centuries the term *zelus* appeared alongside references to crusading with greater frequency. It was linked to two actions: first, and predominantly, vengeance, and second, self-sacrifice. Conceptually, the term was associated with love of God and justice, and therefore twelfth-century writers, drawing upon Paul's Epistles, used the term to mitigate the offense. Zeal signified correct intention, even if the subsequent action was wrong. Because of its association with love of God and the pursuit of justice, zeal led individuals to seek vengeance on those deemed evildoers, and this corresponded to the ideology of crusading as vengeance.

Analysis further revealed that the sentiment behind the medieval term was a composite of passionate love, jealous protectiveness, and angry hostility. These emotions tied zeal to crusading as an act of vengeance in a variety of ways. First, because love for God and fellow Christians was conceptually linked with vengeance. Second, the sentiment of jealous protectiveness corresponded with the idea of crusading as just war—in other words, a war of defense. Third, zeal was tied to anger through the concept of virtuous anger at sin, *ira per zelum*.

---

[133] Ibid., p. 201.

[134] H. E. J. Cowdrey, "Martyrdom and the First Crusade," *The Crusades and Latin Monasticism, 11th–12th Centuries* (Aldershot, 1999), p. 53.

Anger was associated with vengeance in medieval texts in two ways. White and Smail demonstrated that there was a "script" of lordly anger and vengeance in place during the Middle Ages, a "script" that understood that a shameful injury to a lord would anger him, and that anger would drive him to seek vengeance. Barton showed that this anger was known as zealous anger. Once vengeance was enacted, anger faded away; if not, it coalesced into the more durable public sentiment of hatred. This "script" corresponded to the evidence for the idea of crusading as vengeance.

Second, there was a Biblical "script," encapsulated in Exodus 20:5–6, which understood that sin angered God, who then sought divine vengeance. God's propensity for anger at sin was ascribed to his characteristic as a "zealous" god. The crusaders, through papal authority, were often described in the texts enacting God's vengeance, possessing his divine zeal.

The study of zeal in crusading texts revealed two further trends. First, the medieval concept of zeal as vengeance seems to have corresponded to the traditional Jewish idea of faith as action. Second, writers of crusading texts used *zelus* and *aemulatio* interchangeably and both in a positive manner, although *aemulatio* was a term with negative connotations of rivalry and hostility and thus (one would think) ill-suited to be virtuous.

The emotion of zeal also led to the action of self-sacrifice. Zeal was love, and Riley-Smith has shown that through love crusaders were willing to die for their fellow Christians, in imitation of Christ. Drawing upon the link between zeal and emulation, there was evidence that some, like Bernard of Clairvaux, sought to harness the negative, rivalrous desire of *aemulatio* to encourage people to be more virtuous, and one example described a Christian seeking to emulate Christ's death. This was, in effect, the same action as that of crusaders seeking the *imitatio Christi* and dying for their fellows, but the sentiment behind the action was subtly different: righteous, angry defiance as opposed to passive, humble conformity.

In this chapter I have outlined several models that may have contributed to the ideology of crusading as vengeance through the emotion of zeal. Because they were patterns of thought and feeling, even minimal, partial reference may have evoked the entire, commonly understood patterns in individual minds. And perhaps, as Christian has suggested, the emotion of zeal worked as a moral signifier, confirming that one who felt zeal was doing God's will. Thus, the ideology of crusading as vengeance may have been understood both intellectually and emotionally. Rather than a root cause, the rhetoric of zeal seems to have been primarily an emotional catalyst for the crusading movement, and particularly for the ideology of crusading as vengeance.

Conclusion

In the past, historians have understood the idea of crusading as vengeance as a socio-political construction related to feuding, honor, and other similar values. Moreover, many have assumed that the idea of crusading as vengeance was most prominent in the early years of the First Crusade and that, as monastic chroniclers took up the task of interpreting the First Crusade, they played down the idea of vengeance and incorporated more fully ideas considered more acceptable to an ecclesiastical readership.

As a result of this study, it is clear that, although the idea of crusading as vengeance did draw upon what we consider secular values, it was also firmly rooted in religious ideas of divine justice and vengeance as moral punishment. The idea of crusading as vengeance grew from an intricate network of associated values drawn from both Old and New Testaments, Christian theology, and canon law, legendary narratives, and inherited forms of social organization. Moreover, although the idea of crusading as vengeance was current in 1095, it was not yet full blown at that point. It began to be cohesively articulated and repeatedly invoked by those very same monastic chroniclers thought to have negated it, working in the early twelfth century. The frequency with which the idea of vengeance was used in crusading texts dramatically increased through the twelfth century, suggesting at least that the idea was viewed as valuable in practical terms, and at most that it was what we might call a popular idea—well liked and widespread.

What in twelfth-century culture facilitated the popularity of the idea of crusading as vengeance? First, tying in with the idea of vengeance as justice was the notion that fellow Christians, even God himself, had been wrongfully injured by Muslims and that, by taking vengeance for those injuries, the crusaders were assuming divine authority and earning divine approval. This theme was often expressed with Biblical quotations and language, invoking the "God of vengeance" found in both the Old and New Testaments.[1]

What "crimes" had the Muslims committed, from the perspective of the sources? There were specific events that clearly fitted the bill for vengeance, from the crusaders' viewpoint: killing Christians, recovering cities like Edessa and

---

[1] For example, Deuteronomy 32:32 (cited by Robert of Rheims, *Historia Iherosolimitana*, in RHCOc. 3 (Paris, 1866), p. 812) and Romans 13:4 (repeatedly cited by multiple authors).

Jerusalem. However, the sources went further in attributing "crimes" or "injuries" to the Muslims. Some texts went so far as to describe the Muslims as, literally, criminals, of the worst sort. As the account of the siege of Lisbon stated:

> But now, with God inspiring you, you bear arms with which murderers and plunderers should be wounded, the devious controlled, the adulterers punished, the impious lost from the earth, the parricides not allowed to live, nor the sons of impiety to go forth. You therefore, brothers, take up courage along with these arms ... Deeds of this kind are the duty of vengeance which good men carry in good spirit ... It is not cruelty but piety for God. With the zeal of justice, do not go forth with anger, [instead] wage just war.[2]

This is a handy way to justify violence—it is not unprovoked aggression, it is just vengeance (what we might call punishment) that is fully deserved by a group of criminals.

Some other texts went further still, suggesting that the inherent nature or status of the Muslims was criminal. Rather than depicting them as individuals who had committed specific unlawful actions that merited vengeance, these sources routinely described Muslims as treacherous and unfaithful—literally, then, *infideles* in both senses of the word. Needless to say, in a world where for the most part your word was your bond, to be treacherous or unfaithful was itself a crime and injury.

In a related line of thought, a number of texts used Islamic aggression in the Holy Land as proof that Muslims, like heretics, were actively resisting, betraying, and/or rebelling against Christian society—that indeed Muslims were heretics, and not pagans.

This is surprising, since there was actually a very clear distinction in canon law regarding violence towards non-Christians. Muslims (as pagans) were outsiders, who should not be attacked unless they were actively attacking Christendom. Jews were perceived as passive and subordinate, and were not to be violently persecuted unless they rebelled against Christian society. In contrast, heretics who refused to recant were always subject to violent punishment, since by their very refusal to accept orthodox belief they were undermining Christian order and were a threat to society. When Christian violence is understood in this context, it is extremely significant that Muslims and Jews were not always clearly distinguished from heretics—because heretics were always legitimate targets of violence. Heretics were seen as criminal members of Christian society—subject to the same laws and punishments. By portraying Muslims in this way, violence

---

[2]   *De Expugnatione Lyxbonensi*, ed. C. W. David (New York, 1936), pp. 76–80.

(violence deemed "just vengeance") was not only acceptable, but positively required.

What is particularly notable about these themes is that they point to a mindset that classified the Christians and Muslims as subordinate to the same divinity, and both accountable to his justice. Christians and Muslims were presented as though part of one large community, both subject to punishment if they offended God. From a broad perspective, then, in the crusading texts the Muslims were not "the others," but rather "those of us who are doing wrong." It was not so much that they were alien in the sense of unknown and unknowable; rather, they were depicted as deviant and criminal, and therefore legitimately subject to vengeance.

Perhaps the least surprising and most anticipated component of the idea of crusading as vengeance drew upon the notion of vengeance as a socio-political obligation. Crusading texts linked taking vengeance with two potent medieval concepts: aid (*auxilium*) and love (*caritas*).

Auxilium was the term often used for one half of the feudal contract between lord and subordinate. The lord had the right to demand *consilium et auxilium*, "counsel and aid," with aid frequently meaning military help in particular. *Caritas* was, of course, Christian love—love for God, love for family, love for fellow Christians. It was not simply a feeling, but a relationship that came with obligations and required certain expressions. One of these obligations was to help fellow Christians in need—and this, it would seem, included avenging them if they were wrongly killed.

This linkage between vengeance, *auxilium*, and *caritas* allowed vengeance to be interpreted as the provision of military aid to embattled lords and allies, and as the expression of Christian love towards fellow Christians, and indeed God himself. The success of this line of rhetoric depended on characterizing the relationships among crusaders in terms that would suggest an obligation to seek vengeance. God the Father was described as a father and lord owed vengeance, Christ as a brother, lord, or comrade begging for help and vengeance, Jerusalem and/or the Church as a wronged mother deserving vengeance. Although this strain of the ideology clearly had roots in socio-political, indeed biological relationships, it mingled with religion and religious concepts in a very productive way:

> I say to fathers and sons and brothers and nephews: for if some stranger struck
> one of your own, would you not avenge your blood [relation]? How much more
> should you avenge your God, your father, your brother, whom you see blamed,

proscribed, crucified; whom you hear crying out and forsaken and begging for aid: *alone I am trampled in the winepress ...*[3]

Importantly, it was not new to refer to God as a father or Christ as a brother—the tendency to use family relationships to identify true believers and to motivate people to action on behalf of their faith is evident in both the Old and New Testaments.

In addition, the sources document two intriguing phenomena: in crusading texts, there was a marked tendency to ignore distinctions between Muslims, Jews and heretics, and there was also a great penchant for invoking the crucifixion. When we look long and hard at the evidence and the context of the evidence, we see that these two phenomena are in fact related—to each other, and to the idea of crusading as vengeance.

There was a strong triangular relationship between Jews, Muslims, and the crucifixion. Muslims wrongly threatened Jerusalem, the city in which the Jews had purportedly killed Christ. A rhetorical emphasis on injuries to Christ in crusading literature and common devotional trends of the twelfth century, as well as the extremely popular legendary tradition of the *Vindicta Salvatoris*, further promoted attention to the crucifixion as a symbolic event linking Christians, Jews, and Muslims through the nexus of Jerusalem. The texts show that Muslims were incorporated into Christian mytho-history alongside the Jews, literally responsible for the crime of the crucifixion. This was intensified by the fact that frequently the crucifixion was depicted as happening in the present, not the past—"even now our Lord is being injured"—and thus requiring immediate vengeance.

Furthermore, heretics, Jews, and Muslims were all accused of crimes of malicious desecration centered on the crucifixion of Christ, at the same time as they were accused of the common "injury" or "crime" of rebellious disbelief, suggesting that the crucifixion represented, or served as a cultural reference point for, the crime of willful infidelity. It was to some degree a symbol of that very worst crime: the crime of willful disbelief, of betraying God, of seeking to undermine Christian society. When writers wrote about the metaphorical injuries of willful disbelief and rebellion, they invoked the crucifixion: they referred back to its legendary traditions, they evoked the pain of the crucifixion, they accused Muslims, Jews, or heretics of desecrating crucifixes, or committing atrocities that replicated certain details of the crucifixion. And these evocations were accompanied by demands for vengeance. It was almost as though there

---

[3]   Baldric of Bourgueil, *Historia Jerosolimitana*, in RHCOc. 4 (Paris, 1879), p. 101. Reference to Isaiah 63:3.

were three layers of injury requiring vengeance: the immediate action; the willful disbelief that inspired the action; and, under it all, the crucifixion, the ever-present symbol of that willful disbelief.

A related phenomenon (cause or consequence or both) to this assimilation of Muslims, Jews, and heretics, and associating them with the denial of the crucifixion's redemptive character, was the encouragement of an "us or them" mentality—either you were with the Christians, or you were against them. As Peter of Blois stated in one text, "it is Christ who says you are either with me or against me, and he who does not unite with me will be scattered."[4]

At the same time as the idea of crusading as vengeance was used more frequently as the twelfth century progressed, so one particularly charged emotion word appeared alongside it: *zelus*. It is a term with no exact modern English equivalent, and can be translated as "zeal" or "jealousy" as befits context. It was primarily associated with the action of vengeance, but also with the action of self-sacrifice. Conceptually the term was associated with love of God and love of justice, and therefore twelfth-century writers, drawing upon Romans 10:2– 3, used the term to signify correct intention, even if a subsequent action was wrong.

The sentiment behind the medieval term was a composite of passionate love, jealous protectiveness, and angry hostility. These emotions related to the idea of crusading vengeance in a number of ways. First, because as already shown, love for God and fellow Christians (*caritas*) was linked with vengeance. Second, the sentiment of jealous protectiveness corresponded with the idea of crusading as just war—that is, a war of defense. Third, *zelus* was understood as part of righteous anger (*ira per zelum*), and vengeance that was pursued against wrongdoers out of righteous anger was seen by the Church as legitimate and morally correct (as opposed to vengeance that was pursued from personal anger). Both Old and New Testament passages were used to bolster the notion that God would become angry and act on that anger when confronted with sin: in the New Testament, Christ's destruction of the Temple, and in the Old Testament, that well-known verse, Exodus 20:5–6. God's propensity for anger at sin was ascribed to his characteristic as a "zealous" God. The crusaders, through papal authority, were often described according to Romans 13:4 as "ministers of God," enacting his vengeance and possessing the same divine zeal. It could be argued that the emotional rhetoric of zeal, and perhaps the emotion itself, functioned in a suggestive way, as a catalyst that promoted, encouraged, and helped make

---

4   Peter of Blois, *Conquestio de Dilatione Vie Ierosolimitane*, ed. R. B. C. Huygens, CCCM 194 (Turnholt, 2002), p. 83. References to Matthew 12:30 and Luke 11:23.

sense of the idea of crusading as vengeance and the actions that proceeded from that ideology.

At the same time that the idea of crusading as vengeance began to appear more frequently, there were always a few writers who did not use the idea. These writers and their sources defy categorization based on genre, chronology, authorship, or language. It is problematic to extrapolate from negative evidence, but the fact that some sources were silent on the question of crusading as vengeance encourages us to proceed with proper caution. There were undoubtedly some who made a considered choice not to invoke the idea. In addition, we must acknowledge the problematic nature of the medieval sources, and the particular role prominent individuals like Pope Innocent III may have played in advancing the ideology of vengeance.

A fuller grasp of the idea of crusading as vengeance impacts our overall understanding of crusade ideology in the twelfth century considerably. Arguably the most significant point to be taken from this study of crusading as vengeance is the emphasis in the sources on vengeance as justice. The idea of vengeance was used precisely because it justified crusading at a foundational moral level. This indicates that there was concern about morality of purpose. I do not simply mean that the sources were whitewashing the crusades with a superficial and hindsighted justification, but that the constantly reiterated emphasis on vengeance indicates the genuine appeal of behaving in a morally correct way in the central Middle Ages. I am not asserting that the crusades actually *were* right in any sense. Certainly the means of doing this particular "right action" were blood-soaked, and it is arguable that this violence was a major part of its appeal. Nevertheless, in addition to whatever appetite for violence and hatred may have been present in the crusades, there was also a clear demand for a moral purpose, for a role in the Christian mytho-historical narrative that was *just*. Historians must grapple with this paradox—that a desire for moral purpose and an interest in promoting justice coexisted with regular, repeated violence and the frequently vicious rhetoric of religious hatred.

Going further, this hunger for a just enterprise emphasizes the communal nature of crusading, since justice is overwhelmingly concerned with actions between human beings—the relationship of one human being (or group) to another. Crusading was not simply the individual pursuit of salvation through penance, or the individual pursuit of riches and power, or indeed any individual pursuit—it was also, perhaps overwhelmingly, a collective pursuit of a just society, one in which Good was rewarded and Wrong was punished. It may seem fantastical (or bitterly ironic) to us that a collective pursuit of a better society should have led to the atrocities of the crusades—nevertheless, we must acknowledge that people may have believed strongly that they were acting positively to promote a just world, no matter how alien their notion of justice looks to us today, and no matter how far they wound up straying from that idea of justice on the battlefield. And while it is important to study individual motivations for crusading, it is also vital to remember the collective, social motivations for crusading as well.

Second, it is important to note that the idea of crusading as vengeance was invoked regardless of the targets of crusading hostility: violence against Muslims, Jews, heretics, and even on some occasions eastern Christians, was described in terms of vengeance. This constitutes further support for a pluralist understanding of crusading as an activity that encompassed events outside, as well as within, the Holy Land. It also emphasizes that, while understanding the intricacies of canon law on legitimate violence may well be helpful, nevertheless many at the time of the crusades, lay and clergy alike, did not themselves always acknowledge those intricacies. And, at its furthest limits, it suggests that there was, at the least, a tendency for Christian violence to lose its distinctions in favor of general hostility towards any non-Christian.

Third, on a related point, it is clear that crusading was perceived as vengeance due to a powerful combination of concepts and values that were rooted in "secular" society, religious culture, and—this is crucial—both.[5] The whole gamut of ideas—vengeance for family, vengeance as divine chastisement, vengeance for the crucifixion—were present in virtually the whole range of sources. Even the importance accorded to family members was rooted not merely in the social fabric of the times, but in the social fabric of the Bible, as well. The ideas that made crusading as vengeance plausible, and the voices that expressed the construct of vengeance, cannot be classified as purely "secular" or purely "religious."[6]

This raises the question of whether it is legitimate to distinguish other aspects of crusading ideology as "secular" or "religious," and suggests it is not. By identifying concepts according to modern divisions or categories, we may well make the crusades easier for us to understand. But we also risk obscuring the fundamental power of the idea of crusading, the way it combined secular and religious elements into the all-encompassing "rightness" of crusading that swayed those who responded to the appeal of Urban II and his successors. Historians have rightly concluded that crusading was successful precisely because it integrated the laity and the Church, because it gave the laity a significant religious role that

---

[5]   Indeed, the very distinction between "secular society" and "religious culture" is deceptive, and arguably anachronistic.

[6]   This issue is related to, though distinct from, the broader question of the relative dominance of material versus ideological motivations. For more on this debate, see Norman Housley, *Contesting the Crusades* (Oxford, 2006), especially pp. 75–98.

did not require them to give up their worldly lives altogether—it would surely be misleading to study the phenomenon of crusading ideology in binary terms.

A similar point must be made about the study of "elite" versus "popular" ideas or beliefs. Without doubt, the evidence for the idea of crusading as vengeance does not support a division between "elite" and "popular." If both the vernacular epic *Chanson d'Antioche* and the theorist Gratian supported the premise that it was just to wage war to avenge an injury, was that premise elite or popular? If Bernard of Clairvaux wrote to Pope Eugenius III that he must take care to show his strength by avenging injuries or else he will be judged weak, and Raimbaut of Vaqueiras mocked the Marquis Albert Malaspina for his weak inability to take vengeance, were they expressing an elite or popular idea?

There may have been some occasions, or contexts, where there really was a drastic split between the ideas of the upper echelons of the Church and the ideas of the Christian masses.[7] But, for much of the time, when scholars discuss "elite" and "popular" ideas, we are really talking about a social characteristic of the people thought to hold the ideas, rather than a difference clearly present in the ideas themselves. It is another, albeit subtler, way to suggest a division of medieval society along lines that resemble our own. It is also a value judgment, since the implication is that "elite" ideas are what many might call "better"— refined, polished, sophisticated, complex, educated, pious, principled; whatever adjective one chooses to define "elite" ideas, it is rarely negative.

Hopefully, this study has clarified the way in which other, only quasi-historical narratives, including the *chansons de geste*, contributed to contemporary understanding of the crusades. Especially in the later twelfth and early thirteenth centuries, writers of what we consider "historical" chronicles referred to contemporary literature and popular history, making potent connections between the events of the crusades and historical or epic stories.[8]

---

[7]   Although John Tolan is surely right to say that close examination of the texts themselves makes it difficult to maintain a firm distinction between the categories of "elite" and "popular" (*Saracens: Islam in the Medieval European Imagination* (New York, 2002), p. 137).

[8]   Arnold of Lübeck referred to the legendary destruction of Jerusalem by Titus and Vespasian (Arnold of Lübeck, *Chronica*, in MGHSS 21 (Hanover, 1869), p. 164). The poet Raimbaut of Vaqueiras compared the Third Crusade to the expeditions of Alexander the Great, Charlemagne, Louis (presumably the Pious), and Roland (Raimbaut of Vaqueiras, *The Poems of the Troubadour Raimbaut de Vaqueiras*, ed. J. Linskill (The Hague, 1964), p. 244). The Cistercian monk Gunther of Pairis wrote at the beginning of his account of the Fourth Crusade: "we have undertaken this with great astonishment, that through brutish men and poor fishmongers and idiots the world have accepted the faith of Christ though [it was] new and unknown [to them] ... [without] the authority of Caesar Augustus or the knowledge of Plato and Demosthenes or the eloquence of Cicero" (Gunther of Pairis, *Hystoria*

These cross-references, in addition to the remarkable overlap in evidence for the idea of crusading as vengeance, make it apparent that literature, particularly the *chansons de geste* but perhaps also romances, should be considered alongside more traditional historical sources when studying medieval perceptions of the crusading movement.[9] These literary genres, and the ideas they contained, were an important part of the context in which crusading was understood and communicated, and some "fictional" epics (for example, *La Venjance de Nostre Seigneur* and the *Historia Karoli Magni et Rotholandi*) contained mytho-historical ideas that clearly related to, or reflected, aspects of the idea of crusading as vengeance. Even the *Chanson de Roland* contained elements that were familiar to readers of crusade histories and were employed by later writers.[10] This suggests great fluidity among the different medieval genres, a point already

---

Constantinopolitana, ed. P. Orth, Spolia Berolinensia: Berliner Beiträge zur Mediävistik 5 (Zurich, 1994), p. 106). *La Chanson de la Croisade Albigeoise* referred both to the *Chanson d'Antioche* and to Raoul of Cambrai, a character from one of the main cycles of *chansons de geste* (*La Chanson de la Croisade Albigeoise*, ed. M. Zink (Paris, 1989), pp. 40 and 65). The preacher James of Vitry drew a moral parallel between crusading and the actions of Roland: "just as we read about a certain knight, that he went to Spain with Charles the emperor against the Saracens" (James of Vitry, *The Exempla*, ed. T. F. Crane (London, 1890), p. 52). The *Canso d'Antioca* likewise referred to the *Chanson de Roland* twice (*Canso d'Antioca*, ed. C. Sweetenham and L. M. Paterson, in *The Canso d'Antioca: An Occitan Epic Chronicle of the First Crusade* (Aldershot, 2003), pp. 228 and 236). It is debatable whether the timing of the evidence suggests that these connections only began to be made in the late twelfth and early thirteenth centuries, or whether they only begin to be visible in the period.

[9]   The genre of romance made an appearance in the account of the Fourth Crusade knight Robert of Clari: "and the women and the demoiselles of the palace [at Constantinople] climbed to the windows, and other people of the city [too], and the women and demoiselles, having climbed onto the walls of the city, watched the battle...and they said among themselves that from the signs [the men] seemed to be angels, if they should prove handsome, for they were so beautifully armed and their horses were so beautifully decorated" (Robert of Clari, *La Conquête de Constantinople*, ed. P. Lauer, CFM 40 (Paris, 1924), p. 49).

[10]   For example, the two alternatives of death and conversion offered to Muslims in crusading accounts were similarly offered to Muslims by Charlemagne in *Roland*: "in the city not a pagan remained/who was not killed, or became Christian" (*La Chanson de Roland*, ed. C. Segre, TLF 968 (Geneva, 2003), p. 98). Similar attitudes were manifest in the *Historia Karoli Magni et Rotholandi*, where "the Saracens, who wished to be baptized, were spared to life, and those who did not, were struck down by the sword" (*Historia Karoli Magni et Rotholandi*, ed. P. G. Schmidt, in *Karollelus atque Pseudo-Turpini Historia Karoli Magni et Rotholandi* (Stuttgart, 1996), p. 16). Moreover, the relationship between aid and vengeance was clear in the *Chanson de Roland* as well. In battle with Charlemagne (who sought vengeance for the slaughter of the Frankish rearguard) the Muslims cried out: "Aid (*aie*) us, Mohammed!/Our god, avenge us on Charles!" (*La Chanson de Roland*, p. 188).

made by Sarah Kay.[11] In turn, this fluidity emphasizes the need for more study of the interplay between crusading ideology and the contemporary literature.

Put simply, the modern distinctions between "literary texts" and "historical sources" are not always relevant when looking for medieval evidence of crusading ideology.[12] To give a pithy example: in a passage from the *Historia Karoli Magni et Rotholandi*, Charlemagne said to his Muslim foe Aygolandus, "our Lord Jesus Christ, creator of heaven and earth, chose our people, namely the Gauls, above all other peoples and placed us in dominion over all peoples of the whole world, to convert your Saracen people to our law, as much as I can."[13] This was not that far removed from James of Vitry's letter of 1218 in which he wrote: "[we go] towards the East, even to the end of the world where there are Christians; whence, if through the mercy of God we are able to obtain that land, we will extend the Christian religion from the West even to the East."[14] The two texts are very different in other ways, no doubt—but some of the ideas they contain are virtually the same.

It is time to adjust our approach, and not simply in respect of crusading history. Crusading was interpreted as an act of vengeance not so much because of its singularity in the minds of contemporaries, but because of the way it fitted into the overall worldview of western European culture at that time. Put another way, crusading was an act of vengeance because crusading resembled the mytho-historical destruction of Jerusalem by Titus and Vespasian, reminded people of the crucifixion of Christ, emphasized the bonds of Christian love and duty that bound society, and evoked contemporary ideas of justice, authority and punishment. Urban II's appeal at Clermont was unique in its combination of ideas, but the ideas themselves had deep roots. The First Crusade and subsequent expeditions were clearly recognizable and comprehensible because they made a good deal of sense in the larger cultural context.

---

[11]   Sarah Kay, *The Chansons de Geste in the Age of Romance* (Oxford, 1995).

[12]   As Brian Stock so eloquently puts it: "The historical is not isolated from the literary as fact and representation. The two aspects of experience work together: the objectivity of the events spills over into the subjectivity of the records, perceptions, feelings, and observations" (*Listening to the Text: On the Uses of the Past* (Philadelphia, 1990), p. 29).

[13]   *Historia Karoli Magni et Rotholandi*, p. 54. Aygolandus II signals his understanding of this, and states that the outcome of the battle will tell whose faith is more pleasing to God. If he is defeated, he will accept baptism (ibid., pp. 56–8). A similar conversation takes place between Roland and a "giant" pagan on p. 94. For further discussion of these episodes, see my article "Combat and Conversation: Interfaith Dialogue in Twelfth-Century Crusading Narratives," in M. Lower (ed.), *Medieval Encounters: Jewish, Christian and Muslim Culture in Confluence and Dialogue* 13:2 (Leiden, 2007), pp. 310–25.

[14]   James of Vitry, *Lettres de Jacques de Vitry*, ed. R. B. C. Huygens (Leiden, 1960), pp. 102–3.

Why, then, do we continue to study crusading apart from that larger context—or, indeed, to study the twelfth century without close attention to the crusades? It would surely be productive to integrate the study of the crusades with broader currents of activity and thinking, especially in the religious sphere. This is especially true because, over time, the idea of crusading, and of crusading as vengeance, became part of the larger cultural context, a cultural reference point that was invoked, interpreted, and altered by future generations.

Studying religious violence in the Middle Ages—and beyond

As a small step in this direction, it should be observed that the growth, over the course of the twelfth century, of the popularity of the idea of crusading as vengeance brings this book into close relation to the work of two other medievalists who have examined medieval persecution, Robert Moore and David Nirenberg. In the late 1980s, Moore challenged the assumption "that it was in some way natural or appropriate, or at any rate inevitable, that the medieval Church should seek to suppress religious dissent by force."[15] Examining the persecution of lepers, Jews, and heretics in particular, Moore argued that, through the eleventh and twelfth centuries, "persecution became habitual ... deliberate and socially sanctioned violence began to be directed, *through* established governmental, judicial and social institutions, against groups of people defined by general characteristics ... and that membership of such groups in itself came to be regarded as justifying these attacks."[16]

In the decade following the publication of Moore's monograph, Nirenberg analyzed interfaith relations and violence, using fourteenth-century Aragon as a case study. Nirenberg was concerned to dissociate the study of violent persecution from the influence of scholars who, in Nirenberg's words, promoted the view that European people "were increasingly governed by an irrational and paranoid 'collective unconscious.'"[17] Nirenberg asked that historians recognize the role of personal choice in historical contexts, emphasizing that negative discourse against minorities was only effective in the Middle Ages because individuals had

---

[15]   Robert I. Moore, *The Formation of a Persecuting Society: Power and Deviance in Western Europe, 950–1250* (Oxford, 1987), p. 2.

[16]   Ibid., p. 5. Moore felt that the ultimate roots of this rise in persecution lay in the "decisions of princes and prelates," because the minority groups that were persecuted represented the assertion of independent thought against "the subordination of religion first to seigneurial and later to bureaucratic power" (ibid., p. 146).

[17]   David Nirenberg, *Communities of Violence: Persecution of Minorities in the Middle Ages* (Princeton, 1996), p. 12.

chosen to find it so.[18] Working from George Simmel's argument that violence is in fact a form of stabilizing social association, Nirenberg argued that annual Holy Week riots in Aragon were "simultaneously a gesture of inclusion and one of seclusion."[19] Violence against Jews was, he proposed, the expression of a competing, subordinate discourse about kingship and Christian society.[20]

In broad terms, my research supports Moore's conclusion that persecution was justified through religious discourse in the twelfth century, as well as Nirenberg's assertion that religious violence functioned as ritual in the Middle Ages. In addition, this study shows that members of medieval society at all levels colluded to promote discourses of violence. The lowest orders may not have written rhetorical texts, but their support made legendary narratives like *La Venjance de Nostre Seigneur* and the *Old French Crusade Cycle* extremely popular. Because one specific aspect of that discourse was founded on Biblical texts, namely the idea of crusading as vengeance, it would seem that persecution narratives had been fundamental in Western religious culture long before those in power chose to promote religious violence actively.

It seems to me that two large works of synthesis would now be very useful for scholars. First, the work of scholars like Moore and Nirenberg (as well as many others) needs to be studied alongside crusading ideology, ideally in a broad, synthesizing work aimed at illuminating the culture of Christian violence in the Middle Ages. Scholars are necessarily limited by time, but for the most part, medieval Christian violence has been analyzed separately according to the victims— violence against Jews, violence against the Muslims, violence against heretics, and so on.[21] I suggest that medieval historians might now attempt the reconstruction of the discourse of Christian violence by an examination of the perpetrators instead, and to attempt to do so on the macro rather than the micro level.

Second, as already noted, the long twelfth century deserves a synthetic treatment on the broadest cultural level. The last century of scholarship have seen the emergence of the twelfth-century "renaissance," "reformation," "revolution,"

---

[18]   Ibid., p. 6.

[19]   Nirenberg, *Communities of Violence*, p. 15. George Simmel, *Conflict* and *The Web of Group Affiliations*, trans. K. H. Wolff and R. Bendix (Glencoe IL, 1955), p. 14. For Nirenberg, the riots that accompanied Passion plays and the Holy Week served to include the Jews in a ritual re-enactment of the history of Jewish–Christian relations, and "argued for the continued existence of Jews in Christian society, while at the same time articulating the possibility of and conditions for their destruction" (*Communities of Violence*, pp. 201–2).

[20]   Ibid., p. 68.

[21]   An obvious and inspiring exception to this statement is Dominique Iogna-Prat's magisterial work on Peter the Venerable and his rhetoric against heretics, Jews, and Muslims (*Order and Exclusion: Cluny and Christendom Face Heresy, Judaism, and Islam*, trans. G. R. Edwards (Ithaca, 2002)).

and, most recently, "crisis."[22] As it happens, the chronology of the development of the idea of crusading as vengeance coincided with a historical period of great intellectual regeneration, religious reformation, increasing Church power, shifting political structures, and increasing violent persecution. No one yet, to my knowledge, has worked to integrate the overall historiography of the twelfth century with our evolving understanding of the twelfth-century crusading movement. The field would benefit from a work on the twelfth century that brings together all the relevant subfields and aims to provide a panoramic picture of western European culture at the time.

In addition to these larger works, a number of smaller, micro-historical studies are needed. First, both the fate of the idea of crusading as vengeance after 1216, and the theme of war as vengeance for God before 1095, beg for attention. Second, a full analysis of the medieval terminology of vengeance is needed, one that answers the question of whether there was in fact any semantic distinction between *vindicta* and *ultio*. Attentive reading revealed them to be roughly equivalent and interchangeable in medieval texts, but it seems probable that a semantic field of related but slightly different medieval Latin vocabulary will emerge, one including *vindicta*, *ultio*, and *retributio*, and paralleled by similar semantic fields in the medieval vernaculars. The task then will be to reconstruct the conceptual foundations of the semantic associations.

Third, my brief discussion of *zelus* opens up the question of what other emotions medieval contemporaries associated with crusading and how those emotions related to the different strains of crusading ideology. Tangentially, it also raises the issue of what characteristic/s (in addition to being zealous) defined the "ideal crusader" in the sources, and if/how the image of the "ideal crusader" changed over time. Examining medieval perceptions of the "ideal crusader" may well help us better understand medieval perspectives on the nature and purpose of crusading, which in turn may illuminate the overall *raison d'être* of the movement.

Of course, twelfth-century crusaders saw the crusade as vengeance in some part thanks to a general human desire for violent retribution, as well as the specific historical context that surrounded them and defined their actions. Working on the problem posed by the yawning gap between terminology and constructed concepts has highlighted the important difference between that which may be universal (chiefly a desire for retribution when injured) and that which seems to be more specifically cultural—namely, how that desire for retribution is

---

[22]   Charles H. Haskins, *The Renaissance of the Twelfth Century* (Boston, 1927); Giles Constable, *The Reformation of the Twelfth Century* (Cambridge, 1996); R. I. Moore, *The First European Revolution c. 970–1215* (Oxford, 2000); Thomas N. Bisson, *The Crisis of the Twelfth Century: Power, Lordship, and the Origins of European Government* (Princeton, 2009).

channeled and restricted by a given society. Like many other societies, twelfth-century western Europe limited retributive violence by creating rules to contain it, rules that governed who was allowed to pursue retributive violence, and in what circumstances. And, again like other societies, twelfth-century western Europe tied the legitimate pursuit of retributive violence to religion, leading to acts of sacred violence.

Moving outside the realm of medieval history, then, this research potentially provides another case study for many theoretical schools concentrated on human behavior, especially the schools of thought based upon the theory of mimetic desire and religious violence argued by René Girard.[23] In Girard's theories, mimetic desire, the desire to possess the object desired by another and ultimately the being of the other itself, is at the root of human nature, drives conflict, and ultimately leads to limitless violence unless restrained by religious prohibition, ritual, and myth. For Girard, the prosecutory nature of Christianity developed from the inaccurate interpretation of the crucifixion as blood sacrifice, which embedded the need for sacred violence within Christian culture. From a Girardian perspective, the only way out of this cycle for humanity is to focus mimetic desire on God alone: "the real escape from violence is to renew the relationship of true transcendence and loving mimesis, which is the ultimate form of external mediation, of the creator who is external to all human systems and relationships, and beyond the possibility of rivalry."[24] But the substitution of *zelus* and *aemulatio* and the way in which *zelus* was portrayed both as persecution of others and as self-sacrifice in twelfth-century crusading texts suggests that even the imperative to imitate the divine can become entrapped in the cycle of violent conflict as a means to social unity and peace. Theorists following Girard might find this study of crusading ideology valuable. The same could be said for social scientists such as Scheff, Baumeister, Leary, Solomon, Greenberg, and Pyszczynski, who are attempting to formulate broad theories of violence and social relations, and their effect and reliance on culture.[25]

---

[23]   Major works by René Girard in English translation: *Violence and the Sacred*, trans. P. Gregory (Baltimore, 1979); *The Scapegoat*, trans. Y. Freccero (London, 1986); *Things Hidden since the Foundation of the World*, trans. S. Bann and M. Metteer (London, 1987).

[24]   Robert G. Hamerton-Kelly, *Sacred Violence: Paul's Hermeneutic of the Cross* (Minneapolis, 1992), p. 22.

[25]   All works by Thomas Scheff, but especially *Bloody Revenge: Emotions, Nationalism and War* (Boulder, 1994). Roy F. Baumeister and Mark R. Leary, "The Need to Belong: Desire for Interpersonal Attachments as a Fundamental Human Motivation," *Psychological Bulletin*, 117 (1995): 497–529. Mark R. Leary, "Affect, Cognition, and the Social Emotions," in J. P. Forgas (ed.), *Feeling and Thinking: The Role of Affect in Social Cognition* (Cambridge, 2000), pp. 331–56. Sheldon Solomon, Jeff Greenberg and Tom Pyszczynski, "A Terror-

The direct relationship between Christian texts and the promotion of violence against non-Christians demands theological exploration, particularly given the continued popularity of religious violence in the twenty-first century. Some Christian theologians, like Timothy Gorringe, have already showed a willingness to explore the historical propensity of Christianity for religious violence and have proposed ways to minimize that propensity, but so far (to my knowledge) Gorringe's work has not been widely disseminated or endorsed within Christian communities.[26] Muslim and Jewish theologians surely share this responsibility. The idea of violence as vengeance ordered by divine authority was clearly a powerful and popular idea in the twelfth century, based as it was upon both religious and secular conceptions of justice, moral authority and love, and I see little reason to think that it no longer feeds religious violence today.

---

management Theory of Social Behavior: The Psychological Functions of Self-esteem and Cultural Worldviews," *Advances in Experimental Social Psychology*, 24 (1991): 93–159.

[26] Timothy Gorringe, *God's Just Vengeance: Crime, Violence and the Rhetoric of Salvation* (Cambridge, 1996).

Appendix 1
Historiographical Overview

In 1945, Paul Rousset published his monograph on the ideology of crusading, *Les Origines et les Caractères de la Première Croisade*. His goal was to explain the First Crusade from the dual perspective of psychology and religious thought. Perhaps due to this focus on *mentalité*, he was among the first to write about the fact that the idea of vengeance was used to explain the First Crusade to medieval contemporaries. However, his observations were limited to noting the use of the idea of vengeance, specifically the idea of collective vengeance for God, and he did not take that aspect of his research any further.

In 1970, Ernest Blake noted that in crusading texts the Knight Templar was portrayed as a *minister Dei*, but he did not comment on the idea, or connect it with the relevant passage discussing vengeance in the New Testament Book of Romans: *minister enim Dei est, vindex in iram ei qui malum agit.*[1] In 1983, Susan Jacoby published a fascinating, if somewhat overambitious, study of the evolution of the idea of revenge within Western culture. She drew attention to the fact that violent revenge for the death of Jesus was used to justify anti-Jewish violence, and nominally connected that idea to the aftermath of the First Crusade.[2] This connection was further reinforced by Jonathan Riley-Smith's treatment of the subject in the following year.[3]

In 1986, Riley-Smith dealt with the idea of crusading as vengeance more than anyone else before him, in *The First Crusade and the Idea of Crusading* and later in a subsequent publication.[4] He argued that the crusaders viewed the events of the crusade within the pre-existing cultural framework of their world: "summoned to help their oppressed brothers and to liberate the patrimony of their father and lord, they thought, as there was always the danger that they would, in family and feudal terms and embarked upon a blood feud in which they found it hard

---

[1]   Ernest O. Blake, "The Formation of the 'Crusade Idea,'" *Journal of Ecclesiastical History*, 21 (1970), p. 27. Romans 13:4.

[2]   Susan Jacoby, *Wild Justice: The Evolution of Revenge* (New York, 1983), p. 103.

[3]   Jonathan Riley-Smith, "The First Crusade and the Persecution of the Jews," in W. J. Sheils (ed.), *Persecution and Tolerance* (Oxford, 1984), pp. 57–72.

[4]   Jonathan Riley-Smith, *The First Crusade and the Idea of Crusading* (London, 1986); and *The First Crusaders, 1095–1131* (Cambridge, 1997).

to distinguish between peoples they identified as 'enemies of Christ.'"[5] The fact that preachers of the crusade drew attention to the occupation of Jerusalem and the East by Muslims more than 400 years previous only exacerbated the potential confusion: "if they were to make good and avenge injuries to Christ which included the occupation of his land four and a half centuries before, why should they not also avenge the crucifixion, an injury to Christ's person?"[6] But, although there can be no doubt that military obligation and an honor culture contributed to the theme of crusading as vengeance, Riley-Smith did not take into account the role of Christian vengeance in the crusades, and in my opinion he distinguished too neatly between the enthusiasm for vengeance among the laity and the opinions of "responsible churchmen."[7]

In 1993, John Gilchrist tackled the crusading ideology of Pope Innocent III and its promotion of violence.[8] Gilchrist argued from the beginning that warfare in the Western tradition is at heart a "theology of war" in which true war is the war against the non-Christian.[9] Gilchrist noticed that Pope Innocent III relied heavily upon the idea of crusading as vengeance, but commented that this idea of divine vengeance stemmed from the Old Testament alone, making the same mistake as Davy.[10] Moreover, Gilchrist hesitated to comment directly on the aggregate idea of crusading as vengeance upon unbelievers, keeping separate the ideas of crusading as vengeance and crusading as war against non-Christians.

The following year, in 1997, Peter Partner published a comparative study of holy wars in Christianity and Islam.[11] Partner devoted two pages to the idea of crusading as vengeance in the Middle Ages, noting that it was a theme in both popular and learned literature of the period, and that vengeance for Christ's death was a key theme. He followed Riley-Smith in linking this ideology to the secular "blood feud."[12] Also in 1997, came the publication of another comparative monograph on holy war in Islam and Christianity, this time by James Johnson.

---

[5]   Riley-Smith, *The First Crusade and the Idea of Crusading*, p. 154.

[6]   Ibid., p. 55.

[7]   Ibid., p. 49.

[8]   John Gilchrist, "The Lord's War as the Proving Ground of Faith: Pope Innocent III and the Propagation of Violence (1198–1216)," in M. Shatzmiller (ed.), *Crusaders and Muslims in Twelfth-Century Syria* (Leiden, 1993), pp. 65–83.

[9]   Ibid., p. 66.

[10]   Marie-Madeleine Davy, "Le Theme de la Vengeance au Moyen Age," in R. Verdier (ed.), *La Vengeance: Études d'Ethnologie, d'Histoire et de Philosophie* (4 vols, Paris, 1980–84), vol. 4, pp. 125–35.

[11]   Peter Partner, *God of Battles: Holy Wars of Christianity and Islam* (London, 1997).

[12]   Ibid., pp. 81–2.

Johnson described how the medieval Christian ruler served as the *minister Dei* in holy war, finally identifying in print the crucial New Testament passage.[13]

Jean Flori published a collection of works titled *Croisade and Chevalerie* in 1998, and in doing so provided the most in-depth examination of the idea of crusading as vengeance since Riley-Smith's 1986 publication.[14] He remarked that the long-running traditions of just war and the punishment of criminals were probably interpreted by knights accustomed to lordship relations as vengeance.[15] He suggested that the idea of crusading as vengeance developed in the later Middle Ages, but also made the important point that the idea of war as vengeance for God predated the First Crusade.[16] Flori also mentioned the role of vengeance in the persecution of the Jews, describing the phenomenon as "natural," and concluded, like others before him, that the popularity of the idea of vengeance was the result of the values of a "feudal," warrior society superimposed upon medieval Christianity. The consequence of this imposition, in Flori's opinion, was the theme of Christ's vengeance against all his enemies, Jews, Muslims, and heretics alike.[17]

In 2002, Tomaz Mastnak published a monograph on how the desire for peace within Christendom led to the crusades and, ultimately, to Western political structures.[18] In the course of his book Mastnak made several key points about the idea of crusading as vengeance, but, as it was not his primary topic, he presented these points as asides. He noted that Anselm of Lucca claimed the right to persecute for the Church, and distinguished between *persecutio* and *vindicta*. Mastnak defined *vindicta* as "material coercion in general,...punishment."[19] He recognized the role of vengeance in anti-Jewish violence surrounding the crusades, but only in passing.[20] Like Flori, and Riley-Smith in part, Mastnak

---

[13]   James T. Johnson, *The Holy War Idea in Western and Islamic Traditions* (University Park PA, 1997), p. 54. Romans 13:4.

[14]   Jean Flori, *Croisade and Chevalerie* (Brussels, 1998).

[15]   Ibid., p. 188.

[16]   Ibid., p. 189.

[17]   Ibid., p. 234.

[18]   Tomaz Mastnak, *Crusading Peace: Christendom, the Muslim World, and Western Political Order* (Berkeley, 2002). M. Gluckman in *Swazi Nation* demonstrated that conflict on one level of society can foster cohesion and stability at other levels, suggesting that a desire for peace and social cohesion leading to violent conflict is not limited to the history of Western societies. For reference and further discussion see Bruce Lincoln, *Discourse and the Construction of Society: Comparative Studies of Myth, Ritual and Classification* (Oxford, 1989), p. 71.

[19]   Mastnak, *Crusading Peace*, p. 30.

[20]   Ibid., pp. 39 and 60.

argued that crusading as vengeance was popular because it was interpreted as a familial "blood feud" and as Christian vassals doing their duty for God.[21]

In 2003, John Cowdrey noted the important fact that Augustine of Hippo himself, although he lacked a cohesive and systematic definition of what constituted a just war, on one occasion defined *iusta bella* as "those that avenged injuries, that is, unlawful acts."[22] Cowdrey then noted that Gratian referred to this Augustinian vision of just war in the mid-twelfth century.[23] William of Tyre's reliance on the idea of crusading as vengeance caught Cowdrey's eye, and he concluded that the archbishop of Tyre must have gotten the idea from a close reading of Gratian.[24] While it would be hard to say that this was not true, Cowdrey was apparently unaware of the corpus of twelfth-century crusading sources that also expressed the idea of crusading as vengeance, some before Gratian was writing.

Most recently, Phillipe Buc and I have looked at the idea of crusading as vengeance.[25] My initial article outlined the evidence for the growing importance of the idea of crusading as vengeance in the twelfth century. Buc has worked from an exegetical perspective, and has suggested links between the medieval theology of vengeance and the First Crusade. He connects apocalyptic Christianity, with its focus on the Last Judgement, with the eschatology of the First Crusade. Moreover, he examines the legendary antecedents of vengeful crusading, Titus and Vespasian's destruction of Jerusalem, and the struggles of the Maccabees. Many of Buc's arguments are accurate and insightful, and his work provides a long overdue and much needed clarification of the relationship between

---

[21]   Flori, *Croisade et Chevalerie*, pp. 188–9. Riley-Smith, *The First Crusaders*, p. 41. Mastnak, *Crusading Peace*, p. 122.

[22]   Augustine of Hippo, *Quaestionum in Heptateuchum liber* 6.10 (cited and translated by H. E. J. Cowdrey, "Christianity and the Morality of Warfare during the First Century of Crusading," in M. Bull and N. Housley (eds), *The Experience of Crusading 1: Western Approaches* (Cambridge, 2003), p. 177).

[23]   Cowdrey, "Christianity and the Morality of Warfare," p. 186.

[24]   Ibid., pp. 187–8.

[25]   Susanna Throop, "Vengeance and the Crusades," *Crusades*, 5 (2006): 21–38; and Phillipe Buc, "La Vengeance de Dieu: De l'Exégèse Patristique à la Réforme Ecclésiastique et à la Première Croisade," in D. Barthélemy, F. Bougard, and R. Le Jan (eds), *La Vengeance 400–1200* (Rome, 2006), pp. 451–86. Buc has published more recently on broad themes related to Christian violence and vengeance: "Some Thoughts on the Christian Theology of Violence, Medieval and Modern, from the Middle Ages to the French Revolution," *Rivista di storia del cristianesimo*, 5:1 (2008), 9–28; "Exégèse et violence dans la tradition occidentale," *Annali di Storia moderna e contemporanea* 16 (2010), 131–44; "Martyrdom in the West: Vengeance, Purge, Salvation, and History," in N. H. Petersen, A. B'cker, and E. Oestrem (eds), *Resonances: Historical Essays on Continuity and Change* (Turnhout, 2011), 21–56.

Christian sacred texts and the concept of vengeance. As I note throughout this book, his work is a significant addition to crusade historiography, but the field still lacks a broad survey of the idea of crusading as an act of vengeance.

Appendix 2
Resumé of the Sources

Sources for 1095–1137

For the period from 1095 until 1137 I have utilized eleven Latin histories of the First Crusade, as well as Heinrich Hagenmeyer's edition of First Crusade letters, the so-called Encyclical of Sergius IV, and one Hebrew account in translation (the *Mainz Anonymous*).

The eleven Latin histories divide into the five eyewitness accounts of Peter Tudebode, Fulcher of Chartres, Raymond of Aguilers, Ekkehard of Aura, and the anonymous *Gesta Francorum*; and the six non-participant histories of Albert of Aachen, Baldric of Bourgueil, Guibert of Nogent, Robert of Rheims, Ralph of Caen, and Orderic Vitalis.

The *Gesta Francorum* was composed by an unknown crusader before 1104, and the compositions of Peter Tudebode and Raymond of Aguilers both drew upon the *Gesta Francorum* and were completed between 1104 and 1111. As chaplain of Raymond of St. Gilles, a prominent crusader, Raymond of Aguilers was closely tied to the expedition, and it is thought that Peter Tudebode was also an eyewitness. Fulcher of Chartres, a cleric present at the Council of Clermont in 1095, eventually joined the party of Baldwin of Boulougne in the East and thus did not go to Antioch and Jerusalem himself. He also composed the first part of his account of the crusade between 1104 and 1111, and a later section before 1128. The First Crusade letters, written by the leaders of the First Crusade, Pope Urban II, and Pope Paschal II, date from 1095 to 1101. As Chapter Two demonstrates, there was only a limited amount of material promoting the idea of crusading as vengeance in the letters and eyewitness accounts.[1]

The three monastic accounts of Robert of Rheims, Guibert of Nogent, and Baldric of Bourgueil were composed between 1107 and 1108. Albert of Aachen's history is now believed to have been written in two parts, the first section (which dealt with the First Crusade) sometime in the very early years of the twelfth century, and the second section after 1119, and possibly before 1130.[2] Ralph of Caen composed his tribute to his lord Tancred's actions on the

---

[1] See above pages 44–9.

[2] Albert of Aachen, *Historia Ierosolimitana*, ed. Susan Edgington (Oxford, 2007), pp. xxiv–xxv. See also Susan Edgington, "Albert of Aachen and the *Chansons de Geste*," in

First Crusade between 1108 and 1118, possibly in Antioch after Ralph himself participated in the crusade of 1108. Ekkehard of Aura, who was briefly in the East in 1101, set down his account between 1102 and 1106. Orderic Vitalis may have begun writing his ecclesiastical history as early as 1114, but the bulk of his history (including the section on the First Crusade) was composed between 1123 and 1137.[3] Ekkehard of Aura and Ralph of Caen emphasized the idea of crusading as vengeance only slightly more than the eyewitness accounts, but the idea was clearly set forth in the accounts of Robert of Rheims, Guibert of Nogent, Baldric of Bourgueil, and Albert of Aachen, though still relatively less than in later twelfth-century texts.[4]

The Hebrew *Mainz Anonymous* was probably written by a single author contemporaneously with the First Crusade, in approximately 1096/97.[5] It must be acknowledged that translations are always problematic, especially when the topic of research has been so limited to specific vocabulary, but Hebrew texts do not form the backbone of my argument. The Hebrew terms that were translated by Eidelberg as "vengeance" in all of the Hebrew sources seem to be closely related to the root *nâqam*, traditionally translated from the Hebrew as "vengeance."[6] Like the First Crusade histories written by non-participants, the *Mainz Anonymous* contained the idea of crusading as vengeance to a certain degree; again, relatively less so than in later twelfth-century Hebrew texts.[7]

The so-called Encyclical of Sergius IV has been the object of scrutiny and debate for more than a century now. Some historians have argued for the

---

J. France and W. G. Zajac (eds), *The Crusades and Their Sources* (Aldershot, 1998), pp. 23–38.

[3]   Orderic Vitalis, *The Historia Aecclesiastica of Orderic Vitalis*, ed. Marjorie Chibnall (6 vols, Oxford, 1969–80), vol. 1, p. 32.

[4]   See above pages 49–52.

[5]   *Hebräische Berichte über die Judenverfolgungen während des Ersten Kreuzzügs*, ed. Ever Haverkamp, MGHHT 1 (Hanover, 2005), p. 231. See also Anna Sapir Abulafia, "The Interrelationship between the Hebrew Chronicles on the First Crusade," in A. S. Abulafia (ed.), *Christians and Jews in Dispute* (Aldershot, 1998), p. 238. Robert Chazan concurs with Abulafia on the dating of the *Mainz Anonymous* (*God, Humanity, and History: The Hebrew First Crusade Narratives* (London, 2000)). Chazan also posits that part of the *Solomon bar Simson Chronicle*, which he deems the "Trier unit," was also written contemporaneously with the First Crusade. I am not completely convinced by his argument, but, in any case, the section Chazan calls the "Trier unit" contains no references to vengeance.

[6]   I am very grateful to Miri Rubin for her help comparing the English translations of the Hebrew sources with the edited Hebrew texts. For the translations, see Shlomo Eidelberg, *The Jews and the Crusaders* (Madison WI, 1977). For the edited Hebrew texts, see *Hebräische Berichte*.

[7]   For more on these later texts, see below page 199.

authenticity of the document, whilst others have posited a dating in the late eleventh or early twelfth century.[8] One scholar has even declared that the Encylical must date from the late twelfth century due to its apparent ideological link with the papal propaganda of Pope Innocent III.[9] In my opinion, Hans Schaller's argument relied overmuch on incorporating the Encyclical within an earlier tradition of pious pilgrimage and underplaying links between the Encyclical and the ideology of Pope Urban II.[10] To date, Alexander Gieszytor's arguments remain the most in-depth and convincing, drawing upon a wealth of material and textual evidence to conclude that the Encyclical most likely dates from the late eleventh or early twelfth centuries. His argument for tracing the document to Pope Urban II's visit to the Abbey of Moissac in 1095 is much less convincing, but that does not alter the validity of his core argument. The Encyclical strongly emphasized the idea of crusading as vengeance, contrasting with the remainder of the sources for the period and suggesting that further research on the Encylical is needed. Strictly speaking, according to my own criteria the Encyclical was a non-participant text since presumably its monastic author did not go on the First Crusade. However, it was composed before the expedition, suggesting it would be most appropriately grouped alongside the letters and eyewitness accounts.

Sources for 1138–97

For the period from 1138 to 1197 I have looked at fifteen Latin narrative accounts; a variety of other Latin sources including letters, theological tracts, the correspondence of Popes Eugenius III, Hadrian IV, Alexander III, Gregory VIII and Celestine III; three Hebrew accounts in translation; and a number of vernacular crusading songs and epics.

As the major preacher of the Second Crusade, the works of Bernard of Clairvaux were exceptionally pertinent to this section of my research, and I have examined all of his letters, as well as his advice to Pope Eugenius III in *De Consideratione* and his well-known epistle to the Knights Templar, the *Liber*

---

[8]   The former position argued by Hans M. Schaller, "Zur Kreuzzugsenzyklika Papst Sergius' IV," in H. Mordek (ed.), *Papsttum, Kirche und Recht im Mittelalter* (Tübingen, 1991), pp. 135–53; the latter position most recently by Alexander Gieysztor, "The Genesis of the Crusades: The Encyclical of Sergius IV (1009–1012)," *Medievalia et Humanistica*, 5 (1948): 3–23; and 6 (1948): 3–34.

[9]   U. Schwerin, *Die Aufrufe der Päpste zur Befreiung des Heiligen Landes von den Anfangen bis zum Ausgang Innocenz III* (cited by Gieysztor, "The Genesis of the Crusades," vol. 5, p. 8).

[10]   Schaller, "Zur Kreuzzugsenzyklika Papst Sergius' IV," pp. 148–9.

ad Milites Templi de Laude Novae Militiae. Bernard was a contemporary of Peter the Venerable, who was Abbot of Cluny from 1122 until his death in 1156. Peter corresponded with Bernard, which fact alone might make his letters of interest, but he also travelled to Spain in 1142 and subsequently wrote his *Summa Totius Haeresis Saracenorum* and *Liber Contra Sectam sive Haeresim Sarracenos*, and corresponded with King Louis VII about the treatment of Jews in France during the preparations for the Second Crusade. Both Bernard of Clairvaux and Peter the Venerable promoted the idea of crusading as vengeance.

Several narrative accounts written during the period also strongly emphasized the idea of crusading as vengeance, in particular the *De Expugnatione Lyxbonensi*, written by a Frankish priest named Raol who accompanied the Anglo-Norman contingent that took the city of Lisbon and composed his account shortly thereafter in 1147, and the *Gesta Stephani Regis Anglorum*, believed to have been written in two stages, beginning in 1148, by a secular cleric.[11]

William of Tyre relied on the idea of crusading as vengeance in his *Chronicon*, which was composed between 1170 and 1184, when he wrote the preface to the entire work.[12] Having been born in Jerusalem and studied in Europe, William was Archbishop of Tyre from 1175 and was close to King Amaury of Jerusalem until the latter's death in 1174 and subsequently to his heir, Baldwin IV of Jerusalem.[13] This put him in a unique position to record and comment on events almost up to the disastrous battle of Hattin in 1187. William of Tyre's sources for the period around the First Crusade included the accounts of Albert of Aachen, Raymond of Aguilers, Fulcher of Chartres, Baldric of Bourgueil, and the *Gesta Francorum*, making his history interesting from a comparative point of view. The smaller, anonymous *De Expugnatione Civitatis Acconensis*, which included the ideology of crusading as vengeance to a lesser degree, was authored later.

Additional narratives indirectly linked to the crusading movement also relied upon the idea of vengeance. Gervase of Canterbury, a monk of Christ Church, Canterbury, from 1163 to 1210, included the idea in his *Chronica*, which was written from approximately 1185 onwards.[14] Similarly, Gerald of Wales, archdeacon of Brecknock from 1175 and a favorite of King Henry II of England, accompanied Archbishop Baldwin of Canterbury while he preached the Third

---

[11]   Harold Livermore, "The 'Conquest of Lisbon' and its Author," *Portuguese Studies*, 6 (1990), p. 6; Antonia Gransden, *Historical Writing in England c. 550 to c. 1307* (London, 1974), p. 186.

[12]   Peter W. Edbury and John G. Rowe, *William of Tyre: Historian of the Latin East* (Cambridge, 1988), p. 26.

[13]   Ibid., pp. 15–22.

[14]   Gransden, *Historical Writing in England*, pp. 253 and 247.

Crusade in Wales, and wrote his *Itinerarium Kambriae* between 1188 and 1192.[15] Peter of Blois, a man strongly committed to religious reform and twelfth-century spirituality, wrote the *Passio Raginaldi*, a hagiographical account of the death of Reynald of Châtillon, in 1187 while at the papal court in Rome.[16] He composed a second work related to the crusades, the *Conquestio de Dilatione Vie Ierosolimitane*, between 1188 and 1189 and revised the text between 1190 and 1191.[17] Both of these works employed the concept of vengeance to explain crusading.

Chronicles of the deeds of kings were also a fertile group of sources for the idea of crusading as an act of vengeance at the end of the twelfth century. Richard of Devizes, a monk of St. Swithun's at Winchester, wrote his highly satirical *Cronicon de Tempore Regis Richardi Primi* between roughly 1192 and 1198.[18] The second redaction of Rigord's well-known *Gesta Philippi Augusti* was arguably completed by 1206, in order to be presented to Prince Louis (the future Louis VIII) in 1207.[19] Roger of Howden, clerk to King Henry II of England, wrote his *Chronica* between 1148 and 1201. He then used the *Chronica* to rewrite the crusading portions of the earlier *Gesta Regis Henrici Secundi* (previously attributed to Benedict of Peterborough) in or shortly after 1190.[20]

Equally inclusive of the idea of crusading as vengeance were the Old French crusading songs *Chevalier, mult estes guariz* and *Pour lou pueple rescon forteir* and the Occitan poems dating from 1130 to 1149 by the author known as Marcabru.[21] I have also looked at five vernacular crusading narratives. The first two have been used frequently by crusade historians in the past. The late twelfth- and early thirteenth-century text published in 1871 as the *Chronique d'Ernoul et de Bernard le Trésorier*, commonly known as "Ernoul," is in fact a collection of sources, rather than one source.[22] *L'estoire de la guerre sainte* was written by the Norman "Ambroise" between 1194 and 1199, after the return of King Richard

---

[15]   Ibid., pp. 242–5.

[16]   Michael Markowski, "Peter of Blois and the Conception of the Third Crusade," in Benjamin Z. Kedar (ed.), *The Horns of Hattin* (Jerusalem, 1992), p. 263.

[17]   Ibid., p. 265.

[18]   Gransden, *Historical Writing in England*, p. 247.

[19]   *Rigord : Histoire de Philippe Auguste*, ed. Élisabeth Carpentier, Georges Pon, and Yves Chauvin (Paris, 2006), p. 67.

[20]   David Corner, "The *Gesta Regis Henrici Secundi* and *Chronica* of Roger, parson of Howden," *Bulletin of the Institute of Historical Research*, 56 (1983): 126–44. Gransden, *Historical Writing in England*, p. 222.

[21]   *Les Chansons de Croisade*, ed. Joseph Bédier and P. Aubry (Paris, 1909), pp. 5 and 78–9. Marcabru, *Marcabru: A Critical Edition*, ed. Simon Gaunt, Ruth Harvey, and Linda Paterson (Cambridge, 2000), pp. 2–5.

[22]   Margaret R. Morgan, *The Chronicle of Ernoul and the Continuations of William of Tyre* (Oxford, 1973).

I's Third Crusade army.[23] Both texts make some reference to the idea of crusading as vengeance.

There is less of a precedent for my use of the remaining four vernacular texts as historical sources. Although historians have recognized the validity of two out of the three founding epics of the *Old French Crusade Cycle*, the *Chanson de Jérusalem* has traditionally been accorded less worth as a historical source and has been deemed more appropriate for literary studies than for historical analysis. But, given that this study is concerned with investigating ideology and culture, these sources are all very appropriate, since they express ideas about the crusades that were current in the twelfth and thirteenth centuries.

The original trilogy of the *Old French Crusade Cycle* comprised *La Chanson d'Antioche*, *La Chanson de Jérusalem*, and *Les Chétifs*. Although the poems were probably composed orally and independent of each other, they first appeared together in manuscript form circa 1180, having been purportedly redacted by an author known only as "Graindor of Douai." Like the Encyclical of Sergius IV, they have been the subject of debate for many years, as scholars have tried to pinpoint dates of origin and authorship for various poems and parts of poems. In 1962 and 1976, Suzanne Duparc-Quioc argued that the material contained within the *Chanson d'Antioche* could be divided into "original" material from "Richard the Pilgrim" that dated from the beginning of the twelfth century, and material added by "Graindor of Douai" in 1180.[24]

In 1980, Robert Cook intelligently challenged this view, arguing that there was no evidence for the existence of "Richard the Pilgrim," and that "Graindor of Douai" was likewise a name commonly used in the period to lend credibility to *chansons*.[25] For Cook, the search for "Richard" and "Graindor" and the attempt to distinguish between "original" and "secondary" material was a wild goose chase that could never be proved and in fact added little to the historical value of the account. Susan Edgington has pointed out more recently that Cook failed to address the relationship between the account of Albert of Aachen and the *Chanson*, and supported Duparc-Quioc's arguments on the basis that, since Albert of Aachen's account contained more detail than the *Chanson*, the *Chanson* must have served as its source, rather than vice versa. She also noted that *Les Chétifs* and the *Chanson de Jérusalem* do not contain material from

---

[23]   Ambroise, *The History of the Holy War: Ambroise's Estoire de la Guerre Sainte*, ed. Marianne Ailes and Malcolm Barber (2 vols, Woodbridge, 2003), vol. 2, pp. 2–3.

[24]   Suzanne Duparc-Quioc, "La Composition de la Chanson d'Antioche," *Romania*, 83 (1962): 1–29 and 210–47; and Suzanne Duparc-Quioc (ed.), *La Chanson d'Antioche: Étude Critique*, in DHC 11 (2 vols, Paris, 1976–78).

[25]   Robert F. Cook, *"Chanson d'Antioche," Chanson de Geste: Le Cycle de la Croisade est-il Épique?* (Amsterdam, 1980).

Albert of Aachen's account, a surprising fact in her mind if Graindor of Douai was drawing upon it for inspiration.[26] Of course, these arguments are only valid if one accepts that a more detailed text must have been composed later than one with less detail, and believes in the existence of an actual historical person who reworked all three epics.

Following Cook, I accept that speculation on earlier origins of the poems is simply that: speculation. The earliest extant texts of these works date from the very late twelfth and early thirteenth centuries, and as such are creatures of that era, despite the correct assumption that related oral compositions predated the written epics.[27] But while Cook discounted the Crusade Cycle as historical sources because they were not reliably factual and were written *post factum*, the very fact that these epics "reflètent des préoccupations, manifestent des tendences qui sont celles de la vie de saint, de la chanson de geste, du roman, en somme, de la littérature narrative à la date de leur elaboration" makes them invaluable sources for the historian of culture.[28] The *Chanson d'Antioche* and the *Chanson de Jérusalem* heavily relied on the idea of crusading as vengeance, although *Les Chétifs* did not.

Three Hebrew sources (read in translation) also strongly emphasized the idea of crusading as vengeance. The *Eliezer bar Nathan Chronicle* included not only historical material but also four poetic lamentations over the Jewish deaths, and dates to before 1146. The *Solomon bar Simson Chronicle* was a compilation of reports of Jewish persecution before the First Crusade, including the *Mainz Anonymous*, and has been dated to 1140.[29] The *Sefir Zekhirah*, or Book of Remembrance, of Rabbi Ephraim of Bonn recounted the persecution of the Jews on the eve of the Second Crusade. It is unclear whether this account was written before or after the mid-1170s, but since Rabbi Ephraim was alive and present during one of the Second Crusade persecutions, his account was that of a limited eyewitness; he may have personally witnessed one episode of violence, but it is physically impossible for him to have witnessed all of them.[30]

A few crusading texts from the period did not explicitly refer to the ideology of crusading as vengeance. Henry, Archdeacon of Huntingdon, composed the very popular *Historia Anglorum* between roughly 1133 and 1154 at the

---

[26] Edgington, "Albert of Aachen and the *Chansons de Geste*."

[27] For a different viewpoint, arguing against Cook's dismissal of hypothetical (and now non-existent) textual antecedents, see Susan Edgington, "The First Crusade: Reviewing the Evidence," in J. Phillips (ed.), *The First Crusade: Origins and Impact* (Manchester, 1997), pp. 55–77.

[28] Cook, "*Chanson d'Antioche*," pp. 9 and 11–12.

[29] *Hebräische Berichte*, p. 231.

[30] Eidelberg, *The Jews and the Crusaders*, pp. 117–18.

request of Alexander of Blois; this included a description of the First and Second Crusades.[31] Around the same time Helmold, Deacon of Bosau began the *Chronica Slavorum*, covering the period from the conversion of the Saxons through the mid-twelfth century; this work was later used by Arnold of Lübeck.[32] These two texts did not highlight the idea of crusading as vengeance. Likewise, Caffaro of Caschifelone, a patrician who not only was involved in the military and politics of Genoa, but was also in the Latin East for some period of time, did not refer to crusading as vengeance in his account of the First Crusade, *De Liberatione Civitatium Orientis*, written in the mid-1150s, probably circa 1155.[33] Neither did portions of the *Gesta Abbatum Lobbiensium*, the *Annales* of Vincent of Prague and the *Annales Herbipolenses*.

The accounts of the Second Crusade written by Odo of Deuil and Otto of Freising also did not emphasize the ideology. Odo of Deuil, a monk of St. Denis who went on to become abbot in 1152, accompanied King Louis VII of France on the Second Crusade as his chaplain. Sometime before his death in 1162, almost certainly while on the march between 1145 and 1148, Odo recorded the first portion of the Second Crusade in the form of a letter to Abbot Suger of St. Denis, *De Profectione Ludovici VII in Orientem*.[34] Otto, Bishop of Freising, accompanied his nephew Frederick Hohenstaufen on the Second Crusade and included the disastrous events of that expedition in his *Gesta Frederici seu rectius Cronica* before his death in 1158. Otto of Freising also wrote a monumental history of the world, *Chronica sive Historia de Duabus Divitatibus*. Following in the tradition of Augustine and Orosius, and written before 1152, the *Chronica sive Historia* interpreted human existence from a Christian perspective.[35] Both Otto of Freising and Odo of Deuil were most concerned with explaining the outcome of the Second Crusade, rather than its origins and motivations, and both emphasized that its failure was God's vengeance upon the Christians *peccatis exigentibus hominum*.

---

[31]   Gransden, *Historical Writing in England*, pp. 187 and 194.

[32]   Helmold of Bosau, *Chronica Slavorum*, ed. H. Stoob AQDGM 19 (Berlin, 1963), p. 17. More on Arnold of Lübeck in the following section.

[33]   Richard D. Face, "Secular History in Twelfth-Century Italy: Caffaro of Genoa," *Journal of Medieval History*, 6 (1980), p. 172.

[34]   Odo of Deuil, *De Profectione Ludovici VII in Orientem*, ed. Virginia G. Berry (New York, 1948), pp. xiv–xvi. Jonathan Phillips, "Odo of Deuil's *De Profectione Ludovici VII in Orientem* as a Source for the Second Crusade," in M. Bull and N. Housley (eds), *The Experience of Crusading 1: Western Approaches* (Cambridge, 2003), p. 80.

[35]   Charles C. Mierow and Richard Emery (eds), *The Deeds of Frederick Barbarossa* (New York, 1953), p. 5.

Moreover, although the correspondence of Bernard of Clairvaux and Peter the Venerable referred to the idea, other correspondence from the period did not. Suger of St. Denis, Abbot from 1122–51 and Regent of France during the Second Crusade from 1147 to 1149, who corresponded with King Louis VII while Louis was on the crusade, did not focus on the idea of crusading as vengeance, nor on crusading ideology in general, but rather on the affairs of the realm.[36] Likewise, although Pope Eugenius III was Bernard of Clairvaux's former pupil, he did not discuss crusading as vengeance, even in his Second Crusade bull, *Quantum praedecessores*. Neither did three of the four popes who followed him—Hadrian IV, Alexander III, and Gregory VIII.[37]

Sources for 1198–1216

Above all, the letters of Innocent himself (or, at least, the letters issued by his curia) promoted the idea of crusading as vengeance. These letters repeatedly described the Fourth Crusade, the crusades against the Cathars, and the proposed Fifth Crusade as acts of vengeance.

Some texts from the period used the idea of crusading as vengeance to describe crusades from earlier in the twelfth century. I employed the Occitan *Canso d'Antioca*, believed to have been reworked in the late twelfth century and appearing in manuscript form in the early thirteenth century, as a counterpoint to the Old French *Chanson d'Antioche*.[38] The *Canso d'Antioca* did refer to the First Crusade as vengeance, but nowhere nearly as frequently as did the *Chanson d'Antioche*. Many writers of historical narratives described the Third Crusade as vengeance, including Arnold, Abbot of St. John's of Lübeck, who drew upon Helmold of Bosau when composing his *Chronica* before his death in 1212.[39] Similarly, the *Itinerarium Peregrinorum et Gesta Regis Ricardi*, apparently a Latin

---

[36]   Lindy Grant, *Abbot Suger of St-Denis: Church and State in Early Twelfth-Century France* (Harlow, 1998), pp. 156–78.

[37]   Eugenius III, *Epistolae*, in *RHGF* 15 (Paris, 1878). Eugenius III, *Epistolae*, ed. J.-P. Migne, *PL* 180 (Paris, 1855). Alexander III, *Epistolae*, ed. J.-P. Migne, *PL* 200 (Paris, 1855). Hadrian IV, *Epistolae*, ed. J.-P. Migne, *PL* 188 (Paris, 1890). Gregory VIII, *Epistolae*, ed. J.-P. Migne, PL 202 (Paris, 1855). It is interesting to note, however, that the Byzantine emperor Manuel I did refer to the idea of crusading as vengeance in one letter to Pope Eugenius III in 1146. Manuel wrote in Greek, of course, but his letter was promptly translated into Latin by the papal curia (Manuel I, *Epistolae*, RHGF 15 (Paris, 1878), p. 440).

[38]   *Canso d'Antioca: An Occitan Epic Chronicle of the First Crusade*, ed. Carol Sweetenham and Linda M. Paterson (Aldershot, 2003), pp. 48–9.

[39]   Johannes Schilling (ed.), *Arnold von Lübek: Gesta Gregorii Peccatoris* (Göttingen, 1986).

reworking of the vernacular *Estoire de la guerre sainte*, was compiled by Richard, an Augustinian canon in London, between 1216 and 1222.[40] Also in this group of sources that emphasized the ideology were the texts ascribed to Robert of Auxerre (d. 1212); Otto of St. Blasien (d. 1223), who followed in the footsteps of Otto of Freising until 1209 in the *Chronici ab Ottone Frisingensi Episcopo*; Ralph, Abbot of the Cistercian abbey of Coggeshall from 1207 to 1218, who left us his original copy of his *Chronicon Anglicanum*; and the anonymous English writer of the Third Crusade account *De Expugnatione Terrae Sanctae per Saladinum*.[41]

When it came to the Fourth Crusade, some writers, such as Gunther of Pairis, a Cistercian monk who wrote an account circa 1205 based on the reminiscences of his abbot who was on the Crusade, ascribed to the Fourth Crusaders the initial desire to take vengeance and also described the eventual sack of Constantinople as vengeance.[42] Robert of Clari, a poor Picard knight, likewise applied the idea of vengeance to both the initial motivations of the fourth crusaders and the sack of Constantinople. Geoffrey of Villehardouin, Marshal of Champagne, distinguished between the initial motivation of crusaders and the events of 1204, deeming that the former included the desire to avenge God and that the latter reflected the desire to avenge Christian allies and themselves.

Conon of Béthune, a man associated with the longtime crusading family of Artois that participated in both the Third and Fourth Crusades, used the idea of crusading as vengeance in two of his songs. But Raimbaut of Vaqueiras, who was in the household of the crusader Boniface I of Montferrat, did not refer to the idea of crusading as vengeance in his poetry. Robert of Auxerre, who confidently described the Third Crusade as vengeance, visibly declined to do so for the Fourth Crusade. And three other accounts of the Fourth Crusade did not refer to the Fourth Crusade as vengeance: the *Gesta* written by the so-called Anonymous of Halberstadt, based on the experiences of Bishop Conrad of Halberstadt; the *Devastatio Constantinopolitana*, an anonymous source probably written by a low-ranking cleric from the German Rhineland; and the text known as the "Anonymous of Soissons," most likely the work of a canon of Soissons cathedral, based on the experiences of Nevelon of Chérisy, Bshop of Soissons and chief prelate in the army.[43]

Many accounts of the crusades against the Cathars date to much later in the thirteenth century, and thus have not been used for this project. But two accounts

---

[40]　　Gransden, *Historical Writing in England*, p. 240.

[41]　　Ibid., p. 323. Ambroise, *History of the Holy War*, vol. 2, p. 17.

[42]　　Alfred J. Andrea, "Essay on Primary Sources," in D. E. Queller and T. F. Madden (eds), *The Fourth Crusade: The Conquest of Constantinople* (2nd edn, Philadelphia, 1997), p. 304.

[43]　　Andrea, "Essay on Primary Sources," pp. 306, 303 and 307.

that were contemporary show, again, differing uses of the ideology of crusading as vengeance. Peter of Les Vaux-de-Cernay's *Hystoria Albigensis*, an account written in early 1213 for Pope Innocent III, was awash with references to crusading as vengeance for both human deaths (like that of the papal legate Peter Castelnau) and injuries done to Christ. On the other hand, although the early portion of *La Chanson de la Croisade Albigeoise*, written between 1210 and 1213, implied that the death of the papal legate was followed up by violent retribution from the Church, it did not state this explicitly with the vocabulary of vengeance.

James of Vitry, Bishop of Acre from 1216, enthusiastically preached for both the crusades against the Cathars and the Fifth Crusade, and many of the letters and *exempla* from his early career are readily available.[44] But, although on many occasions he described humans taking vengeance (both authorized and therefore just, and the opposite), and although he depicted divine vengeance unleashed on the sinful, he only once and briefly described crusading as an act of vengeance. Thus the sources for the early thirteenth century are polarized between the rhetoric of Pope Innocent III, Peter of Les Vaux-de-Cernay, and some Latin historians on the one hand, and the works of others like James of Vitry and the Anonymous of Soissons on the other.

Two vernacular epics related to crusading were also useful sources for early thirteenth-century crusading ideology, and both incorporated the idea of crusading as vengeance. The origins of the popular Christian legend that the Roman destruction of Jerusalem in 70 C.E. was vengeance for the crucifixion lay in the fourth-century translation of Josephus, the *De Excidio Urbis Hierosolymitanae* of Hegesippus.[45] The legend continued to grow and was used in the preaching tradition of popes such as Gregory the Great, evolving into legendary narratives, often titled the *Vindicta Salvatoris*, as early as 700.[46] By the end of the twelfth century these narratives were appearing in a variety of written forms, even including a Germanic two-part romance entitled "Veronica and Vespasian." In the fourteenth and fifteenth centuries the legend was popularized in a number of medieval plays that survive in at least six different languages—only the dramatization of the Passion of Christ was performed more frequently.[47]

---

[44] James of Vitry, *Lettres de Jacques de Vitry*, ed. R. B. C. Huygens (Leiden, 1960). James of Vitry, *The Exempla*, ed. T. F. Crane (London, 1890). I also examined some of his edited sermons, to see if perhaps the ideology surfaced in his writings from later in life, but with very limited success; see above p. 119 (James of Vitry, *Sermones*, in C. T. Maier (ed.), *Crusade Propaganda and Ideology* (Cambridge, 2000)).

[45] Stephen K. Wright, *The Vengeance of our Lord: Medieval Dramatizations of the Destruction of Jerusalem* (Toronto, 1989), p. 21.

[46] Ibid., pp. 23–9.

[47] Ibid., p. 1.

The Roman destruction of Jerusalem, and the notion that Christ prophesied the city's destruction on the cross, featured in crusading texts from the very beginning of the twelfth century onwards.[48] Often parallels were drawn in these sources between various crusades and the actions of the Romans, and I have found evidence of almost identical plot points and phrases in the oldest version of the *Venjance de Nostre Seigneur* and the *Chanson d'Antioche*.[49] The evolving legendary tradition of the *Venjance* was closely linked in medieval minds with the crusading movement, and as such the earliest textual version, dated to roughly 1200, has proved a highly useful source.[50]

Equally useful was the text commonly known as the "Pseudo-Turpin," the *Historia Karoli Magni et Rotholandi*. Although it is believed that this narrative, written as though from the perspective of Archbishop Turpin, was originally composed in the first half of the twelfth century, it was first written down circa 1200, placing it within this period.[51] It was a text concerned with influencing lay morality, and with its frequent emphasis on taking vengeance and converting the Muslims it is highly relevant for this discussion.[52]

Ideally, for this period I would also have read the *Rolandslied*, the *Millstätter Exodus*, and a number of additional *chansons de geste*, such as *La Chanson d'Aspremont*. Time, and in the case of the Old German texts ignorance of the language, prevented me.

---

[48]   Albert of Aachen, *Historia Ierosolimitana*, p. 432. Baldric of Bourgueil, *Historia Jerosolimitana*, in *RHCOc.* 4 (Paris, 1879), p. 11. Saewulf, "A Reliable Account of the Situation of Jerusalem," in J. Wilkinson (ed.), *Jerusalem Pilgrimage 1099–1185* (London, 1988), p. 101. Otto of Freising, *Chronica sive Historia de Duabus Divitatibus*, ed. A. Schmidt, *AQDGM* 16 (Darmstadt, 1961), pp. 248–50. *La Chanson d'Antioche*, ed. J. Nelson, OFCC 4 (Tuscaloosa, 2003), pp. 53–5. Arnold of Lübeck, *Chronica*, in *MGHSS* 21 (Hanover, 1869), p. 164.

[49]   Compare lines 138 and 1231 of *La Venjance de Nostre Seigneur*, in L. A. T. Gryting (ed.), *The Oldest Version of the Twelfth-Century Poem La Venjance Nostre Seigneur* (Ann Arbor, 1952) and lines 4422 and 37 of *La Chanson d'Antioche*. Both poems deal with vengeance being taken for the death of Christ and the seizure of Jerusalem; in both cases the city in question is besieged, there is widespread starvation, and the city is betrayed by a traitor inside the gates.

[50]   There are many later versions readily available, but due to the chronological limits of this project I have not incorporated that textual evidence. See *La Venjance Nostre-Seigneur: the Old and Middle French Prose Versions*, ed. Alvin E. Ford (2 vols, Toronto, 1984–93).

[51]   Paul G. Schmidt (ed.), *Karollelus atque Pseudo-Turpini Historia Karoli Magni et Rotholandi* (Stuttgart, 1996), pp. v–vi.

[52]   For an example of the moralizing tendencies of the text, see *Historia Karoli Magni et Rotholandi*, in Schmidt, *Karollelus atque Pseudo-Turpini Historia Karoli Magni et Rotholandi*, p. 34.

Bibliography

Sources

Albert of Aachen, *Historia Ierosolimitana*, ed. S. Edgington (Oxford, 2007).

Alexander III, *Epistolae*, ed. J.-P. Migne, PL 200 (Paris, 1855).

Ambroise, *The History of the Holy War: Ambroise's Estoire de la Guerre Sainte*, ed. M. Ailes and M. Barber (2 vols, Woodbridge, 2003).

Annales Herbipolenses, in MGHSS 16 (Hanover, 1859).

Anonymous of Halberstadt, *Gesta*, in MGHSS 23 (Hanover, 1874).

Anselm of Canterbury, *Cur Deus homo*, ed. F. S. Schmitt, S. Anselmi Opera Omnia 2 (Edinburgh, 1946).

Arnold of Lübeck, *Chronica*, in MGHSS 21 (Hanover, 1869).

Baldric of Bourgueil, *Historia Jerosolimitana*, in RHCOc. 4 (Paris, 1879).

Bernard of Clairvaux, *De Consideratione ad Eugenium Papam*, ed. J. Leclerq and H. M. Rochais, SBO 3 (Rome, 1963).

Bernard of Clairvaux, *Epistolae*, ed. J. Leclerq and H. M. Rochais, SBO 7–8 (Rome, 1974–77).

Bernard of Clairvaux, *Liber ad Milites Templi de Laude Novae Militiae*, ed. J. Leclerq and H. M. Rochais, SBO 3 (Rome, 1963).

Bernard of Claivaux, *Sermones super Cantica Canticorum*, ed. J. Leclerq and H. M. Rochais, SBO 1–2 (Rome, 1957–58).

Caffaro of Caschifelone, *De Liberatione Civitatum Orientis*, ed. L. T. Belgrano, *Annali Genovensi di Caffaro e de'suoi continuatori* 1 (Genoa, 1890).

Canso d'Antioca, ed. C. Sweetenham and L. M. Paterson, in *The Canso d'Antioca: An Occitan Epic Chronicle of the First Crusade* (Aldershot, 2003).

Celestine III, *Epistolae*, ed. J.-P. Migne, PL 206 (Paris, 1855).

Christine de Pizan, *The Book of Deeds of Arms and of Chivalry*, ed. C. C. Willard, trans. S. Willard (University Park PA, 1999).

Chronique d'Ernoul et de Bernard le Trésorier, ed. M. L. de Las Matrie (Paris, 1871).

Conon of Béthune, *Les Chansons de Conon de Béthune*, ed. A. Wallensköld, CFM 24 (Paris, 1921).

De Expugnatione Civitatis Acconensis, in RS 51.3 (London, 1870).

De Expugnatione Lyxbonensi, ed. C. W. David (New York, 1936).

De Expugnatione Terrae Sanctae per Saladinum, ed. J. Stevenson, RS 66 (London, 1875).

Ekkehard of Aura, *Hierosolymita*, in RHCOc. 5 (Paris, 1895).

Eliezer bar Nathan Chronicle, trans. S. Eidelberg, *The Jews and the Crusaders* (Madison WI, 1977).

Encyclical of Sergius IV, ed. H. M. Schaller, "Zur Kreuzzugsenzyklika Papst Sergius' IV," in H. Mordek (ed.), *Papsttum, Kirche und Recht im Mittelalter* (Tübingen, 1991), pp. 150–53.

Epistulae et Chartae ad Historiam Primi Belli Sacri Spectantes, ed. H. Hagenmeyer (New York, 1973).

Eugenius III, *Epistolae*, ed. J.-P. Migne, *PL* 180 (Paris, 1855).

Eugenius III, *Epistolae*, in RHGF 15 (Paris, 1878).

Fulcher of Chartres, *Historia Hierosolymitana*, ed. H. Hagenmeyer (Heidelberg, 1913).

Geoffrey of Villehardouin, *La Conquête de Constantinople*, ed. E. Faral (2 vols, Paris, 1938).

Gerald of Wales, *Itinerarium Kambriae*, ed. J. F. Dimock, RS 21.6 (London, 1868).

Gervase of Canterbury, *Chronica*, in RS 73:1 (London, 1879).

Gesta Abbatum Lobbiensium, in MGHSS 21 (Hanover, 1869).

Gesta Francorum et Aliorum Hierosolimitanorum, ed. R. Hill (Oxford, 1962).

Gesta Regis Henrici Secundi, ed. W. Stubbs, RS 49 (2 vols, London, 1867).

Gesta Stephani Regis Anglorum, ed. K. R. Potter (Oxford, 1976).

Gratian, *Corpus Iuris Canonici*, ed. A. E. Richteri (2nd edn, 2 vols, Lipsiae, 1879).

Gregory VIII, *Epistolae*, ed. J.-P. Migne, PL 202 (Paris, 1855).

Guibert of Nogent, *De Vita Sua*, ed. E.-R. Labande (Paris, 1981).

Guibert of Nogent, *Dei Gesta per Francos*, ed. R. B. C. Huygens, CCCM 127A (Turnholt, 1996).

Gunther of Pairis, *Hystoria Constantinopolitana*, ed. P. Orth, Spolia Berolinensia: Berliner Beiträge zur Mediävistik 5 (Zurich, 1994).

Hadrian IV, *Epistolae*, ed. J.-P. Migne, PL 188 (Paris, 1890).

Hebräische Berichte über die Judenverfolgungen während des Ersten Kreuzzugs, ed. E. Haverkamp, MGHHT 1 (Hanover, 2005).

Helmold of Bosau, *Chronica Slavorum*, ed. H. Stoob, AQDGM 19 (Berlin, 1963).

Henry of Huntingdon, *Historia Anglorum*, ed. T. Arnold, RS 74 (London, 1879).

Historia Karoli Magni et Rotholandi, ed. P. G. Schmidt, in *Karollelus atque Pseudo-Turpini Historia Karoli Magni et Rotholandi* (Stuttgart, 1996).

Innocent III, *De Miseria Condicionis Humane*, ed. R. E. Lewis (London, 1980).

Innocent III, *Die Register Innocenz' III*, ed. O. Hageneder and A. Haidacher (Vols 1–8, Graz, 1964–2001).

Innocent III, *Epistolae*, ed. J.-P. Migne, PL 214–16 (Paris, 1890–91).

Itinerarium Peregrinorum et Gesta Regis Ricardi, ed. W. Stubbs, RS 38:1 (London, 1864).

James of Vitry, *The Exempla*, ed. T. F. Crane (London, 1890).

James of Vitry, *Lettres de Jacques de Vitry*, ed. R. B. C. Huygens (Leiden, 1960).

James of Vitry, *Sermones*, ed. C. T. Maier, *Crusade Propaganda and Ideology* (Cambridge, 2000).

La Chanson d'Antioche, ed. J. Nelson, OFCC 4 (Tuscaloosa, 2003).

La Chanson de la Croisade Albigeoise, ed. M. Zink (Paris, 1989).

La Chanson de Jérusalem, ed. N. R. Thorp, OFCC 6 (Tuscaloosa, 1992).

La Chanson de Roland, ed. C. Segre, TLF 968 (Geneva, 2003).

La Vengeance de Nostre-Seigneur, ed. A. E. Ford, *La Vengeance de Nostre-Seigneur: The Old and Middle French Prose Versions* (2 vols, Toronto, 1984–93).

La Venjance de Nostre Seigneur, ed. L. A. T. Gryting, *The Oldest Version of the Twelfth-Century Poem La Venjance Nostre Seigneur* (Ann Arbor, 1952).

Les Chansons de Croisade, ed. J. Bédier and P. Aubry (Paris, 1909).

Les Chétifs, ed. G. M. Myers, OFCC 5 (Tuscaloosa, 1981).

Mainz Anonymous, trans. S. Eidelberg, *The Jews and the Crusaders* (Madison WI, 1977).

Manuel I, *Epistolae*, in RHGF 15 (Paris, 1878).

Marcabru, *Marcabru: A Critical Edition*, ed. S. Gaunt, R. Harvey, and L. Paterson (Cambridge, 2000).

Odo of Deuil, *De Profectione Ludovici VII in Orientem*, ed. V. G. Berry (New York, 1965).

Orderic Vitalis, *Historia Aecclesiastica*, ed. M. Chibnall (6 vols, Oxford, 1969–80).

Otto of Freising, *Chronica sive Historia de Duabus Divitatibus,* ed. A. Schmidt, AQDGM 16 (Darmstadt, 1961).

Otto of Freising, *Gesta Frederici seu rectius Cronica*, ed. F.-J. Schmale, AQDGM 17 (Darmstadt, 1965).

Otto of St. Blasien, *Chronici ab Ottone Frisingensi episcopo conscripti continuatio auctore..Ottone Sancti Blasii monacho*, MGHSS 20 (Hanover, 1868).

Peter of Blois, *Conquestio de Dilatione Vie Ierosolimitane*, ed. R. B. C. Huygens, CCCM 194 (Turnholt, 2002).

Peter of Blois, *Passio Raginaldi Principis Antiochie*, ed. R. B. C. Huygens, CCCM 194 (Turnholt, 2002).

Peter of Les Vaux-de-Cernay, *Hystoria Albigensis*, ed. P Guébin and E. Lyon (3 vols, Paris, 1926–39).

Peter the Venerable, "Epistola ad Archiepiscopos Arelatensem et Ebredunensem, Diensem et Wapincensem Episcopos," RHGF 15 (Paris, 1878).

Peter the Venerable, "Epistola Petri Pictavensis," ed. J. Kritzeck, *Peter the Venerable and Islam* (Princeton, 1964).

Peter the Venerable, *Liber contra Sectam sive Haeresim Saracenorum*, ed. J. Kritzeck, *Peter the Venerable and Islam* (Princeton, 1964).

Peter the Venerable, *Summa Totius Haeresis Saracenorum*, ed. J. Kritzeck, in *Peter the Venerable and Islam* (Princeton, 1964).

Peter the Venerable, *The Letters of Peter the Venerable*, ed. G. Constable (2 vols, Cambridge MA, 1967).

Peter Tudebode, *Historia de Hierosolymitano Itinere*, ed. J. H. Hill and L. L. Hill, DHC 12 (Paris, 1977).

Pseudo-Augustine, *De Vera et Falsa Poenitentia*, ed. J.-P. Migne, PL 40 (Paris, 1845).

Raimbaut of Vaqueiras, *The Poems of the Troubadour Raimbaut de Vaqueiras*, ed. J. Linskill (The Hague, 1964).

Ralph of Caen, *Gesta Tancredi in Expeditione Hierosolymitana*, in RHCOc. 3 (Paris, 1866).

Ralph of Coggeshall, *Chronicon Anglicanum*, ed. J. Stevenson, RS 66 (London, 1875).

Raymond of Aguilers, *Liber*, ed. J. H. Hill and L. L. Hill, DHC 9 (Paris, 1969).

Richard of Devizes, *Cronicon de Tempore Regis Richardi Primi*, ed. J. T. Appleby (London, 1963).

Rigord, *Gesta Philippi Augusti,* in *Rigord : Histoire de Philippe Auguste*, ed. E. Carpentier, G. Pon and Y. Chauvin, Sources D'Histoire Médiéval 33 (Paris, 2006).

Robert of Auxerre, *Chronicon*, MGHSS 26 (Hanover, 1882).

Robert of Clari, *La Conquête de Constantinople*, ed. P. Lauer, CFM 40 (Paris, 1924).

Robert of Rheims, *Historia Iherosolimitana*, RHCOc. 3 (Paris, 1866).

Roger of Howden, *Chronica*, ed. W. Stubbs, RS 51 (4 vols, London, 1868–71).

Saewulf, "A Reliable Account of the Situation of Jerusalem," ed. and trans. J. Wilkinson, *Jerusalem Pilgrimage 1099–1185* (London, 1988).

Sefir Zekhirah, trans. S. Eidelberg, in *The Jews and the Crusaders* (Madison WI, 1977).

Solomon bar Simson Chronicle, trans. S. Eidelberg, in *The Jews and the Crusaders* (Madison WI, 1977).

Suger of St. Denis, *Epistolae*, RHGF 15 (Paris, 1878).

Thomas of Chobham, *Summa Confessorum*, ed. F. Broomfield (Paris, 1968).

Vincent of Prague, *Annales,* MGHSS 17 (Hanover, 1861).

William of Tyre, *Chronicon*, ed. R. B. C. Huygens, CCCM 63 (Turnholt, 1986).

Secondary literature

Abramsky, Sasha, *American Furies: Crime, Punishment, and Vengeance in the Age of Mass Imprisonment* (Boston, 2007).

Abulafia, Anna Sapir, *Christians and Jews in the Twelfth-Century Renaissance* (London, 1995).

Abulafia, Anna Sapir, "The Intellectual and Spiritual Quest for Christ and Central Medieval Persecution of the Jews," in A. S. Abulafia (ed.), *Religious Violence between Christians and Jews: Medieval Roots and Modern Perspectives* (Basingstoke, 2002), pp. 61–85.

Abulafia, Anna Sapir, "The Interrelationship between the Hebrew Chronicles of the First Crusade," in A. S. Abulafia (ed.), *Christians and Jews in Dispute* (Aldershot, 1998), pp. 221–39.

Alfonso, Isabel, "Vengeance, Justice et Lutte Politique dans l'Historiographie Castillane du Moyen Âge," in D. Barthélemy, F. Bougard and R. Le Jan (eds), *La Vengeance, 400–1200* (Rome, 2006), pp. 383–419.

Andrea, Alfred J., "Essay on Primary Sources," in D. E. Queller and T. F. Madden (eds), *The Fourth Crusade: The Conquest of Constantinople* (2nd edn, Philadelphia, 1997), pp. 299–313.

Anspach, Mark R., "Penser la Vengeance," *Esprit*, 128 (July 1987): 103–11.

Axelrod, Robert, *The Evolution of Cooperation* (New York, 1984).

Barthélemy, Dominique, "Knightly Feud in Tenth-Century France," in S. Throop and P. Hyams (eds), *Vengeance in the Middle Ages: Emotion, Religion and Feud* (Ashgate, 2010), pp. 105–13.

Barton, Richard E., "'Zealous Anger' and the Renegotiation of Aristocratic Relationships in Eleventh- and Twelfth-Century France," in B. H. Rosenwein (ed.), *Anger's Past: The Social Uses of an Emotion in the Middle Ages* (Ithaca NY, 1998), pp. 153–70.

Baumeister, Roy F. and Mark R. Leary, "The Need to Belong: Desire for Interpersonal Attachments as a Fundamental Human Motivation," *Psychological Bulletin*, 117 (1995): 497–529.

Beal, Timothy K., "The White Supremacist Bible and the Phineas Priesthood," in J. Bekkenkamp and Y. Sherwood (eds), *Sanctified Aggression: Legacies of Biblical and Post-Biblical Vocabularies of Violence* (New York, 2004), pp. 120–31.

Bisson, Thomas, "Medieval Lordship," *Speculum*, 70 (1995): 743–59.

Bisson, Thomas, *The Crisis of the Twelfth Century: Power, Lordship, and the Origins of European Government* (Princeton, 2009).

Blaise, Albert, *Le Vocabulaire Latin des Principaux Thèmes Liturgiques* (Turnholt, 1966).

Blake, Ernest O., "The Formation of the 'Crusade Idea,'" *Journal of Ecclesiastical History*, 21 (1970): 11–31.

Borkenau, Franz, *End and Beginning: On the Generation of Cultures and the Origins of the West* (New York, 1981).

Bossy, John, *Christianity in the West 1400–1700* (Oxford, 1985).

Bougard, François, "Les Mots de la Vengeance," in D. Barthélemy, F. Bougard, and R. Le Jan (eds), *La Vengeance 400–1200* (Rome, 2006), pp. 1–6.

Bower, Gordon H., "How Might Emotions Affect Learning?," in S.-A. Christianson (ed.), *The Handbook of Emotion and Memory: Research and Theory* (Hillsdale NJ, 1992), pp. 3–31.

Brownlee, Marina, "Verbal and Physical Violence in the *Historie of Aurelio et Isabell*," in S. Throop and P. Hyams (eds), *Vengeance in the Middle Ages: Emotion, Religion and Feud* (Aldershot, 2010), pp. 137–50.

Buc, Phillipe, "La Vengeance de Dieu: De l'Exégèse Patristique à la Réforme Ecclésiastique et à la Première Croisade," in D. Barthélemy, F. Bougard, and R. Le Jan (eds), *La Vengeance 400–1200* (Rome, 2006), pp. 451–86.

Bull, Marcus, "Views of Muslims and of Jerusalem in Miracle Stories, c. 1000–c. 1200: Reflections on the Study of First Crusaders' Motivations," in M. Bull and N. Housley (eds), *The Experience of Crusading 1: Western Approaches* (Cambridge, 2003), pp. 13–38.

Chadwick, Henry, "Symbol and Reality, Berengar and the Appeal to the Fathers," in P. Ganz, R. B. C. Huygens, and F. Niewöhner (eds), *Auctoritas und Ratio* (Göttingen, 1990), pp. 25–46.

Chazan, Robert, "Emperor Frederick I, the Third Crusade, and the Jews," *Viator*, 8 (1977): 83–93.

Chazan, Robert, "Ephraim ben Jacob's Compilation of Twelfth-Century Persecutions," *Jewish Quarterly Review*, 84:4 (1994): 397–416.

Chazan, Robert, "From the First Crusade to the Second: Evolving Perceptions of the Christian-Jewish Conflict," in M. A. Signer and J. Van Engen (eds), *Jews and Christians in Twelfth-Century Europe* (Notre Dame IN, 2001), pp. 46–62.

Chazan, Robert, *God, Humanity, and History: The Hebrew First Crusade Narratives* (London, 2000).

Chazan, Robert, "The Anti-Jewish Violence of 1096: Perpetrators and Dynamics," in A. S. Abulafia (ed.), *Religious Violence between Christians and Jews: Medieval Roots, Modern Perspectives* (Basingstoke, 2002), pp. 21–43.

Chodorow, Stanley, *Christian Political Theory and Church Politics in the Mid-Twelfth Century: The Ecclesiology of Gratian's Decretum* (Los Angeles, 1972).

Christian, William A., *Apparitions in Late Medieval and Renaissance Spain* (Princeton, 1981).

Claassens, Geert H. M., "The Cycle de la Croisade: Vernacular Historiography," in B. Besamusca, W. P. Gerritsen, C. Hogetoorn, and O. S. H. Lie (eds), *Cyclification: The Development of Narrative Cycles in the Chansons de Geste and the Arthurian Romances* (Amsterdam, 1994), pp. 184–8.

Clark, David, "Revenge and Moderation: The Church and Vengeance in Medieval Iceland," *Leeds Studies in English*, new series, 36 (2005): 133–56.

Cohen, Jeremy, "Christian Theology and Anti-Jewish Violence in the Middle Ages: Connections and Disjunctions," in A. S. Abulafia (ed.), *Religious Violence Between Christians and Jews: Medieval Roots and Modern Perspectives* (Basingstoke, 2002), pp. 44–60.

Cohen, Jeremy, "The Jews as Killers of Christ in the Latin Tradition, from Augustine to the Friars," *Traditio*, 39 (1983): 1–28.

Cohen, Ronald, "Warfare and State Formation: Wars make States and States make Wars," in R. B. Ferguson (ed.), *Warfare, Culture, and Environment* (London, 1984), pp. 329–58.

Collins, Adela Y., "Persecution and Vengeance in the Book of Revelation," in D. Hellholm (ed.), *Apocalypticism in the Mediterranean World and the Near East* (Tübingen, 1983), pp. 729–49.

Colson, Elizabeth, "Social Control and Vengeance in Plateau Tonga Society," *Africa*, 23 (1953): 199–211.

Constable, Giles, *The Reformation of the Twelfth Century* (Cambridge, 1996).

Constable, Giles, *Three Studies in Medieval Religious and Social Thought* (Cambridge, 1995).

Cook, Robert F., *"Chanson d'Antioche," Chanson de Geste: Le Cycle de la Croisade est-il Epique?* (Amsterdam, 1980).

Corner, David, "The *Gesta Regis Henrici Secundi* and *Chronica* of Roger, Parson of Howden," *Bulletin of the Institute of Historical Research*, 56 (1983): 126–44.

Cottingham, John, "Varieties of Retribution," in A. Duff (ed.), *Punishment* (Aldershot, 1993), pp. 75–84.

Courtois, Gerard, "La Vengeance, du Désir aux Institutions," in R. Verdier (ed.), *La Vengeance: Études d'Ethnologie, d'Histoire et de Philosophie* (4 vols, Paris, 1980–84), vol. 4, pp. 7–45.

Cowdrey, H. E. J., "Christianity and the Morality of Warfare during the First Century of Crusading," in M. Bull and N. Housley (eds), *The Experience of Crusading 1: Western Approaches* (Cambridge, 2003), pp. 175–92.

Cowdrey, H. E. J., "Martyrdom and the First Crusade," *The Crusades and Latin Monasticism, 11th–12th Centuries* (Aldershot, 1999), pp. 46–56.

Daniel, Norman, "Crusade Propaganda," in H. W. Hazard and N. P. Zacour (eds), *A History of the Crusades 6: The Impact of the Crusades on Europe* (Madison WI, 1989), pp. 39–97.

Davis, R. H. C., "Introduction," *Gesta Stephani*, ed. and trans. K. R. Potter (Oxford, 1976).

Davy, Marie-Madeleine, "Le Theme de la Vengeance au Moyen Age," in R. Verdier (ed.), *La Vengeance: Études d'Ethnologie, d'Histoire et de Philosophie* (4 vols, Paris, 1980–84), vol. 4, pp. 125–35.

De Waal, Frans, *Good Natured: The Origins of Right and Wrong in Humans and Other Animals* (Cambridge MA, 1996).

De Waal, Frans, *Peacemaking among Primates* (Cambridge MA, 1989).

Delaborde, Henri-François, *Notice sur Rigord et sur Guillaume le Breton* (Paris, 1885).

Derbes, Anne, "The Frescoes of Schwarzheindorf, Arnold of Wied and the Second Crusade," in M. Gervers (ed.), *The Second Crusade and the Cistercians* (New York, 1992), pp. 141–54.

Desjardins, Michel, *Peace, Violence and the New Testament* (Sheffield, 1997).

Dobson, R. Barrie, *The Jews of Medieval York and the Massacre of March 1190* (York, 1974).

Douglas, Mary, *Purity and Danger* (London, 1966).

Du Cange, Charles, *Glossarium Mediae et Infimae Latinitatis* (7 vols, Paris, 1840–50).

Duparc-Quioc, Suzanne, ed., *La Chanson d'Antioche: Étude Critique*, DHC 11 (2 vols, Paris, 1976–78).

Duparc-Quioc, Suzanne, "La Composition de la Chanson d'Antioche," *Romania*, 83 (1962): 1–29 and 210–47.

Durkheim, Emile, "Review of E. Kulischer 'Untersuchungen über das primitive strafrecht'," trans. W. D. Halls, in A. Giddens (ed.), *Durkheim on Politics and the State* (Stanford, 1986), pp. 167–70.

Edbury, Peter W. and John G. Rowe, *William of Tyre: Historian of the Latin East* (Cambridge, 1988).

Edgington, Susan, "Albert of Aachen and the *Chansons de Geste*," in J. France and W. G. Zajac (eds), *The Crusades and Their Sources* (Aldershot, 1998), pp. 23–38.

Edgington, Susan, "The First Crusade: Reviewing the Evidence," in J. Phillips (ed.), *The First Crusade: Origins and Impact* (Manchester, 1997), pp. 55–77.

Edwards, J. Goronwy, "The *Itinerarium Regis Ricardi* and the *Estoire de la Guerre Sainte*," in J. G. Edwards, V. H. Galbraith, and E. F. Jacob (eds), *Historical Essays in Honour of James Tait* (Manchester, 1933), pp. 59–77.

Erdmann, Carl, *The Origin of the Idea of Crusading*, trans. M. W. Baldwin and W. Goffart (Princeton, 1977).

Face, Richard D., "Secular History in Twelfth-Century Italy: Caffaro of Genoa," *Journal of Medieval History*, 6 (1980): 169–84.

Falls, M. Margaret, "Retribution, Reciprocity, and Respect for Persons," in A. Duff (ed.), *Punishment* (Aldershot, 1993), pp. 27–54.

Ferguson, R. Brian, "Explaining War," in J. Haas (ed.), *The Anthropology of War* (Cambridge, 1990), pp. 26–55.

Ferguson, R. Brian, "Introduction: Studying War," in R. B. Ferguson (ed.), *Warfare, Culture, and Environment* (London, 1984), pp. 1–81.

Flori, Jean, *Croisade and Chevalerie* (Brussels, 1998).

French, Peter, *The Virtues of Vengeance* (Lawrence KS, 2001).

Funkenstein, Amos, "Basic Types of Christian Anti-Jewish Polemics in the Later Middle Ages," *Viator*, 2 (1971): 373–82.

Gieysztor, Alexander, "The Genesis of the Crusades: The Encyclical of Sergius IV (1009–1012)," *Medievalia et Humanistica*, 5 (1948): 3–23; and 6 (1948): 3–34.

Gilchrist, John, "The Lord's War as the Proving Ground of Faith: Pope Innocent III and the Propagation of Violence (1198–1216)," in M. Shatzmiller (ed.), *Crusaders and Muslims in Twelfth-Century Syria* (Leiden, 1993), pp. 65–83.

Gildea, Marianna, *Expressions of Religious Thought and Feeling in the Chansons de Geste* (Washington D.C., 1943).

Gillingham, John, "Conquering the Barbarians: War and Chivalry in Twelfth-Century Britain," *The Haskins Society Journal*, 4 (1992), pp. 67–84.

Girard, René, *The Scapegoat*, trans. Y. Freccero (London, 1986).

Girard, René, *Things Hidden since the Foundation of the World*, trans. S. Bann and M. Metteer (London, 1987).

Girard, René, *Violence and the Sacred*, trans. P. Gregory (Baltimore, 1979).

Glasse, Robert M., "Revenge and Redress among the Huli: A Preliminary Account," *Mankind*, 5 (April, 1959), pp. 273–89.

Goddard, Hugh, *A History of Christian–Muslim Relations* (Edinburgh, 2000).

Gorringe, Timothy, *God's Just Vengeance: Crime, Violence and the Rhetoric of Salvation* (Cambridge, 1996).

Gransden, Antonia, *Historical Writing in England c. 550 to c. 1307* (London, 1974).

Grant, Lindy, *Abbot Suger of St-Denis: Church and State in Early Twelfth-Century France* (Harlow, 1998).

Greenspan, Patricia S., *Emotions and Reasons: An Inquiry into Emotional Justification* (New York, 1988).

Greimas, Algirdas J., *Dictionnaire de l'Ancien Français* (Paris, 1999).

Hamerton-Kelly, Robert G., *Sacred Violence: Paul's Hermeneutic of the Cross* (Minneapolis, 1992).

Häring, Hermann, "Working Hard to Overcome Violence in the Name of Religion," in W. Beuken and K.-J. Kuschel (eds), *Religion as a Source of Violence* (London, 1997), pp. 93–109.

Haskins, Charles H., *The Renaissance of the Twelfth Century* (Boston, 1927).

Heckman, Christina, "*Imitatio* in Early Medieval Spirituality: *The Dream of the Rood*, Anselm, and Militant Christianity," *Essays in Medieval Studies*, 22 (2005): 141–53.

Helvétius, Anne-Marie, "Le Récit de Vengeance des Saints dans l'Hagiographie Franque (Vie–IXe siècle)," in D. Barthélemy, F. Bougard, and R. Le Jan (eds), *La Vengeance 400–1200* (Rome, 2006), pp. 421–50.

Herlihy, David, "Family," *American Historical Review*, 96 (1991): 1–16.

Horowitz, Mardi J., "Self-righteous Rage and the Attribution of Blame," *Archives of General Psychiatry*, 38 (1981): 1233–38.

Housley, Norman, *Contesting the Crusades* (Oxford, 2006).

Housley, Norman, *Fighting for the Cross: Crusading to the Holy Land* (New Haven, 2008).

Houtart, François, "The Cult of Violence in the Name of Religion: A Panorama," in W. Beuken and K.-J. Kuschel (eds), *Religion as a Source of Violence* (London, 1997), pp. 1–10

Hyams, Paul R., *Rancor and Reconciliation in Medieval England* (Ithaca NY, 2003).

Iogna-Prat, Dominique, *Order and Exclusion: Cluny and Christendom Face Heresy, Judaism, and Islam*, trans. G. R. Edwards (Ithaca NY, 2002).

Jacoby, Susan, *Wild Justice: The Evolution of Revenge* (New York, 1983).

Johnson, James T., *The Holy War Idea in Western and Islamic Traditions* (University Park PA, 1997).

Johnson, Máire, "'Vengeance is Mine': Saintly Retribution in Medieval Ireland," in S. Throop and P. Hyams (eds), *Vengeance in the Middle Ages: Emotion, Religion and Feud* (Aldershot, 2010), pp. 5–50.

Johnstone, Ronald L., *Religion and Society in Interaction: The Sociology of Religion* (Englewood Cliffs NJ, 1975).

Kaeuper, Richard W., *Chivalry and Violence in Medieval Europe* (Oxford, 1999).

Kahl, Hans-Dietrich, "Crusade Eschatology as seen by St. Bernard in the years 1146–1148," in M. Gervers (ed.), *The Second Crusade and the Cistercians* (New York, 1992), pp. 35–47.

Katzir,Yael, "The Second Crusade and the Redefinition of *Ecclesia, Christianitas* and Papal Coercive Power," in M. Gervers (ed.), *The Second Crusade and the Cistercians* (New York, 1992), pp. 3–11.

Kay, Sarah, *The Chansons de Geste in the Age of Romance* (Oxford, 1995).

Kedar, Benjamin Z., *Crusade and Mission: European Approaches toward the Muslims* (Princeton, 1984).

LaMonte, John L., ed., *The Crusade of Richard Lion-heart*, trans. M. J. Hubert (New York, 1941).

Langmuir, Gavin I., "At the Frontiers of Faith," in A. S. Abulafia (ed.), *Religious Violence between Christians and Jews: Medieval Roots and Modern Perspectives* (Basingstoke, 2002), pp. 138–56.

Leach, Edmund, *Culture and Communication* (Cambridge, 1976).

Leary, Mark R., "Affect, Cognition, and the Social Emotions," in J. P. Forgas (ed.), *Feeling and Thinking: The Role of Affect in Social Cognition* (Cambridge, 2000), pp. 331–56.

Lemaire, Andre, "Vengeance et Justice dans l'Ancien Israel," in R. Verdier (ed.), *La Vengeance: Études d'Ethnologie, d'Histoire et de Philosophie* (4 vols, Paris, 1980–84), vol. 3, pp. 13–33.

Lewis, Charlton T., *An Elementary Latin Dictionary* (Oxford, 1977).

Lincoln, Bruce, *Discourse and the Construction of Society: Comparative Studies of Myth, Ritual, and Classification* (Oxford, 1989).

Livermore, Harold, "The 'Conquest of Lisbon' and its Author," *Portuguese Studies*, 6 (1990): 1–16.

Macy, Gary, "Berengar's Legacy as Heresiarch," in P. Ganz, R. B. C. Huygens, and F. Niewöhner (eds), *Auctoritas und Ratio* (Göttingen, 1990), pp. 47–67.

Manselli, Raoul, "De la 'persuasio' a la 'coercitio'," in E. Privat (ed.), *Le Crédo, la Morale et l'Inquisition* (Ariège, 1971), pp. 175–97.

Mansfield, Mary C., *The Humiliation of Sinners: Public Penance in Thirteenth-Century France* (Ithaca NY, 1995).

Markowski, Michael, "Peter of Blois and the Conception of the Third Crusade," in B. Z. Kedar (ed.), *The Horns of Hattin* (Jerusalem, 1992), pp. 261–9.

Mastnak, Tomaz, *Crusading Peace: Christendom, the Muslim World, and Western Political Order* (Berkeley, 2002).

Mayer, Hans E., *The Crusades*, trans. J. Gillingham (2nd edn, Oxford, 1988).

McCauley, Clark, "Conference Overview," in J. Haas (ed.), *The Anthropology of War* (Cambridge, 1990), pp. 1–25.

Mead, George H., "The Psychology of Punitive Justice," *The American Journal of Sociology*, 23 (1918): 577–602.

Mendenhall, George E., *The Tenth Generation: The Origins of the Biblical Tradition* (Baltimore, 1973).

Mierow, Charles C. and Richard Emery (eds), *The Deeds of Frederick Barbarossa* (New York, 1953).

Miller, Robert I., *The First European Revolution c. 970–1215* (Oxford, 2000).

Miller, William I., *Bloodtaking and Peacemaking: Feud, Law and Society in Saga Iceland* (Chicago, 1990).

Miller, William I., *Humiliation* (Ithaca NY, 1993).

Moore, Robert I., *The Formation of a Persecuting Society: Power and Deviance in Western Europe, 950–1250* (Oxford, 1987).

Morgan, Margaret R., *The Chronicle of Ernoul and the Continuations of William of Tyre* (Oxford, 1973).

Morris, Colin, *The Papal Monarchy* (Oxford, 1989).

Muldoon, James, "Tolerance and Intolerance in the Medieval Canon Lawyers," in M. Gervers and J. M. Powell (eds), *Tolerance and Intolerance: Social Conflict in the Age of the Crusades* (Syracuse NY, 2001), pp. 117–23.

Newman, Martha G., *The Boundaries of Charity: Cistercian Culture and Ecclesiastical Reform, 1098–1180* (Stanford, 1996).

Niermeyer, Jan F., *Mediae Latinitatis Lexicon Minus* (Leiden, 1997).

Nietzsche, Friedrich, *Human, All Too Human*, trans. C. Diethe, in K. Ansell-Pearson (ed.), *On the Genealogy of Morality* (Cambridge, 1994), pp. 131–41.

Nietzsche, Friedrich, *On the Genealogy of Morality*, ed. K. Ansell-Pearson, trans. C. Diethe (Cambridge, 1994).

Nirenberg, David, *Communities of Violence: Persecution of Minorities in the Middle Ages* (Princeton, 1996).

Noorani, Abdul G., *Islam and Jihad* (London, 2002).

Pancer, Nira, "La Vengeance Féminine Revisitée: Le Cas de Grégoire de Tours," in D.

Barthélemy, F. Bougard, and R. Le Jan (eds), *La Vengeance 400–1200* (Rome, 2006), pp. 307–24.

Partner, Peter, *God of Battles: Holy Wars of Christianity and Islam* (London, 1997).

Peels, H. G. L., *The Vengeance of God: The Meaning of the Root NQM and the Function of the NQM-texts in the Context of Divine Revelation in the Old Testament* (Leiden, 1995).

Peleg, Samuel, *Zealotry and Vengeance: Quest of a Religious Identity Group* (Lanham MD, 2002).

Peters, Rudolph, *Jihad in Classical and Modern Islam: A Reader* (Princeton, 1996).

Phillips, Jonathan, "Ideas of Crusade and Holy War in *De Expugnatione Lyxbonensi (The Conquest of Lisbon)*," in R. Swanson (ed.), *Holy Land, Holy Lands, and Christian History*, Studies in Church History 36 (2000), pp. 123–41.

Phillips, Jonathan, "Odo of Deuil's *De Profectione Ludovici VII in Orientem* as a Source for the Second Crusade," in M. Bull and N. Housley (eds), *The Experience of Crusading 1: Western Approaches* (Cambridge, 2003), pp. 80–95.

Primoratz, Igor, "Punishment as Language," in A. Duff (ed.), *Punishment* (Aldershot, 1993), pp. 57–74.

Purkis, William, "Elite and Popular Perceptions of *Imitatio Christi* in Twelfth-Century Crusade Spirituality," in K. Cooper and J. Gregory (eds), *Elite and Popular Religion*, Studies in Church History 42 (Woodbridge, 2006), pp 54–64.

Reddy, William M., *The Navigation of Feeling: A Framework for the History of Emotions* (Cambridge, 2001).

Reynolds, Susan, *Fiefs and Vassals: The Medieval Evidence Reinterpreted* (Oxford, 1994).

Riley-Smith, Jonathan, "Christian Violence and the Crusades," in A. S. Abulafia (ed.), *Religious Violence between Christians and Jews: Medieval Roots, Modern Perspectives* (Basingstoke, 2002), pp. 3–20.

Riley-Smith, Jonathan, "Crusading as an Act of Love," *History*, 65 (1980): 177–92.

Riley-Smith, Jonathan, *The Crusades: A History* (2nd edn, New Haven, 2005).

Riley-Smith, Jonathan, *The First Crusade and the Idea of Crusading* (London, 1986).

Riley-Smith, Jonathan, "The First Crusade and the Persecution of the Jews," in W. J. Sheils (ed.), *Persecution and Tolerance* (Oxford, 1984), pp. 57–72.

Riley-Smith, Jonathan, *The First Crusaders, 1095–1131* (Cambridge, 1997).

Riley-Smith, Jonathan, "The Latin Clergy and the Settlement in Palestine and Syria, 1098–1100," *Catholic Historical Review*, 74 (1988): 539–57.

Riley-Smith, Jonathan, "The Military Orders and the Orient, 1150–1291," unpublished (n.d.).

Rivers, Kimberly, "The Fear of Divine Vengeance: Mnemonic Images as a Guide to Conscience in the Late Middle Ages," in A. Scott and C. Kosso (eds), *Fear and Its Representations in the Middle Ages and Renaissance* (Turnholt, 2002), pp. 66–91.

Roche, Thomas, "The Way Vengeance Comes: Rancorous Deeds and Words in the World of Orderic Vitalis," in S. Throop and P. R. Hyams (eds), *Vengeance in the Middle Ages: Emotion, Religion and Feud* (Aldershot, 2010), pp. 115–36.

Rosenwein, Barbara H., *Emotional Communities in the Early Middle Ages* (Ithaca NY, 2006).

Rosenwein, Barbara H., "Les Emotions de la Vengeance," in D. Barthélemy, F. Bougard and R. Le Jan (eds), *La Vengeance 400–1200* (Rome, 2006), pp. 237–57.

Rousset, Paul, *Les Origines et les Caractères de la Première Croisade* (Neuchâtel, 1945).

Rubin, Miri, *Gentile Tales: The Narrative Assault on Late Medieval Jews* (New Haven, 1999).

Rubin, Miri, "Mary and the Jews," paper given in Cambridge, 30 March 2004.

Ruether, Rosemary R., *Faith and Fratricide: The Theological Roots of Anti-semitism* (New York, 1979).

Schaller, Hans M., "Zur Kreuzzugsenzyklika Papst Sergius' IV," in H. Mordek (ed.), *Papsttum, Kirche und Recht im Mittelalter* (Tübingen, 1991), pp. 135–53.

Scheff, Thomas, *Bloody Revenge: Emotions, Nationalism and War* (Boulder, 1994).

Scheff, Thomas, "Emotions and Identity: A Theory of Ethnic Nationalism," in C. Calhoun (ed.), *Social Theory and the Politics of Identity* (Oxford, 1994), pp. 277–303.

Scheff, Thomas, *Microsociology: Discourse, Emotion, and Social Structure* (Chicago, 1990).

Scheff, Thomas, "Shame and Conformity: The Deference-Emotion System," *American Sociological Review*, 53 (1988): 395–406.

Scheff, Thomas, "The Taboo on Coarse Emotions," in P. Shaver (ed.), *Review of Personality and Social Psychology*, 5 (Beverly Hills, 1984): 146–69.

Schilling, Johannes, ed., *Arnold von Lübek: Gesta Gregorii Peccatoris* (Göttingen, 1986).

Schmandt, Raymond H., "The Fourth Crusade and the Just-War Theory," *Catholic Historical Review*, 61 (1975): 191–221.

Schwinges, Rainer C., "William of Tyre, the Muslim Enemy, and the Problem of Tolerance," in M. Gervers and J. M Powell (eds), *Tolerance and Intolerance: Social Conflict in the Age of the Crusades* (Syracuse NY, 2001), pp. 124–32.

Siberry, Elizabeth, *Criticism of Crusading, 1095–1274* (Oxford, 1985).

Simmel, George, *Conflict and The Web of Group Affiliations*, trans. K. H. Wolff and R. Bendix (Glencoe IL, 1955).

Smail, Daniel L., "Hatred as a Social Institution in Late-Medieval Society," *Speculum*, 76 (2001): 90–126.

Smail, Daniel L. and Kelly Gibson (eds), *Vengeance in Medieval Europe: A Reader* (Toronto, 2009).

Solomon, Robert C., *A Passion for Justice: Emotions and the Origin of the Social Contract* (London, 1995).

Solomon, Sheldon, Jeff Greenberg, and Tom Pyszczynski, "A Terror-management Theory of Social Behavior: The Psychological Functions of Self-esteem and Cultural Worldviews," *Advances in Experimental Social Psychology*, 24 (1991): 93–159.

Staub, Ervin, *The Roots of Evil: The Origins of Genocide and Other Group Violence* (Cambridge, 1989).

Stock, Brian, *Listening for the Text: On the Uses of the Past* (Philadelphia, 1990).

Stock, Brian, *The Implications of Literacy: Written Language and Models of Interpretation in the Eleventh and Twelfth Centuries* (Princeton, 1983).

Strickland, Debra H., *Saracens, Demons and Jews* (Princeton, 2003).

Thomas, Yan, "Se Venger au Forum: Solidarité Familiale et Procès Criminel à Rome," in R. Verdier (ed.), *La Vengeance: Études d'Ethnologie, d'Histoire et de Philosophie* (4 vols, Paris, 1980–84), vol. 3, pp. 65–100.

Throop, Susanna, "Combat and Conversation: Interfaith Dialogue in Twelfth-Century Crusading Narratives," in M. Lower (ed.), *Medieval Encounters: Jewish, Christian and Muslim Culture in Confluence and Dialogue* 13:2 (Leiden, 2007), pp. 310–25.

Throop, Susanna, "Vengeance and the Crusades," *Crusades*, 5 (2006): 21–38.

Throop, Susanna, "Zeal, Anger and Vengeance: The Emotional Rhetoric of Crusading," in S. Throop and P. R. Hyams (eds), *Vengeance in the Middle Ages: Emotion, Religion and Feud* (Aldershot, 2010), pp. 177–201.

Tolan, John V., *Saracens: Islam in the Medieval European Imagination* (New York, 2002).

Turney-High, Harry H., *Primitive War: Its Practice and Concepts* (Columbia SC, 1949).

Tyerman, Christopher, *God's War : A New History of the Crusades* (Cambridge MA, 2006).

Verdier, Raymond, "Le Système Vindicatoire," in R. Verdier (ed.), *La Vengeance: Études d'Ethnologie, d'Histoire et de Philosophie* (4 vols, Paris, 1980–84), vol. 1, pp. 13–42.

Voegelin, Eric, *Anamnesis*, trans. G. Niemeyer (Notre Dame IN, 1978).

Watt, John A., *The Theory of Papal Monarchy in the Thirteenth Century* (London, 1965).

White, Stephen D., "The Politics of Anger," in B. H. Rosenwein (ed.), *Anger's Past: The Social Uses of an Emotion in the Middle Ages* (Ithaca NY, 1998), pp. 127–52.

White, Stephen D., "Un Imaginaire Faidal: La Representation de la *Guerre* dans quelques Chansons de Geste," in D. Barthélemy, F. Bougard, and R. Le Jan (eds), *La Vengeance 400–1200* (Rome, 2006), pp. 175–98.

Wright, Stephen K., *The Vengeance of Our Lord: Medieval Dramatizations of the Destruction of Jerusalem* (Toronto, 1989).

Index

Abel 81, 88, 108

Abulafia, Anna Sapir 98n, 101n, 105, 106n, 196n

Acre 29, 69, 74, 111, 205

Adhémar of Le Puy 81

adultery 21, 38–9, 58, 93, 115n, 124, 136, 174

aid 24–5, 51, 59, 61–2, 73, 81, 108, 109, 112–13, 120, 122, 139, 141–3, 147, 175–6, 181n

    auxilium 12, 57, 61, 70, 108–9, 141, 175

Albert of Aachen 23, 31–2, 37, 49, 50n, 52, 53n, 54, 58, 59n, 61n, 62, 64, 67–8, 69n, 106n, 110, 164n, 195–6, 198, 200–201, 206n

Alexander III, Pope 84, 149, 197, 203

Alexandria 117

Alexius I Comnenus 20, 46

Alexius IV Angelus 16n, 117, 128

Alexius V Dukas Mourtzouphlos 16, 117

alliances 13, 20, 25, 32, 37, 175, 204

Amaury of Jerusalem 198

Ambroise 20–21n, 69, 77, 111, 112n, 199, 200n, 204n

Ambrose of Milan 108, 109n, 114

Ananias and Saphira 92

Andronicus I Comnenus 29, 39

Annales Herbipolenses 85, 202

Anonymous of Halberstadt 127, 155, 204

Anonymous of Soissons 127, 204–5

Anselm of Lucca 155, 191

Antichrist 56, 81, 85, 135

anti-Jewish sentiment 64–71, 97–107, 115

anti-Jewish violence 64–71, 73, 80, 97–107, 189, 191

Antioch 1, 23, 30, 36, 38, 43–4, 51, 53–4, 59, 78, 81, 93, 146, 195–6

    fall of 1, 36, 43, 51, 54, 93

Aquinas, Thomas 169

Aragon, Kingdom of 29, 151, 183–4

Arnold Amaury 123, 134

Arnold of Lübeck 26, 30–31, 119–22, 130, 136, 141, 150, 154, 164, 180n, 202–3, 206n

Arnulf of Chocques 14, 63

Arsuf 62, 77

Audita tremendi 73, 149

Augustine of Hippo 16–18, 88, 105n, 131

authorship, issues of 8, 12, 30, 44, 52, 76, 112, 178

authority

    divine 13n, 18–19, 53, 164, 173, 187

    group 15

    moral 12, 19, 34–5, 40, 187

    papal 9, 20, 34, 73, 90, 92, 94–5, 107, 115, 117, 132n, 164, 171, 177

    political 19–31, 40, 108–14, 142, 180n, 182

    see also power

Baldric of Bourgueil 1, 2n, 14, 15n, 23, 36, 49n, 51, 53–6, 58, 60–62, 106n, 110, 163, 176n, 195–6, 198, 206n

Baldwin I of Jerusalem 37, 51

Baldwin II of Jerusalem 147

Baldwin IV of Flanders 16, 122

Baldwin IV of Jerusalem 74, 198

Barton, Richard 158n, 161, 168, 171

Becket, Thomas 27, 30

Bede 105, 153, 165

Berengar of Tours 61

Bernard of Clairvaux 18–20, 33, 35, 73, 76,
    83, 85, 88n, 92, 96–7, 99, 100n,
    114, 147, 152, 154–6, 160, 161n,
    163–5, 167, 171, 180, 197–8, 203
Béziers 123–4, 136–7
Bible *see* Old Testament; New Testament
biology 6, 59, 175
blasphemy 88, 95, 106–7, 132, 136, 141 *see
    also* sacrilege
blood 59, 81
    blood feud 189–90, 192
    blood sacrifice 186
    of Christians 34, 36, 67, 78, 83, 89,
        108, 120, 125, 130–32, 141, 147,
        150–51
    of family 25, 32, 51, 67, 78, 108, 175
    unclean 56, 103
    see also Christ, blood of
Bohemond of Taranto 19, 48, 58–9
Boniface I of Montferrat 30, 142, 204
Buc, Phillipe 2n, 57n, 149n, 192
Byzantine Church 135
Byzantines 18, 48, 75, 117, 128, 132n, 135,
    147, 150, 203n

Caffaro of Caschifelone 8, 19, 20n, 85, 202
cannibalism 39, 98
canon law 17–18, 88–96, 99, 107, 115, 128,
    131, 173–4, 179
Canso d'Antioca 118–19, 132n, 138, 181n,
    203
Carcassonne 123, 130
Cathars 9, 117–18, 123–5, 127–8, 130,
    132, 134–5, 137, 150–51, 203 *see
    also* heresy; Languedoc
Celestine III, Pope 79, 197
Chanson d'Antioche, La 1–2, 48, 64,
    68–71, 77, 81–3, 93, 107n, 110n,
    138n, 162, 180, 181n, 200–201,
    203, 206
Chanson de Jérusalem, La 38, 77, 78n, 81,
    93, 110n, 111n, 113n, 200–201

Chanson de la Croisade Albigeoise, La 29,
    127, 134, 181n, 205
Chanson de Roland 113, 181
Charlemagne 126–7, 180n, 181n, 182
Chazan, Robert 66n, 97n, 98n, 99, 101,
    196n
Chétifs, Les 93, 111–13, 200–201
Chevalier, mult estes guariz 80, 103, 199
Chodorow, Stanley 26n, 92, 131n
Christ 44–5, 47–8, 56, 59, 61–2, 76, 82,
    91, 100, 102, 121, 123, 133, 152,
    156, 177, 182, 206
    apostles of 20, 47, 53, 156
    as avenger/judge 17–18, 53, 122, 159,
        177
    blood of 44, 65, 81, 98, 108, 119, 127,
        137, 150, 164
    body of 1, 56–7, 61, 81, 98, 101, 137,
        190
    cross of 24, 33, 79–80, 83, 86, 93, 100,
        101n, 106–7, 119–21, 124–5,
        137, 139–40, 153, 164, 206 *see also*
        Crucifixion
    emulation of 4, 167–8
        aemulatio 152, 157n, 165–6, 171,
        186
    enemies of 27, 67, 70, 93, 121, 132,
        135–6, 164, 190–91
    as forgiving 153
    as friend 142–3
    imitation of 3, 49, 167–8, 171
        imitatio Christi 3n, 167, 171
    inheritance of 78, 108, 120, 140, 142,
        148
    injuries to 33n, 51, 56, 77–81, 83,
        88, 100, 110, 115, 119, 121, 122,
        124–5, 131–2, 142, 161, 190, 205
    as kinsman 2, 51, 59–61, 142–3,
        175–6
    knights of 58, 80, 123, 126, 133
    Passion of 59–61, 79, 82, 97, 100–101,
        137, 205 *see also* Crucifixion

Christian reform 57n, 99n, 129, 133, 142, 149n, 169, 184–5, 192n, 199

Christian unity 100, 108, 125, 130–35, 139, 186

Christians, eastern 1, 43, 122, 128, 179 *see also* Byzantines

chronicles, general discussion of 1, 7–8, 118, 143, 180, 199

Chronique d'Ernoul 34, 35n, 39, 199

circumcision 106

Cistercians 80, 83, 88, 99–100, 115n, 180n, 204

Clement III, Pope 120, 139, 141, 150

Clermont, Council of 43, 48, 50, 62, 109, 147, 182, 195

coercion 91, 94–6, 99, 112, 115n, 155, 160, 191

conflict, internal v. external 15

Cologne 64

Concordat of Worms 91

Conon of Béthune 118–19, 120n, 121, 128, 130n, 140, 142, 204

Conrad III Hohenstaufen 73–4

Constable, Giles 33n, 77n, 101n, 147n, 166, 167n, 185n

Constantinople 14, 16, 19, 25, 28–9, 39 1204 conquest of 32, 117, 122, 127–8, 130–31, 135, 181n, 204

conversion 48, 65–8, 70, 97, 127, 132–6, 142, 155–6, 169n, 181n, 182, 202, 206

convertere 134

Cook, Robert 68, 69n, 200–201

counsel 18, 20, 25, 33, 35, 37, 55, 83, 96, 111, 152, 175

cowardice 23–4, 26, 121

Cowdrey, H. E. J. 2n, 3n, 16n, 155n, 170, 192

crime 11n, 13n, 14–17, 20–22, 28, 34, 37–8, 40, 51, 54, 56, 63, 70, 76–7, 82, 91–6, 99, 102–7, 115–16, 123–4, 136, 142, 153, 163–4, 173–4, 176, 187n

betrayal/treachery 1, 13, 23, 40, 63, 93–4, 126, 141, 174, 176, 206n

murder 17, 21, 27–8, 32, 50, 64–6, 77, 84, 93, 98–9, 104, 140, 153–5, 159, 174

see also adultery; sins

criminals 17, 21, 51, 95–6, 154, 191

heretics as 136

see also Muslims, as criminals

Crucifixion 57, 64–5, 115, 176–7, 182, 186

reenactment/imitation of 106–7, 136–7

sign of willful disbelief 105–7, 116, 136, 139, 177

vengeance for 1–2, 60–61, 66–70, 81–2, 97–107, 126, 135–9, 162, 176–7, 179, 190, 205

see also Christ, cross of; Christ, Passion of

crusades

Albigensian 9, 29, 117, 119, 123–4, 127, 130–32, 134–7, 150–51, 164, 181n, 205

Baltic 73, 117

Fifth 118, 127, 133, 151, 203, 205

First 1, 3–5, 8, 9, 14, 15–16, 18, 20, 25, 28, 34, 43–7, 49–62, 64–6, 68–71, 74–5, 77, 81–3, 86–7, 91, 93, 96–7, 99–100, 104, 108, 110–11, 113–14, 117–19, 126, 132n, 146, 148n, 162–3, 165, 170, 173, 181n, 182, 189–92, 195–8, 201–3

Fourth 16, 24, 32, 118, 121–2, 124, 127–8, 130–31, 142, 180n, 181n, 203–4

Iberian 3n, 73, 83, 87, 92n, 106–7, 147, 174, 198

Second 14, 18, 73–6, 78, 83, 85–7, 92, 97, 99, 115n, 147, 153, 197–8, 201–3

Third 3n, 69, 74, 77, 86, 97, 111, 114, 121, 127, 135, 148, 150, 180n, 199n, 200, 203–4

crusading
  as an act of love 3n, 62–3, 109, 158n,
    166, 171
  criticism of 23, 52n, 53n, 85n, 96n
  study of ideas of 3n, 192n, 190, 178–83
Cyprus 24, 74

Damascus 31, 73, 81, 147
De Expugnatione Lyxbonensi 3n, 83, 88n,
    92–4, 106–9, 136, 147n, 174n, 198
De Expugnatione Terrae Sanctae per
    Saladinum 119–20, 130, 134,
    139–40, 204
De Waal, Frans 25n, 60
defense 4, 124, 130–31, 170, 177
  of the Church 3
  self-defense 14n, 140
  and vengeance 141
  weapons of 133
Devastatio Constantinopolitana 127, 204
Din, al–, Nur 22, 114
Din, al–, Salah 73–4, 77, 87, 111, 114, 117,
    119, 130–31, 134, 140
dishonor 14, 36, 55
disloyalty 93, 128 *see also* loyalty
Dorylaeum, Battle of 59
Du Cange, Charles 11, 156–7, 165
Durkheim, Emile 15
duty 182, 192
  of kings 27
  see also vengeance, duty to take

Edessa 73, 76, 85–8, 93, 147, 162, 173
Edgington, Susan 23n, 50n, 69n, 106n,
    164n, 195n, 200, 201n
Ekkehard of Aura 46–7, 64, 66–7, 146,
    152, 154, 156, 165, 195–6
Eliezer bar Nathan 64, 84, 201
emotional communities 169
emotions 3, 6–7, 12n, 17, 18n, 19–31, 38n,
    39n, 40, 49, 58, 61, 101, 109, 114n,
    139, 145–71, 177, 185, 186n

anger 12n, 17, 19n, 29, 37, 38, 59,
    61, 65, 68, 70, 93, 98, 119, 145n,
    147–8, 152–8, 162, 164, 169–70,
    174
  divine 50, 54, 83, 89, 96, 123, 159,
    162, 163–5, 168, 171, 177
  ira per vitium 158–9
  ira per zelum 158–99, 170, 177
  ira regis 21, 37, 40
  lordly 21–4, 29, 161, 168, 171
  righteous 152, 156, 159–60, 163,
    168, 177
anxiety 31, 53, 89–90
contempt 23–4, 28, 31, 33, 100, 112,
    137, 164
fear 14–15, 22, 24, 28, 30–31, 36, 99,
    103, 121, 151, 164, 169
hatred 13n, 29, 50, 98–100, 104,
    106–7, 114, 122, 124, 137, 157–64,
    168, 171, 178
jealousy 157–8, 165, 170, 177
joy 22, 45, 80, 96, 134, 169
love 3, 38, 90, 152–65, 175, 187
  caritas 3, 12, 57, 62, 70, 108, 141,
    143, 154n, 175, 177
  for fellow Christians 57, 62, 125–6,
    139, 141, 161, 166–8, 171
  for God 1, 62, 81, 99, 101, 114–15,
    142, 156, 158, 160–61,
    166–70, 177
  of God 50, 54, 122, 155
  of justice 154–5, 177
  passionate 101, 156–7, 170, 177
  see also crusading, as an act of love
pity 18, 122
shame 14, 22–4, 26, 30–31, 33n, 34,
    40, 53, 76–7, 89–90, 103, 108,
    119–20, 121–2, 140, 147, 161–2,
    171 *see also* humiliation
emulation *see* Christ, emulation of
Encyclical of Sergius IV 44–7, 52, 68–70,
    195–7, 200

Eucharist, the 39n, 61, 101, 105, 136–7
Eugenius III, Pope 18, 20, 33, 73, 78, 84–5,
　　87, 154, 156, 164, 167, 180, 197,
　　203
excommunication 34–5, 91, 154
executions and capital punishment 11n,
　　16–17, 63, 142
exempla 16, 35, 38n, 39, 118, 127, 132,
　　140n, 142, 151–2, 166–7, 181n,
　　205
eyewitness accounts 43–9

family 2, 13, 57–8, 60–61, 108–16,
　　139–43, 164, 175–6, 179, 189, 204
feud 2, 4, 11, 12n, 15, 38n, 39n, 114n,
　　145n, 173 *see also* blood, blood feud
Flori, Jean 2n, 47n, 191
Frederick I of Germany 26, 74, 97, 120–21,
　　141, 150
friendship 13, 22, 58, 60, 70, 77, 80, 82,
　　108, 110, 116, 125, 139, 142–3
Fulcher of Chartres 46–7, 56n, 195, 198

genres, issues of 7–8, 86, 112, 178, 181
Geoffrey of Joinville 122
Geoffrey of Villehardouin 25, 30, 121, 128,
　　130, 135, 140, 142, 204
Gerald of Wales 38, 90, 109, 198
Gervase of Canterbury 21, 26–30, 34,
　　83–4, 88, 98, 198
Gesta Francorum 46, 48, 195, 198
Gesta Regis Henrici Secundi 77–80, 88–9,
　　148, 199
Gesta Stephani 76, 87, 92, 198
Gieszytor, Alexander 44n, 197
Gilchrist, John 2n, 190
Girard, René 107n, 186
Glossa Ordinaria 153
God
　　agents of 26–7, 28, 40, 54–5, 160, 164,
　　　168
　　enemies of 27, 45, 66, 68, 104

　　as father 58, 60, 70, 109, 139, 143, 148,
　　　167, 175–6
　　as lord 58, 70, 140–41, 175
　　ministers of 14, 19, 83, 156, 167, 177
　　sanction of 17–18, 77, 83, 111
　　servants of 80, 110, 119–20, 140–41, 150
　　of vengeance 2, 46, 50–58, 88–96, 121,
　　　123, 130, 162–4, 171, 173, 177
　　see also Christ
Godfrey of Bouillon 20, 25, 55, 59, 62, 82,
　　110
Graindor of Douai 68–9, 200–201
Gratian 6n, 17, 26, 92, 94, 96, 131, 180, 192
greed 35, 53, 66–7, 132
Greeks *see* Byzantines
Gregory I, Pope 205
Gregory VIII, Pope 73, 149, 197, 203
Guibert of Nogent 28, 49n, 50–51, 55–6,
　　58–9, 64, 68, 165, 195–6
guilt 39, 52, 56, 101n, 105, 107, 109, 153,
　　159, 168
Gunther of Pairis 122–3, 135, 180n, 204

Hadrian IV, Pope 84, 197, 203
Hagenmeyer, Heinrich 44, 46n, 132n, 195
Hattin, Battle of 73, 79, 89, 130, 198
Helmold of Bosau 85, 202–3
Henry I of England 20
Henry II of England 30, 73, 78, 148, 198–9
Henry IV of Germany 22
Henry VI of Germany 26, 29
Henry Dandolo 16, 24, 30, 122
Henry of Huntingdon 85, 878n, 95, 105–6,
　　109, 201
heresy 33, 56, 68, 80, 84, 94–5, 99–100,
　　104, 106, 115, 117, 124–5, 128–9,
　　132–9, 136, 140, 142, 148, 151,
　　155, 164, 174, 176–7, 177, 179,
　　183–4, 191
　　justification of violence against heretics
　　　94–5
　　see also Cathars

hierarchy 32, 34, 40, 86, 108–14, 128,
    141–2, 167
Historia Karoli Magni et Rotholandi 127,
    181–2, 206
Holy Land, vengeance for 1, 47, 77–9, 83,
    87, 105, 109, 119–21, 124, 134,
    140, 150–51, 164, 174, 190 *see also*
    Jerusalem
Holy Sepulchre 45, 78, 84, 138
Honorius III, Pope 133
humiliation 23, 31, 53, 73, 90, 168 *see also*
    emotions, shame
Hyams, Paul 7n, 12n, 13, 23n, 31, 38n, 39n,
    57n, 114n, 145n, 158

identity 21n, 108–14, 160n
    group 61, 109, 139
    religious 31–7, 134–5
imitatio Christi *see* Christ, imitation of
injury 13–14, 23, 40, 83–8, 192
    to Christians 1, 59, 62–3, 65–6, 78,
        109, 123, 130, 140, 173
    to the Church 27, 33, 126, 131, 135
    to the cross 79, 83, 120–21
    communal injury 14, 16–17, 26, 40, 55,
        76, 92, 95, 115, 141, 155
    concealment of 28–9
    to God 14, 21, 26, 33, 40, 44, 80, 90,
        109, 123, 125–6, 132, 143, 151,
        154, 164, 173
    personal injury 17, 26, 92, 110–11, 155
    see also Christ, injuries to; crime; insults
Innocent II, Pope 33, 91, 154
Innocent III, Pope 34, 117–18, 122, 124–5,
    129–30, 132, 135–6, 140, 142–3,
    148, 151, 157, 160, 163–4, 178,
    190, 197, 205
insults 23–4, 29, 48, 122, 148
interpretation, difficulty of 7, 78, 102,
    138n, 160, 186
Iogna-Prat, Dominique 56n, 95n, 100n,
    101n, 104, 105n, 107, 184n

irrationality 145, 183
Isidore of Seville 17
Israel 24, 36, 84, 96, 104, 109, 125n, 140n
Israelites 88, 160
Itinerarium peregrinorum 20, 23n, 31,
    112n, 120, 140, 148–9, 203

Jacoby, Susan 2n, 18n, 189
James of Vitry 16, 35, 37–8n, 39, 118–19,
    127, 132–3, 140, 142, 150–52,
    163–4, 166–9, 181n, 182, 205
Jerusalem 2, 5n, 14, 27, 36–7, 43, 44, 63,
    78, 85–6, 101, 124, 136, 149, 159,
    195, 198
    Christian conquest of (1099) 36, 43,
        47, 51–2, 56, 59–61, 95
    Christian loss of to Salah al-Din 73, 77,
        86–8, 93, 119, 121, 130–31, 140, 162
    Islamic occupation of 45–7, 49–50, 74,
        84, 122, 190
    Kingdom of 74, 117
    as mother 58, 70, 108, 120, 139, 175
    as nexus for idea of crusading as
        vengeance 100, 115, 138, 176
    Roman destruction of 2, 45–6, 69–70,
        82–3, 102, 126, 138–9, 162, 180n,
        182, 192, 205–6 *see also* Titus and
        Vespasian
    see also Holy Land, vengeance for
Jews 59, 61, 64–70, 82, 84, 97–107, 115,
    126–8, 132, 134–9, 142, 146,
    148–9, 152–3, 160, 164–7, 171,
    174, 176–7, 179, 183–4, 187 *see
    also* Anti-Jewish sentiment; Anti-
    Jewish violence
Josephus 69, 205
justice 3, 4, 11, 13–21, 26–7, 31–4, 36n,
    37–40, 50, 54, 57, 61, 67, 70, 76,
    83, 85, 87–9, 90–96, 101n, 103,
    115, 122–3, 125–8, 130, 139, 147,
    150, 154–6, 169–70, 173–9, 182,
    187, 189n

Kedar, Benjamin 3n, 94n, 95n, 96n, 133n,
        153n, 169, 199n
Kerbogha 36, 50–51, 53
Knights Templar 76, 139, 151, 166–7, 189,
        197

Languedoc 84, 118, 123, 125, 135, 150
law 14, 18–19, 36–7, 54, 79, 85, 90–91,
        93–4, 121, 133, 135, 147–9, 151,
        154–5, 159n, 160, 174, 182, 192
        see also canon law
Lisbon *see* De Expugnatione Lyxbonensi
lordship 19n, 21–2, 26, 29–30, 57–61, 70,
        80, 108–16, 128, 139–43, 161, 168,
        171, 175, 185n, 189–91
Louis VII of France 73, 77, 114, 147–8,
        198, 202–3
loyalty 14, 23 *see also* disloyalty

Maccabees 139, 147, 149, 192
Mainz 64–6
Mainz Anonymous 64–70, 84, 195–6, 201
Manuel I Comnenus 30, 203n
Marcabru 80, 88, 96, 199
martyrdom 3n, 48–9, 62, 98, 149, 151,
        167–8, 170, 192n
Mary, mother of Jesus 39, 53, 106n
Mastnak, Tomaz 2n, 191–2
memory 58–60, 70, 139
mercy 18–19, 24, 53, 54n, 62–3, 67, 89–90,
        122–3, 127, 182
Mohammed 126, 133, 136, 181n
Morris, Colin 91n, 129
Moore, R. I. 99n, 183–5
motivations 18, 103, 152–3, 169, 176,
        186n
    for crusading 5n, 45, 52, 58, 63, 85,
        146, 156, 162, 179, 202, 204
    and vengeance 17, 65–9, 105, 141, 155
Muslims
    as allies 37
    as avengers 22, 36, 111–12

as criminals 55–6, 92–4, 115, 135, 164,
        173–4
as heretics 94–5, 104–6, 115, 132–5
as Ishmaelites 80, 84, 104, 164
justification of violence against 70,
        93–4, 104, 179
in the mytho-historical narrative
        102–3, 107, 115, 137–9, 176–7
mytho-history 101–4, 107, 115, 137, 143,
        176, 178, 181

narrative, importance of 1–2, 7–9, 12, 68n,
        74, 101–2, 137, 139, 168, 178, 180,
        182n, 184, 201
negative evidence, problem of 87, 178
New Testament 56, 88, 92, 114n, 160, 173,
        176–7,
    Acts 48n, 156
    Galatians 160
    Hebrews 115n
    John 98n
    1 John 56n, 115n
    Luke 91n, 100n, 177n
    Matthew 100n, 114n, 124, 133n, 137n,
        159n, 177n
    1 Peter 163n
    Romans 26n, 84, 88, 89n, 114–15n,
        152, 156n, 165, 167n, 173n, 177,
        189, 191n
Nicaea 43
Niermeyer, Jan 11, 157, 165
Nirenberg, David 183–4
non-participant accounts 43–4, 49–52

Odo of Deuil 14, 75, 85, 86n, 87n, 147n,
        202
Old Testament 55, 102, 190
    Deuteronomy 50n, 89, 92, 132n, 164n,
        173n
    Exodus 157n, 163–4, 171, 177
    Genesis 157n
    Isaiah 51n, 109, 176n

Jeremiah 90
Job 90
Joshua 96n
Judges 18, 132n
Lamentations 119n
Proverbs 154
Psalms 89n, 100n, 126n, 130n, 161n
Zechariah 51, 55, 57
Orderic Vitalis 12n, 18n, 27, 49n, 50–51,
    53, 54n, 56, 59, 68, 103–4, 110,
    146, 195–6
Otto of Freising 64, 67n, 85–6, 91, 102,
    105, 202, 204, 206n
Otto of St. Blasien 29, 30n, 120n, 121, 123,
    130, 131n, 139, 140n, 141, 142n,
    204

Partner, Peter 2n, 190
Paschal II, Pope 44–5, 47–8, 62, 195
peccatis exigentibus hominum 52, 87, 89,
    202
penance 4, 16, 43, 52, 125, 178
Peter II of Aragon 29, 151
Peter of Blois 3n, 81, 88–9, 90n, 93n, 100,
    108, 164n, 177, 199
Peter of Castelnau 131, 135, 205
Peter of Les Vaux-de-Cernay 123, 124n,
    129, 130n, 131, 132n, 134n, 135n,
    136n, 137, 150, 151n, 164n, 205
Peter the Hermit 36, 49, 53, 162
Peter the Venerable 33, 77, 87, 94–5, 96n,
    99, 101n, 104, 147, 154, 164n,
    184n, 198, 203
Peter Tudebode 46, 47n, 48, 75n, 195
Peter, Bishop of Oporto 83, 92, 108, 114,
    136, 147
Philip II of France 27, 73, 83, 98, 121, 125,
    130, 142, 148, 151
Phineas 160
pilgrimage 3, 43, 48–9, 83, 124–5, 128,
    150, 197, 206n
pollution, concept of 21, 50

Pontius Pilate 59–60, 126
Port St. Symeon 25, 59, 110
power 19–30, 110–14, 116
    material/spiritual 90–92, 115, 125
    papal 34, 88–96, 115, 129
    see also authority
Prague 64, 85, 202
preaching 43, 51, 73, 78, 90, 97, 118, 127,
    132–4, 148, 151–2, 181n, 190,
    197–8, 205 *see also* sermons
Prester John 134
prudence 20, 37, 154
punishment
    as correction/chastisement 53–7,
        130–31, 154, 159, 163
    and vengeance 11–16, 96, 174–5, 191
    see also crime

Quantum praedecessores 73, 84, 203

Raimbaut of Vaqueiras 24, 118, 137, 138n,
    180, 204
Rainald Porcet 1, 48, 106, 110
Ralph of Caen 14n, 15, 49n, 54, 55n, 56,
    195–6
Ralph of Coggeshall 121, 132n, 133, 134n,
    136, 150, 204
Raymond of Aguilers 47–8, 75n, 195, 198
Raymond of St. Gilles 20, 28, 33, 46, 54–5,
    146, 195
Raymond V of Toulouse 83
Raymond VI of Toulouse 125
reciprocal altruism 25
reconciliation 31, 52, 60, 134, 161
Reddy, William 7, 145n
retribution 13n, 26, 33, 36, 38n, 50, 56,
    83, 89, 121, 123, 131, 164, 185,
    205
    retributio 6
Reynald of Châtillon 149, 199
Reynolds, Susan 6n, 61
Rhineland, the 73, 97, 204

Richard I of England 20, 24, 31, 73, 80, 111, 121, 148

Richard of Devizes 20, 24n, 29, 34n, 36n, 80, 199

righteousness 56, 109, 114, 146n, 152–7, 159, 163, 168, 171, 177

Rigord 27n, 83, 98, 103n, 106, 148, 149n, 199

Riley-Smith, Jonathan 2n, 3n, 4n, 43, 49n, 56n, 59n, 60n, 62–3, 66n, 71, 102n, 158, 166n, 171, 189–91, 192n

ritual 22, 25, 29, 98n, 102, 106n, 107n, 139, 161, 184, 186, 191n

rivalry 39, 157, 165–7, 171, 186

Robert of Auxerre 19–20, 121, 127, 135n, 150, 204

Robert of Clari 16, 25n, 29, 30n, 32, 122, 131n, 142, 181, 204

Robert of Rheims 19, 36, 49n, 50, 51, 55, 58–9, 173, 195–6

Roger of Howden 78–80, 88, 148n, 199

Roland 24, 113, 127, 180n, 181, 182n

Rouen 34, 64, 68

Rubin, Miri 101n, 106n, 139, 196n

Rupert of Deutz 101, 106

sacrifice 107n, 186
   self-sacrifice 62–3, 149, 151, 158, 166–8, 170–71, 177

sacrilege 27–8, 33 *see also* blasphemy

St. Ambrose *see* Ambrose of Milan

St. Augustine *see* Augustine of Hippo

St. Francis of Assisi 132, 169n

St. Jerome 92

St. Paul 152, 160, 166, 170, 186n

St. Peter 53

St. Stephen 131

St. Veronica 126, 205

Saladin *see* Din, al–, Salah

Satan 93, 135, 167 *see also* Antichrist

Schaller, Hans 45n, 197

Scheff, Thomas 23n, 186

'scripts' 22, 161–3, 168–71

Second Lateran Council 91

Sefir Zekhirah 80, 86, 97, 201

sermons 43, 51, 61, 78, 83, 90, 92, 100n, 108, 118, 119n, 127, 133n, 136, 142, 156n, 161n, 205n *see also* preaching

Sicily 29, 74, 147

sins 17, 18, 28, 32, 39, 55, 63, 67, 96, 122, 130, 152, 158–60, 164
   and crime 34, 136
   preoccupation with 52–4, 57, 88–9, 162–3, 168–71, 177
   remission of 43, 45, 52, 65, 120, 124–5, 139–40

Smail, Daniel L. 4n, 13n, 159n, 161–2, 168, 171

social relationships *see* family; friendship; lordship

Solomon bar Simson 64, 69, 84, 104–5, 196n, 201

Stephen of Blois 27, 59

Stock, Brian 8n, 58n, 138, 182n

Suger of St. Denis 33, 84, 114, 155, 202–3

Summa Parisiensis 95, 104

swords
   Doctrine of the Two Swords 90–91
   material 79, 92, 94, 125
   of vengeance 18, 22, 27, 30, 50, 79, 83, 89, 126–7, 154, 156, 163

Tancred 14–15, 24n, 31–2, 36–7, 55n, 56n, 110, 195

Thomas of Chobham 16–17, 26n, 55, 141n, 154–5, 158, 159n

Titus and Vespasian 82–3, 102, 180n, 182, 192 *see also* Jerusalem, Roman destruction of

Toulouse 29, 83, 123, 125, 164

translation, issues of 5, 11, 14, 19, 146, 154n, 177, 196

treachery *see* crime, betrayal/treachery

Trier 64
'Trier unit' 196n
Twelfth-century Europe, historical
    approaches to 4–5, 8, 178–85

unfaithfulness 52–7, 93, 95, 99, 103, 107,
    123, 132–4, 143, 153, 164, 174
    see also Crucifixion, sign of willful
    disbelief
Urban II, Pope 1, 43–4, 47–50, 58, 62, 109,
    132n, 147, 154, 179, 197
Urban III, Pope 73

Venetians 117, 122, 130
vengeance
    absence of 46–8, 84–8, 127–9
    dangers of taking 28–30
    desire for 20, 28–30, 36, 37n, 46, 48,
        55, 64–7, 162, 164, 168
    duty to take 21, 27, 93, 108–9, 131,
        143, 155, 174
    ethnicity and 37–40
    failure to take 23, 40, 63, 121
    ius talionis 57
    licit/illicit 17
    nâqam 5, 196
    non-violent 34–5
    predisposition for 40
    as primitive 3–4
    as private 13, 15
    threat of 30, 39n
    vocabulary of 5–6
    women and 37–40
    see also Crucifixion, vengeance for;
        God, of vengeance; Holy Land,
        vengeance for; motivations, and
        vengeance; Muslims, as avengers;

punishment, and vengeance;
    swords, of vengeance; war, and
    vengeance, distinction between
Venice 16, 24
Venjance de Nostre Seigneur, La 2, 5, 46,
    64, 68–71, 126, 138–9, 181, 184,
    204, 206
Verdier, Raymond 15, 36n, 190n
Vincent of Prague 85, 202
Vindicta Salvatoris 5, 69, 176, 205

war
    holy war 3, 47, 92n, 190–91
    just war 3, 16–18, 32, 83, 88, 93, 131,
        135, 147, 170, 174, 177, 191–2
    penitential war 3, 125
    and vengeance, distinction between 15
willful disbelief *see* Crucifixion, sign of
    willful disbelief
William of Malmesbury 94
William of Tyre 16, 20, 22, 25n, 27–8, 31n,
    34, 78n, 89, 93, 103n, 109–10, 147,
    157, 192, 198, 199n
White, Stephen D. 13n, 19n, 21, 22n,
    161–2m 168, 171
women 29, 38–40, 89–90, 149, 181n
wounds 11, 55, 63, 81–2, 90, 93, 97, 101,
    103, 109, 137, 174

Zadar 24–5, 117, 122, 131
zeal
    of God 55, 162–5
    and intention 152–3
    ira per zelum 158–62
    and justice 17, 93, 154–6
    zelus, meaning of 146, 156–7, 165–6
Zengi 73, 114